Many Such as She:

Victorian Australian

Women Poets of World War One

© Copyright 2018 Michael Sharkey

Published by Walleah Press
PO Box 368
North Hobart
Tasmania 7002
Australia

http://walleahpress.com.au
ralph.wessman@walleahpress.com.au

This book is copyright. Apart from any fair dealing for the purposes of study and research, criticism, review, or as otherwise permitted under the Copyright Act, no part may be reproduced in any manner without first gaining written permission from the author.

Revised edition copyright 2019
ISBN 978 1 877010 89 7

Many Such as She:

Victorian Australian

Women Poets of World War One

An anthology edited by Michael Sharkey

CONTENTS

Introduction and Acknowledgements   1

Margery Ruth Betts [1892 UK—c. 1950 UK]   11
- The Laggard   17
- The Dreamers   19
- Called   21
- The Fulfilment   24
- Liebknecht   25
- The Maimed   26
- Busy as Newtown   27
- The Ghost   29
- The Reckoning   30

Beatrice Vale Bevan [1876 Vic—1945 Melbourne]   31
- Previously Reported Dead   39
- Passed—With Honour!   41
- The Worn-Out Sentry: A Vision'   42
- Untitled ['Lord God of Empires, now we raise']   44
- Untitled ['I wonder are there many (such)']   45

Marion Bray [c. 1885 Vic—1947 Rosanna, Vic]   47
- Peace   50
- Socks   51

Mary Bright [1869 Bendigo —1942 Bendigo]   52
- Blinded by a Shell   59
- The Song of the Women   60
- Pozières   61
- Credo   62

Muriel Beverley Cole [1882 Armadale, Vic —1947 Melbourne]	63
The Allied Dead	68
In Memory. 63rd Regimental Ball	69
Oh! Come on Australia!	70
The Sign of Anzac	71
The Journey's End	73
1918	74
Martha Coxhead [Bet Bet, Vic 1864—1947 Footscray]	75
The Friend of the Wounded	80
Belgium	83
Violet B. Cramer (1879 Brighton—1968 Horsham)	84
The Lusitania	87
Death of Miss Cavell	88
Fight! Be Men!	89
In Memorium J.C.T.	90
The Conquest of Jerusalem	92
Surrender of German Ships	94
Enid Derham [1882 Hawthorn—1941 Kew, Vic]	96
Gallipoli 1917	105
The Return	106
'E' (Mary Fullerton) [1868 Glenmaggie, Vic—1946 London]	107
The Targets	115
The Gippslander	118
Next Door	120
War Time	121
A Man's a Sliding Mood	122

Lesbia Harford [1891 Brighton, Vic—1927 Melbourne]   123
    The Troop-ships   128
    The people have drunk the wine of peace   129
    Ours was a friendship in secet, my dear   130
    To Leslie   131

Gertrude Hart [1873 Williamstown, Vic—1965 Ferntree Gully]   132
    We Must Do More   135
    April and After   137
    Armistice Day   139

Capel Boake (Doris Boake Kerr) [1889 Sydney—1944 Melbourne]   140
    Stitchin' Seams   143
    Anzac Day 1927   144

Marion Miller Knowles [1865 Woods Point, Vic—1949 Camberwell]   146
    A Tribute to the Memory of Campbell Peter   152
    His Mother   154
    O Wondrous Love!   156
    Jack   157
    Father Finn (Sedd-El-Bahr)   158

Phyllis Lewis [1894 Elsternwick, Vic—1986 Hobart]   160
    1918   166

Dorothy Frances McCrae [1878 Melbourne—1937 Sydney]   171
    The Empire's Call   177
    The Shawl   178
    Second Thoughts   179
    Geoffrey   180
    Gaba Tepe   181

My Soldier	184
The Hero	185
The Gift	186

Grace Ethel Martyr [1888 Ballarat—1934 Bendigo]   187

The Soldier	193
Rain	195
Follow On	196
To the Stretcher-Bearers	197
Returned	198

Myra Morris [1893 Boort, Vic—1966 Frankston Vic]   199

The Old Mother	206
To the Glorious Dead	208
England	209
Remembrance. Anzac Day	210
Going Home	211

Nina Murdoch [1890 North Carlton, Vic—1976 Victoria]   212

Socks	223
Unfit	225
Army Nurses	226
Colored Bows	227
A Toast	229
The News	230
The Two That Strayed	231

Joyce M. NanKivell [1887 Qld—1982 Ouranopolis, Greece]   232

To You Who Should Follow	240
We Are Not Schooled in Vengeance	241
Where Are You Going To?	232
Lake Narocz	233

Nettie Palmer [1885 Bendigo—1964 Hawthorn]   245
    The Mother   251
    The Barrack Yard   252
    The Birds   253
    The Hero   255

Clara Leonor Patey [? Bendigo—1926 Seaford, Vic]   256
    Welcome All   261
    Boys in the Navy Blue   262
    Remembrance Day   263

Marie E.J. Pitt [1869 Bulumwaal—1948 Kew]   266
    The Mercy   271
    With the Guns at Charleroi   273
    The Ringers   276
    Transports   277

Philadelphia Nina Robertson [1886 Wangaratta—1950 South Yarra]   278
    More Men, and Yet More Men are Wanted   284
    Killed at Gallipoli   285

Joan Torrance [1873 Stanraer Scotland—1943 Abbotsford, Vic]   286
    The Call to Arms   294
    Lines Suggested on Viewing Mount Macedon   296
    An Invocation   297
    Christmastide, 1919   298

Select Bibliography   300

INTRODUCTION

Years ago, when I taught literature in universities, I was sometimes invited to talk to high school students about Wilfred Owen's poetry and its relationship to World War One. The syllabus committees who prescribed such a topic were doubtless well intentioned in wanting young readers to understand the impact of wars on men who had fought in them, but in light of Owens's cultural, historical and geographical remoteness from the students' current concerns, the undertaking struck me as having limited appeal or effect. Many students voiced a heartfelt sentiment, when they optimistically asked me, 'What should I say about this or that poem in the exam?' After a couple of experiences of this sort, I knocked back invitations to repeat anything like discussion under such conditions.

My greater interest lay in the ways civilian poets, and especially the women poets, reacted to that War. Addressing that question involved literary archaeology. Understandably, given the nature of custodianship of the memory of that event, anthologies of Australian writing relating to the War tended to favour work by soldier poets, but two collections stood out as acknowledging women's responses. J.T. Laird's 1971 *Other Banners: An anthology of Australian Literature of the First World War* (1971) contained 48 poems by eighteen male poets and 6 poems by four women poets, and David Holloway's *Dark Somme Flowing: Australian Verse of the Great War 1914-1918* featured 114 poems by fifty-one males and 25 poems by fifteen women poets.

The book I wanted to read, containing more responses by women poets to World War One, and something of their status as real people, did not exist, so I began, in a roundabout way, to collect a broader sampling of poems that might reflect their authors' lives and attitudes. I don't assume that any poem that appears in print can be taken as an unmediated or 'pure' utterance, independent of the rhetorical factors of argument appealing to logic, selective shared beliefs, and other clues to the writer's sense of role and purposeful identification with readers. Poems on patriotic occasions are particularly slippery, so I expect readers of the poems in this collection will be alert to and wary of poets' invocations of customs, manners, folkways and traditions. A short poem by the Queensland-born writer Lala Fisher, first published in the *Australian Worker* in 1915 and subsequently in her book, *The Grass Flowering* (Sydney:

The author, 1915), memorably epitomised the problematic nature of the weasel word 'sincerity' in public discourse:

> Sincerity?
> The cross, the rack, the bloody thong,
> The cruel right, the stubborn wrong,
> These to sincerity belong.

I was already familiar with books by some of the better known poets, such as Mary Gilmore, Zora Cross, Marion Miller Knowles, and a few of the less renowned or long forgotten: Emily Coungeau, Mary E. Fullerton ('E'), Gertrude Hart and others. Some books came my way from second-hand bookshops and the poetry shelves of university libraries, but I thought, rather grandly, of trying to read every Australian woman poet's book published during or shortly after World War One. It's not so daunting if one's prepared to spend time in far-flung Rare Book rooms of State and university libraries. I can't claim to have covered every publication even now, but since the arrival of TROVE, the National Library's digital resource of bygone newspapers and magazines, and the wider availability of digitally copied archives, the pursuit is appreciably easier.

The very number of women who had written and published verse, much of it admirable in its technical competency and depth of reflection, impressed me. I was perplexed why their work should continue to remain hidden at a time when patriotic nostalgia was being worked up toward what would eventually be an orgy of commercialised fervour associated with the anniversary of the War.

It was evident, of course, that poetry was a convenient and popular mode of expressing emotions and ideas in earlier times. Compulsory universal education in Australia added impetus: the poems offer eloquent testimony to the high standards of late Victorian and early twentieth century primary and secondary education. It also testifies to the degree to which Empire patriotism was inculcated and absorbed, notwithstanding the ways some of the poets later questioned its practice and results. Obviously, not all the poetry written between 1914 and 1918 was concerned directly with the War. The usual suspect topics related to death, love, the frustrations and pleasures associated with work, home, exile, or separation, along with questions of faith and endurance continued to appear. So too, the tenor of occupations, social conditions, beliefs and related matters of class. From what the women had to say concerning the war, however, it was apparent that the overriding temper of their poetry was more contemplative than gung-ho. An anthology reflecting the range would, I thought, reveal the changes in outlook from Empire enthusiasm or chagrin all the way to abiding sorrow.

The project received another provocation. Invited to lead a seminar at a Summer School on the New Literatures in English at the University of Osnabrück in 1998, I broached the topic of Australia's wartime poets. The place and timing were significant. 1998 marked the three hundred and fiftieth anniversary of the Peace of Westphalia—the series of treaties that marked the conclusion of the ruinous Thirty Years War, a struggle exacerbated by sectarian elements, and as global in its way as the First World War two hundred and sixty-six years later.

Osnabrück's subtle approach to commemoration appealed to me. The city combined the anniversary with other civic and religious events and ceremonies to honour victims of war that was still present in many memories. The memorial to the painter Felix Nussbaum, arrested and killed while fleeing Nazi persecution as a 'degenerate' artist and Jew, bore striking testimony to the city's sense of sorrow. In another building, an exhibition honoured the life and work of Erich Maria Remarque, author of *All Quiet on the Western Front* and other novels based on his experience of World War One. Remarque had left Germany to settle in the USA as a result of attacks on his 'degenerate' pacifism. Part of the show was a display of editions in several languages of his most famous novel, which had been banned in many countries. Alphabetically, Australia led the pack of nations that found the book's anti-war sentiments so offensive as to merit suppression. Yet it had been an Australian, Arthur Wesley Wheen, who had first translated the book into English. Like Remarque, Wheen was a veteran of the War. So my seminar on the poetry of Australians poets who were variously pro- or anti-war resonated with the commemorative events occurring in Osnabrück in 1998.

Ten years after Osnabrück, I published an essay on some of the women's war poetry that I had further collected. Leaving aside the question of quality, the sheer quantity of poetry pointed to a catastrophic intellectual and emotional crisis experienced by the poets.

I approached some publishers with the idea of a commemorative anthology, and again met with the response that it was a non-starter. What was wanted was anything to do with Gallipoli and other feats of Australian chivalry. It wasn't hard to see the way Australian war nostalgia was tending.

Another ten years has passed, in which I have been fascinated by the extent of opportunism associated with the First World War: from organised tourist excursions to Gallipoli, all the way down to the khaki-clad soft toys and other commemorative Kitsch cluttering the shelves of Post Office shops.

Now that the anniversary of Gallipoli has departed with all its civic hoorays, I can think that this book will mark the anniversary of the end of hostilities, much as those thoughtful commemorative events I saw in Germany marked the end of an earlier war to end wars.

§

Between 2008 and 2016, I had abandoned my initial grandiose plan and narrowed my focus to one Australian State, rather than the entire nation. The primary reason was in a sense arbitrary: compared with other States, Victoria published more single books by women poets. I'd also discovered the mobility of many poets of the period—those born elsewhere but who spent a significant time in Victoria even while continuing to publish in their 'home' States and even internationally, as well as in Victoria. Further, several Victorian-born poets had moved to other States where they also published, in some cases, most of their output. Ultimate selection would not be straightforward.

My selection is based on the criterion of 'significant' Victorian association or identification: some combination of birth, education, work experience including child-rearing, literary and other activity associated with the State during the War. The decision to include or exclude was not always tidily resolved. Typical dilemmas arose. What should I do concerning Alexandra Seager? Born at Ballarat in 1870, Alexandrine Laidlaw (also called Ina) married Captain Clarendon J. Seager, a former British Army cavalry officer. The couple had three sons and three daughters and moved to Adelaide around 1910. There, Alexandra ran an agency to supply governesses, domestic helpers and other workers on rural properties. Her sons enlisted in the Army as soon as war was declared. Edward George, the youngest son, was killed at Gallipoli. The older brothers, Major Harold William Seager MC, and Lieutenant Edward Clarendon Seager DCM, returned to Australia in January 1919.

Alexandra Seager wrote poetry throughout the War and was a founding member, Honorary Secretary and Organiser of the 'Cheer-Up

Our Boys Society' that provided supper, concerts and conversation for enlisted men before their embarkation. She was also a founder, in 1915, of Violet Day, a day on which every member of the public was asked to wear a violet in memory of the fallen. She called the first meeting of men returned from Gallipoli, urged them to form an association, and contributed fifty pounds from the Cheer-Up Society. It was subsequently claimed that she was the founder of the RSL. Her poetry appeared in many places, including Edith S. Abbott's *Violet Verses* anthology in 1917, and her poem 'Our Soldier's Song' was set to music by Louis William Yemm and sung at patriotic concerts in South Australia. Was she a Victorian poet, then? Her exemplary personal, creative and humanitarian investment in Australia's contribution to World War One is in no doubt, but alas, I left her out of a representative collection of poets who had more formative and sustained literary association with Victoria during the War. One such was Victorian-born Beatrice Vale Bevan, whose poems appeared nationwide, and especially in Victoria, even though she spent much of her life as a Congregational minister's wife in China and Adelaide. Bevan's life followed an arc of departure and return to her native State: after years in China and South Australia, she returned to Victoria to live among her siblings in a Melbourne bayside suburb.

§

I do not claim greatness for every poem I've chosen, but I think some, and not always those by the most celebrated authors, are outstanding. I have included many earnest efforts by writers who were famous in their time, as well as many by more obscure practitioners. Many of the poets published at least one book or modest chapbook of verse that has to do with the subject of war. Several—Lesbia Harford, Gertrude Hart, Clara Leonar Patey, Marie E.J. Pitt—published predominantly in regional, State or national newspapers, and their work was collected, if at all, long after the War.

Unsurprisingly, several of the poets had begun publishing in newspapers and journals while still very young and long before 1914. Gertrude Hart (born in 1873) and Marie E.J. Pitt (born in 1869) first published at age fourteen; Nettie Palmer (born in 1885) and Myra Morris (born 1893) also published while still at school. Some poets were particularly encouraged when young by literary elders.

'Cinderella' (Mary Grant Bruce), editor of the children's letters section of the Melbourne *Herald* newspaper, encouraged Joice NanKivell to keep up her contributions of letters and stories and poems, much as Zora Cross was encouraged by 'Dame Durden' (Ethel Turner) of the *Town and Country Journal* to keep sending material for publication. By 1902, Cross (born in 1890) and NanKivell (born in 1887) were published writers in whom love of country and love of Empire ran strong.

The effusions of such precocious young writers were constrained by the prevailing tastes and expectations of editors and readers as much as by the poets' self-inclusion in the English tradition. Rhythmic poetry was a staple of public performance and entertainment. English, Irish and Scottish lyricism and narrative poetry, and such nineteenth century Australian or American works of which many wartime poets saw themselves the heirs, inevitably contributed to the sometimes lilting or lolloping effects of the World War One women's (and men's) poetry.

Colonial, State and national education systems endorsed such conventional influence. The nation's newspapers and quarterlies were chiefly edited by journalists whose tastes reinforced traditional practice. The exceptions were so few as to have had a negligible effect on mainstream readers. Harford, Palmer, Fullerton and others who inhabited advanced political circles were familiar with contemporary American and English practice that would eventually result in a shift in sensibility, but beyond the occasional little magazine or fugitive experimental pamphlet, where could the poets have obtained encouragement and sustenance? If any reader believes that the poetry of these women's civilian male contemporaries represented a seismic shift away from a shared outlook or received stylistic form, a perusal of Christopher Brennan's poem *A Chant of Doom* or Henry Lawson's 'England Yet' and other wartime verse will find cause to reconsider. This said, sometimes the women's poetry has some surprises. Archaic expressions and reliance on overly poetical effects like insistent rhyme are variously rejected, adapted or exploited in the poetry of Harford and Grace Ethel Martyr. Sometimes emphatic rhyme is relieved by a sudden denouement, as in the poem 'Stitchin' Seams' by Capel Boake (Doris Kerr), or Martyr's poem 'Rain'. Nina Murdoch's jaunty poems, 'Socks', and 'Colored Bows', also reveal the variety of cadence possible in received forms.

The tone of the poetry is just as varied, and is sometimes evident in the work of a single poet. As one example, the jingoistic fervour in the early effusions of Dorothy Frances McCrae was soon replaced by grief and sacred awe that followed the death of her younger brother. So many of the earliest wartime poems were shaped by the literary conventions and Imperial patriotism of the poets' counterparts in Great Britain, but this is a commonplace observation. We cannot expect the literary taste of one generation to be long maintained let alone respected by that which follows.

Dissident women poets of World War One who published extensively are relatively scarce, a reflection on the difficulty of achieving mass circulation in a period of stringent censorship of printed matter. Lesbia Harford, Nettie Palmer, Mary E. Fullerton ('E') and Marie E.J. Pitt stand out as writers whose work appeared in radical papers, though all appear to have understood the pressure on and compulsion of men to enlist even while they opposed conscription. Fullerton and Margery Ruth Betts are hardly to be thought of as congruent in their careers and political aims—the former a prominent anti-conscription speaker and activist, the latter a devout wife of a Congregational minister and college principal, yet both lamented the destruction of what they considered civilised values—in Betts' case extending to an almost unique poem of sympathy for the maimed, and a truly unique poem expressing sympathy for the German opponent of war, Karl Liebknecht, whose treatment by the German government she compares to Christ's under Pilate. Betts' poem 'The Maimed' is a masterpiece of controlled rhetorical argument, building by anaphora (liturgy-like repetition of a particular word to open each line of a list of war's horrors) to an irresistible claim that calls into question the ability of all 'these things numberless and measureless', that is, words alone, to truly signify what the 'sacrifice' of actual lives can mean to those who have not experienced them, as the dead and maimed have, in the flesh. It is as if the words, to Betts' mind, carry the weight of actions and of human lives, as the Eucharist is said to do. The poem pushes against the restrictions of language and seems to question the power of poetry itself, and it is all the more extraordinary for doing so.

Perhaps, too, Betts' poem, like many others in this collection, might show something of the subtle undertow of incipient modernism in certain poets' works. The poems are not all so formally derivative of Romantic and mid-to-late Victorian stylistics as a glance at Australian anthologies covering a longer historical overview of Australian men's and women's poetry might suggest. The experimental impulse is present in poets as different in background and temperament as Harford, Betts, Martyr, and Capel Boake (Doris Kerr).

The women's occupations reflect their sense of world events. Their professions and daily activities include law, postal work, journalism, school and university teaching, clerical work, Red Cross and charity organising, banking, factory work, librarianship, travel writing, fiction writing, political activism, music teaching and dramatic performance. The elocutionary and rhetorical standards are uniformly high, befitting an educated, aspirational, democratic and talented citizenry.

The poems in this collection relay the experiences of such women as felt compelled to come to terms with the effects of war on their lives. Not every poet, female or male, felt driven to do the same. Some poets wrote sparingly of war. Those women who were already publishing at the outset of the War continued to write of other experiences and scenes as well as war-related matters throughout the conflict. Landscape, travel, women's roles and the convulsions of faith, love and loss beyond those associated with war continued to dominate much of their work. It's noteworthy that where they employ rural or native Australian references, their purpose is often quite ambiguous. In many poems, springtime brings memories of happier times with now-absent friends, lovers, siblings, children and colleagues, or a bitter reminder that for some of their loved ones there would be no more springs, and for themselves no consolation could ever come with the return of the seasonal flowers. And many poets did ensure that the flowers they referred to were native to the country.

I initially considered arranging the poems in chronological order of their first appearance in print but have opted for simpler organisation in alphabetical order of the poets' names. This collection focuses on some of the poets associated with just one representative Australian State. Where details of the poets' lives were on public record, I've added brief biographical sketches—as much as one can glean from materials on public record, without lapsing into what Richard Holmes calls the fatal 'past subjunctive' speculations of biography. In every case, I have also cited sources of information. Nothing is so infuriating as unsubstantiated hearsay concerning a poet's life. I have checked and counterchecked facts recorded in this book, but any errors or bias can be sheeted home to me.

At all accounts, I hope a better sense of the range of under-appreciated Australian poetry of the period will become somewhat clearer from the examples that follow.

Michael Sharkey
Castlemaine, 2018

ACKNOWLEDGMENTS

I'm grateful to the following institutions and individuals for permission to reproduce photographic and other images:

State Library Victoria: for photographs of Beatrice Vale Bevan, Doris Kerr ('Capel Boake'), Mary E. Fullerton ('E'); Nettie Palmer and Joan Torrance;
National Library of Australia: for photographs of Enid Derham, Marion Miller Knowles and Nina Murdoch;
State Library of New South Wales and Micheal Lester: for photograph of Marie E. J. Pitt;
Clarke Elwood Studios (101-102 Hatton Gardens, London EC and 34-36 Oxford Street, London), Hachette Australia, Hachette (UK), Kirsty McHugh and the John Murray archive, National Library of Scotland; also Ron Cosens, cartedevisite.co.uk, and State Library Victoria: for Joice NanKivell Loch;
Maxwell Coxhead, for photograph of Martha Coxhead;
Penny Lade, for photograph of Lieutenant Raymond Lade and Phyllis Lewis;
The Wallwork family (Christchurch), for permission to reproduce Elizabeth Wallwork's pencil portrait of Dorothy Frances McCrae held by the State Library Victoria.

I acknowledge the generosity of the Equity Trust Committee, Equity Trustees Ltd, Level 1, 575 Bourke Street, Melbourne Victoria 3000, for the Janet Palmer Estate, for permission to reprint a poem by Nettie Palmer, and I thank the following; Dennis Oliver for advice relating to copyright status of the poems of Lesbia Harford; Anthony Black, State Library and Archive Service, LINC Tasmania for information relating to Lt Owen Lewis; Anton Lade for information and contact with members of the Lade family of Launceston, Hobart and Devonport; Jane Grosvenor, Rebecca Free and Mrs Dora Bramich, members of the Country Women's Association In Tasmania for further information concerning Phyllis Lade; Sylvia Martin for advice concerning Mary E. Fullerton's publications; Susanna De Vries, for permission to reprint poems by Joice NanKivell Loch.

Sources of poems are noted in the brief biographical and bibliographical introductions to individual poets. Every effort has been made to locate copyright owners of poems subject to the copyright Act. I would like to hear from copyright claimants to works by the following: Violet B. Cramer: for poems published between 1916 and 1922; Gertrude Hart: for poems published between 1915 and 1926; Myra Morris: for poems published between 1917 and 1919; and Nina Murdoch, for poems published between 1914 and 1922. Any person claiming copyright to any poem should contact me in writing via the publisher, at the same time providing legal evidence of possession of copyright.

I'm grateful to Rory Cooke, Des Cowley, Lilly O'Gorman, Kevin Molloy, and other staff of the State Library Victoria, and to staff of the State libraries noted above, and staff of the Goldfields Library Corporation. Thanks also to the National Library for hosting the TROVE search engine, and the University of Queensland for hosting the Australian online literary database AUSTLIT.

Many thanks also to Melbourne University for an invitation to give a public lecture on Australian Women Poets of the First World War in 2011, and to Ian Greenhalgh and the staff of the Armidale-Dumaresq War Memorial Library in Armidale, New South Wales, who invited me to speak on the same topic, on 11 November 2011.

A note on the second edition

Readers of the first edition who drew my attention to oversights or omissions have my thanks, and I especially record my gratitude to my publisher, Ralph Wessman of Walleah Press, who took on this project when others hesitated. For this, all my readers owe him an enormous debt.

Michael Sharkey
Castlemaine, July 2019

MARGERY RUTH BETTS

Margery Ruth Betts, known in her family as Ruth, was born in England, one of three daughters of the Rev. Robert Arthur Betts (1859-1913) and his wife Catherine Mary Noyes (1856-1945). Ruth's life and writings were distinguished by her commitment to the Congregational values of her forebears.

The lives and character of the male grandparents and parents are relatively well documented, but those of the daughters are largely unrecorded. Ruth's father's parents were Louisa Betts (née Taplin, 1827-1902) and the Rev. Robert Wye Betts (1825-1868). The latter had served from 1853 as assistant minister at the Hanover Chapel at Peckham in Surrey, where he helped set up the Surrey Congregational Union. A history of Congregationalism in Surrey speaks of him as a man who delighted in open-air preaching but one who did not enjoy good health: he died, 'after much suffering', in his forty-fourth year.

Ruth's father was also to experience poor health and die relatively young in the course of a career that in some aspects mirrored his father's. Educated at Peckham and Hackney, he married Catherine Mary Noyes, daughter of a Congregationalist minister, at Lewisham in Kent, in 1887, and the couple had three daughters, the second of whom was Margery Ruth. Her older sister (born at St Thomas in Devon, 1890) was named Catherine Jane, and her younger sister was known as Molly.

Ruth's maternal uncles Henry and Edward Noyes had migrated to Australia with their sister Jane around 1856 and established Noyes Brothers, an engineering firm in Sydney and Melbourne. The latter branch became a prominent electrical engineering concern.

In the 1890s, Ruth's parents also migrated to Australia, where Ruth's father commenced as pastor at Kew Independent (Congregational) Church and remained at that post for seventeen years. In 1900, he preached in Adelaide as well as in Melbourne, and from 1902, he was chairman of the Congregational Union of Victoria, serving as chairman of the Congregational College, where he taught as a professor under Dr Gosman. On retiring in 1912, Dr Gosman expressed a strong wish that Betts should succeed him as principal of the College, and Betts was subsequently elected to the post. He resigned from his pastorate to devote himself to the College, which he sought to expand to include a students' residence. In the course of preaching a sermon at Prahran on 2 November 1913, however, he became so ill that the service was abandoned. The Rev. Robert never recovered from the attack, and he died nine days later. His medical adviser had long before urged him to spend as much time in the open air as possible, but Betts was enthusiastic about his work for the College and the Congregational Union. Until shortly before his death, he also enjoyed chess, at which he was a player of inter-State ranking. He had played on four occasions against New South Wales, and on his death, the Melbourne *Leader* newspaper published a telegraphic match that he had played and won against a New South Wales opponent in September 1900.

Other members of Ruth's extended English family had Australian connections. One such was Ruth's cousin Robert Wye Betts, born in Lewisham in Kent in 1886, a farmer who had worked as an apprentice to a Gloucestershire farmer. Migrating to Australia in 1908, he worked as a fruit grower at Mildura until enlisting as a Private in the AIF on 7 December 1914. He survived Gallipoli unscathed and served with the Second Field Artillery until his death from wounds at the age of twenty-eight in France on 20 April 1917. Ruth's poem 'The Fulfilment' has a particular poignancy in light of the death of her older relative. Vivien Newman, author of *Tumult and Tears: An Anthology of Women's First World War Poetry,* states that Betts spent time in England as a student in 1920. She came back to Australia but sometime after 1928, returned to England, and her name disappears from the Kooyong (Melbourne) electoral roll. Her mother, whose name is listed on the roll for the last time in 1924, died at Kew in Melbourne on 8 October 1931.

Ruth's sisters Catherine and Molly remained in Victoria, Catherine dying in Melbourne in 1945; her funeral notice indicates Ruth's address as England.

§

Margery Ruth Betts contributed poems to the *Australasian* newspaper and the Congregationalist journal *Victorian Independent* from 1915, and continued to do so until late 1918. Her poetry was characteristically infused with evangelical sentiment, inflected with images of blossoming trees and flowers such as that in 'The Little Brother':

And you—oh laddie, in Heaven can memories find you?
Comes there a Spring to those shining fields and fair,
Do primroses, violets, and daffodils grow to remind you?
Are snowflakes and little forget-me-nots blossoming there?

The theological scholar Kerrie Handasyde has remarked on the prevalence of such imagery in the poetry of both Betts and Beatrice Bevan, for both of whom the flowering of plants (predominantly European in Betts's poetry, Australian 'native' flowers and trees in Bevan's) is symbolic of the flowering into manhood of the young men who are the subject of much of their verse. Betts's 1915 poem 'The Dreamers' concludes with the lines, 'But while there's still a flag to love, a love song to be sung, / The winds of spring shall sigh and sing of nought but you—the young'.

Of Betts's sole poetry collection (*Remembering and Other Verses*) a volume 'dedicated to the mothers of Australian soldiers who have died in battle', the reviewer for *The Graphic of Australia* newspaper wrote on 23 November 1917, 'Throughout the verse there is a sincere pathetic feeling, and we can not but feel that the authoress has been deeply pierced by the anguish she so poignantly describes. Great sorrow is here clothed in lyrical language of great beauty, yet the note is not hopelessness, but rather victory, as for example, "The First Australian Casualty List"'. A fortnight earlier, a reviewer in the *Age* newspaper had commented that

> With so much minor poetry being published at the present time, it would be unfortunate if Miss Betts's verses were overlooked. They are not ambitious or arresting in craftsmanship, but they are obviously written in the attempt to express something that is worth expressing. The commonest fault of minor poets is to write for the sake of making poetry. Miss Betts merely uses the poetic form because it best suits her thoughts and the message she would convey. Of the 27 poems in the volume, there are at least a dozen that deserve a place in any anthology of Australian war poetry.

The *Age* reviewer nominated 'Killed in Action' as the best poem in the volume.

The Sydney *Sun* review of the collection, on 30 December 1917, remarked on the 'note of melancholy' that ran though the volume and supposed that some direct references to suffering 'which may have been that of sympathy or experience' lay at the root. The reviewer perceptively noted that the 'joyous uplift that speaks of consciousness of a great cause and a knowledge that the deaths died leave their memories undying' constituted 'forget-me-nots in a garden of grief'. The *Sun* newspaper chose to reprint the entire short quasi-humorous poem 'Busy as Newtown', which had been reprinted in a slew of newspapers following its first appearance in Betts's volume.

The reviewer for the Sydney *Sunday Times* in January 1918 took an unkinder view of the 'hackneyed' nature of subject matter generally prevalent in martial (and other) topics by that stage of the War, but in the event chose to publish a poem titled 'Spring' and concluded with a confident announcement:

> Miss Margery Ruth Betts is the latest of Australian woman-poets. In her case the word poet, frequently abused, may be employed reasonably. With some charm of song she has the true poetic instinct; she sees and feels in music, in her own being throbs to the pulse of the world. The verses in this first little volume are nearly all about soldiers and the war. It is a pity, because that theme becomes rather hackneyed, and needs to be revitalised by some flaming pen of genius. We choose rather to cite some verse of Miss Betts on another subject. The theme is again hackneyed, but it is one of those subjects that no hard usage can stale. [...]
>
> There is, in point of fact, nothing more difficult to write than war-verse written well. The splendour and tremendous sublimity of the theme well might daunt a master poet; but all the little rhymesters of the suburbs are turning out war-verses by the bushel. Miss Betts ranks far above these and all their like. In her verse there is much of pure beauty, much of sincerity, much that persuades and remains. There is throughout the resolute yet pleading note that never comes undiluted save from a woman's heart. There is also—a thing unusual in a young poet—a fine sense of form, a nice sense of word-values. Of its kind, this is the best book of the woman's year in Australia. The next book will be better still, of course; but it may be taken that now, already, Miss Margery Ruth Betts has definitely arrived.

Betts's emphasis on the soldier's 'calling', directly referred to in the title of the poem 'Called', underlines the religious aspect of her verse overall, and of the religious nature of the engagement of mothers and sons in the struggle. Both are 'called' to follow a sacred bidding. In the reviews referred to above, the hackneyed nature of the poetry's themes is averred, but both reviewers neglect the rich allusiveness of the ecclesiastical and biblical language that reinforces both Christian destination and implicit consolation, for those who remain, that the dead and the living are ultimately called to a home that is not of this earth.

Publication
Remembering and Other Verses, Melbourne: Australasian Authors Agency, 1917.

References

Edward E. Cleal and T.G. Crippen, *The Story of Congregationalism in Surrey*, London: James Clarke & Co, 1908, https://archive.org/stream/storyofcongregat00clea/storyofcongregat00clea_djvu.txt. Accessed 31 May 2016.

The Warn Family in Tetbury from 1722, *Phil Warn's Family Tree*, Person Page 135 [Betts and Noyes families]
http://homepage.ntlworld.com/philwarn/FamHist1/p135.htm#i5660 Accessed 1 June 2016

'Stow Memorial Church [Adelaide] Evening service "Jehoiada" by Rev. R.A. Betts', *South Australian Register*, Saturday 20 January 1900, p. 2.

F.G.A. Barnard, *The Jubilee History of Kew, Victoria: Its Origin and Progress 1803-1910*. Kew: E.F.G. Hodges, Mercury Office, 1920,
http://www.biostats.com.au/Kew/s16-churches.html Accessed 7 January 2016

'Chess Items', *Otago Witness,* 16 August 1900, p. 56 (T.H. Kirkpatrick vs Rev. R. Betts).

'Robert Betts', Edo Historical Chess Ratings, http://www.edochess.ca/players/p.178html
Accessed 1 June 2016 [Betts won against NSW in 1899 and 1900, and against Perth in 1900].

Argus, Thursday 24 October 1912, p. 12 [Rev. Robert Arthur Betts, A.T.S. appointed post of principal of the Congregational College].

'Death of the Rev. R.A. Betts', *Argus*, Wednesday 12 November 1913, p. 16.

Argus, Wednesday 12 November 1913, p. 1 [Death notice of Robert Arthur Betts].

Ballarat Star, Thursday 13 November 1913, p. 7 [Death of Rev. Robert A. Betts].

'The Rev. Robert A. Betts', *Leader,* Saturday 22 November 1913, p. 59.

Argus, Wednesday 10 January 1945, p. 2, and *Age,* Wednesday 10 January 1945, p. 6 [Death notice of Catherine Betts, eldest daughter of the late Rev. Robert Arthur Betts and Catherine A. Betts, on 8 January 1945].

'Betts Robert Wye: SERN 3604', Discovering Anzacs, http://discovering-anzacs.naa.gov.au/browse/records/104720 Accessed 2 June 2016 [AIF record of Robert Wye Betts].

Betts, Robert Wye, Lewisham War Memorials, by Local History and Archives Centre, Lewisham. http://lewishamwarmemorials.wikidot.com/person:betts-robert-wye Accessed 2 June 2016.

'Faithful Unto Death, Memorial Tablet Unveiled at St Andrews', *Mildura Cultivator,* Wednesday 6 February 1918, p. 5 [Memorial to Robert Wye Betts].

Graphic of Australia, Friday 23 November 1917, p. 14 [Review of *Remembering and Other Verses*].

Age, Saturday 10 November 1917, p. 6 [Review of *Remembering and Other Verses*].

Sun (Sydney), Sunday 30 December 1917, p. 15 [Review of *Remembering and Other Verses*].

Anonymous review, 'Some Charm of Song', *Sunday Times* (Sydney), 13 January 1918, p. 10 [Review of *Remembering and Other Verses*].

Margery Ruth Betts, 'The Little Brother', *Australasian,* Saturday 9 February 1918, p. 38.

Age, Saturday 10 October 1931, p. 4 [Death notice of Catherine Mary Betts, widow of Rev. Robert Betts].

Nosheen Khan, *Women's Poetry of the First World War.* Lexington: University Press of Kentucky, 1988, pp. 65-66.

Kerrie Handasyde, 'Anzac Theology and Women Poets Under the Southern Cross', *Colloquium,* vol. 49, no. 1, 2017, pp. 17-30, especially p. 25.

Vivien Newman, *Tumult and Tears: The Story of the Great War Through the Eyes and Lives of its Women Poets,* Barnsley: Pen & Sword History, 2016, pp. 161-162.

Mary Ruth Betts
The Laggard

They set their sails, and they sailed away,
For ever and ever and half a day,
Into the blue of the sunlit bay,
      The blue, of the sunlit bay.

But ere they went they spoke to me
Of a wonderful land beyond the sea,
With valleys peaceful and mountains, steep,
And rivers silent and swift and deep,
And flower-blest meadows and stars untold,
And mornings rosy and evenings gold,
And people happy and calm and wise,
And numberless babies with friendly eyes.
And that is the laud where the dreams come true,
Where stars, are silver, and days are blue;
Flowers underfoot, and (stars overhead.
Oh! follow, and come with us, they said.

But under my window a rose-tree grew
1 loved and tended the whole year through.
And a longing seized me, fraught with pain,
To see my rose-tree bloom again.
So I bade them leave me, and sail away;
Yet come again on another day.
And they sang as they went a light refrain,
That rose and fell and lifted again,
And their sails were as white as the driven snow,
And I loved them well as I watched them go
And a wind awaked on the golden sand.
And danced with the sea-poppies stately and grand.

The clouds are low, and the clouds are grey,
And a wind awakes o'er the moaning bay;
My watch is lonely and sad and long,
And I cannot remember the lilt of the song
Oh! boat of mine, come back again,
'Twixt lifting seas and drifting rain,
I'll follow over the sobbing tide—
The roses have budded and blossomed and died.
Never again—ah! well I know,
Though I fain must watch where I saw them go
For they've set their sails, and they've sailed away,
For ever and ever and half a day.
       For ever and ever and half a day.

Source: *Australasian,* Saturday 22 May 1915, p. 44.

Margery Ruth Betts
The Dreamers

Some have died for honour's sake, and some for love have died,
And all are gallant gentlemen, and all have shared our pride,
And each one has his token meet, and each one has his pay
The laurel or the blood-red rose we pluck for him to-day;
For one the laurel, one the rose, and cypress for them all,
All the gallant gentlemen who fight and laugh and fall.
But what the token, what the pay, and what the flower or bud
For those who died for just a dream that stirred their eager blood?

Oh! the world is fair to-day, to-day's the spring begun,
Sun-kissed winds that talk of flowers and winter past and done,
Happy roads that lead adown between the happy fields,
Earth adream of spring-time and all her brown breast shields.
The dear white heath's in bud again, the violet's nearly done,
Wattle-blossom's out again, forget-me-not's begun
Forget-me-not so blue for hope, and heath so white for truth,
And violet for the hue of kings, and wattle gay for youth.

All the flowers of spring for you, then royal hearts and young,
Who beat in gallant, fearless time to some sweet song unsung.
All the flowers of spring for you, oh, feet so shod in flame.
That went not forth at pride's command or passion's clarion claim.
And all the flowers of spring for you, who drew your dying breath
With lips unstained tor mother's kiss, whose first sweet love was death,
Who dared to stretch your young hands forth and take the Wine and Bread,
Of Him who through the ages long the hosts of youth has led.

Oh! the spring is here again, and all the ways are fair,
The wattle-blossom's out again, and do you know it there?
Does its scent wind through the night, the trembling stars between,
And breathe a sigh at heaven's gates for earth so dear and green?
Wattle-blossom is for youth whose songs are yet to sing.
Forget-me-not is blue for hope, and violet for a king,
And heath, the dearest of them all, she goes in white for truth—
And red for dreams unsilenced yet, the bleeding dreams of youth.

Some have died for honour's sake, and some for truth have died.
And all are gallant gentlemen, and all have shared our pride,
And each one has the token meet, and each one has his pay,
In poet's song, or woman's tears, or England's faith to-day.
For one the laurel, one the rose, and glory for them all,
All the gallant gentlemen who fight and laugh and fall—
But while there's still a flag to love, a love song to be sung,
The winds of spring shall sigh and sing of nought but you—the young.

Source: *Australasian*, Saturday 2 October 1915, p. 51.

Margery Ruth Betts
Called

'Oh, shining eyes, what have you seen?
And dusty boots, where have you been?
Coming up the valley-road, with twilight closing in,
There's the whispering road before,
Here's the lighted-open door;
Hasten, you, and cross the threshold
ere the goblin-hours begin.

Now tell me, laddie, where you took
For your mouth that stranger look.
Did you touch the rowan, boy? The little folk are strong.
Perhaps a little flight of wings
Brushed your lips, the happy things,
Set that way 'twixt words and silence
like the ending of a song.'

'I saw the bracken wet with dew
When the morning hills were blue;
I stooped and kissed it lightly in the silence of the morn.
Here's the very truth, I wis,
Naught has touched my lips but this.
Since I kissed you, mother, when I said
good-bye at dawn.'

'Oh, the shining eyes of him,
Like to turn the candle dim!
Tell your, mother, laddie, where your dear eyes stole that sheen.
Was it the little people now
You met upon the mountain's brow?
Speak, and tell your mother, boy,
what elfin thing you've seen.'

       'Mother, such a long way back
       Before I left the mountain-track,
I knew you set the candle high and opened wide the door,
       And when the last bend came in sight
       I knew I'd see the watching light,
If my eyes are shining, mother,
       that's the thing they saw.'

       'Now his cheeks are cold to kiss,
       Laddie, tell your mother this;
What strange thing befell you on the lonely way to-day?
       Did some elfin lady cold
       Steal your heart with fairy gold,
Fairy gold of her lone hair a gleaming
       through the twilight grey?'

       'Foolish mother mine, be still.
       Dusk is lone and grey and chill;
She has kissed me, darling, from the mountain-track to here.
       With her breath my cheeks are cold,
       Now you have my story told.
Does that content you, mother sweet,
       does that content you, dear?'

       'If it was but the dusk you saw,
       If it was but the lighted door,
If it was but the bracken that you lightly kissed to-day,
       Why should you kneel beside me so,
       Why should you bend your head so low;
Why should that sob catch up your breath
       and steal your words away?

  Oh, boy, the holding hands of you!
  It is your mother's dream come true;
She knew the way your hands would hold when you were grown a man.
  Look up and tell the truth to me,
  Oh, son of mine, look up and see,
Your mother's eyes can face the truth.
  Look up and know they can.'

  'Then, mother, take the truth you seek,
  For now it is the truth I speak;
It was the dead men kissed me as I came, adown the hill,
  The blessed dead who saw the Flag,
  And did not pause and did not lag.
It was the dead men's kisses, dear,
  that made my cheek so chill.

  And if my eyes have learnt to shine,
  Then here's the reason, mother mine;
Down mountain track and valley-road I heard the bugles blow.
  I saw the Flag all crossed with red—
  Oh, mother, I have blood to shed;
Oh, mother, where my heart has gone
  my feet are fain to go.'

Source: *Australasian,* Saturday 19 August 1916, p. 42.

Margery Ruth Betts
The Fulfilment

Most strange it is to think that you, my dear,
>   Who were so young, might bear for England's sake
The final pain and loneliness and fear,
>   The awful last renunciation make;
And in the surging passion of the fight,
>   And through the after-hours most dark and long,
Should in your body bear the pangs of right,
>   Broken against the wrong.

Could I have looked on you when you were dead,
>   When all the fight was fought and victory won,
Before the dust received your hands and head,
>   And sealed your eyes for ever from the sun,
I think I would have seen your eager face,
>   Still in a look of triumph, hushed and high,
And haughty in its final deathly grace,
>   As you were proud to die.

So sweet, so strange it was that God should take
>   The proud boy's dreams that thrilled your nights and days,
And pierced and left you, yet again to break
>   Like storm and singing down the dusty ways;
That He should claim those thoughts but known to you,
>   Those shining things, that were your trembling joy,
And in your very flesh should prove them true,
>   While you were still a boy.

Source: Margery Ruth Betts, *Remembering and Other Verses*, Melbourne: Australasian Authors' Agency, 1917, p. 12. [First appearance in 'The Victorian Independent'; also later reprinted in Mary E. Wilkinson, *Gleanings from Australian Verse: Poems of Manhood*, Melbourne: Whitcombe and Tombs, 1919, 1920.

Margery Ruth Betts
Liebknecht

Since Liebknecht, the German Socialist, was imprisoned for speaking the truth to his countrymen, he has three times attempted to commit suicide, leading one to wonder what treatment could have reduced a man of so fearless a temper to such a condition. The latest report states that he is now dying in a prison hospital.

And this is truth, oh Pilate! Truth to me
    Was as the sword with which I smote the wrong.
    It was my staff when ways were steep and long.
It was my dream, which yet should come to be
My pilot star above a stormy sea,
    The song which rang above my hours of strife
    And bound the broken measures of my life,
    The flag I followed while my feet were free.

And this is truth, oh Pilate! this at last—
    This cross by which I am upraised to die,
Above my Germany, by nails made fast,
    Hung with my wounds against the changing sky,
Upheld to sun and stars till lies be past,
    Higher than all the flags of earth are high.

Source: Margery Ruth Betts, *Remembering and Other Verses*, Melbourne: Australasian Authors' Agency, 1917, p. 23.

Margery Ruth Betts
The Maimed

By black, immeasurable hours of pain,
By terrors faced in silence and alone,
By strengths despoiled and weakness proved and known,
By clean, strong joys that will not come again,
By dreams forgone and horrors that remain,
By young desires laid low and hopes let go,
By all you know and all you have to know,
By stifled cry and slowly spreading stain,
By deep and sullen nights most slow to end,
By awful vigils kept in No Man's Land,
By these things numberless and measureless.
So far does this your sacrifice transcend,
All we can know or understand,
All we can reckon, measure, dream, or guess.

Source: Margery Ruth Betts, *Remembering and Other Verses,* Melbourne: Australasian Authors' Agency, 1917, p. 25.

Margery Ruth Betts
Busy as Newtown

The busy business man was trying to put a deal through on the 'phone on Christmas eve, but although he became impatient at the delay caused by the rush of work in the city exchange, he did not lose his temper. 'Busy?' he asked the girl who had answered in a work-weary voice. 'Busy's no name for it,' she answered. 'I'm as busy as Newtown.' The girl offered no explanation of her strange remark, and it was not for half an hour that the busy businessman awoke to a realisation of its meaning. Newtown is L on the automatic exchange.—Sydney *Sun*.

His wounded wait his saving help, 'midst smoke and shell and shot,
His mules are grazing at their will, their master heeds them not;
He's done his final mile with them, and all that he could do,
And now he is at Heaven's gates, helping soldiers through.

What though the way from here to there is strange and very far,
Beyond the outposts of the dawn, beyond the furthest star;
You need not fear the silences if, at the journey's end,
There waits a comrade's hail for you, the challenge of a friend.

Oh, new and lonely stranger-souls, who fare beyond the stars,
Who fought your way from out the flesh through bleeding battle-scars,
A comrade's voice shall call you friend, a comrade challenge you,
For Murphy is at Heaven's gates, helping soldiers through.

Source: *Richmond Guardian,* Saturday 5 January 1918, p. 6.

The poem also appeared in the following:
Port Fairy Times and Macarthur News, Thursday 10 January 1918, p. 4.
Gordon, Egerton and Ballan Advertiser, Friday 11 January 1918, p. 5.
Graphic of Australia, Friday 11 January 1918, p. 6.
Mildura Telegraph and Darling and Lower Murray Advocate, Friday 11 January 1918, p. 6.
Woodend Star, Saturday 12 January 1918, p. 4.

Narracan Shire Advocate, Wednesday 13 January 1918, p. 4.
Violet Town Sentinel, Tuesday 15 January 1918, p. 4.
Tungamah and Lake Rowan Express and St James Gazette, Thursday 17 January 1918, p. 8.
Upper Murray and Mitta Herald, Thursday 17 January 1918, p. 4.
Rosedale Courier, Thursday 17 January 1918, p. 4.
Bealiba Times, Friday 18 January 1918, p. 4.
Lismore, Derrinallum and Cressy Advertiser, Wednesday 23 January 1918, p. 9.
Myrtleford Mail and Whorouly Witness, Thursday 24 January 1918, p. 2.
Beulah Standard and Mallee and Wimmera Advertiser, Thursday 24 January 1918, p. 4.
Yea Chronicle, Thursday 24 January 1918, p. 6.

These newspaper printings of the poem carried the following introduction: This simply-written, levelly-cadenced Australian verse is from the pen of Margery Ruth Betts, a Victorian writer, who founds it upon the story of a sergeant reporting the death of Anzac's deathless 'Murphy' by saying: 'Murphy is at Heaven's gate, helping the soldiers through'. And it is too fine a story for any real Australian to question its accuracy.

Margery Ruth Betts
The Ghost

In August evening when the wattle's coming back
There on the Flanders fields, for one fair head they fold!
Oh the valley's dark, and the track's dark; but the farthest peak is gold.

Call to him, oh! call to him, beside the bend he knew.
Beneath the fairy wattle-tree, and there I shall be for you
May be on the Flanders flowers, for two blue eyes they hide!
The wattle's kiss, the wind's kiss, and another kiss beside.

Source: *Australasian,* Saturday 2 August 1919, p. 49.

Margery Ruth Betts
The Reckoning

Drown the weeping with the guns, never heed or hark,
    Talk in millions if you will, yet you must come to one,
You must hear a woman's voice, wailing down the dark,
    'Kaiser of Germany, give me back my son!'

Kaiser of Germany, let the guns boom out,
    Cling to all your panoply, crown and sword and throne,
Go where the crowds are waiting, go where people shout,
    Yet her voice shall follow you when you are alone.

Talk of tactics if you will, proclaim and justify,
    Talk of needful measures and of empire on the sea;
Through the martial music there shall ring a woman's cry:
    'Kaiser of Germany, give back my son to me!'

Ah! you could not hear it then, the bugles blew so loud.
    Martial splendour hath a voice more strong than woman's pain.
Stand up and take your meed, the shouting of the crowd,
    Let the banners float on high, the bugles sound again.

Yes, escape it while you may, for hear at length you must,
    Yet your sins shall find you out, the hour of lies be past,
'The spirit to the God who gave, the body to the dust,'
    Just as any man's, your doom shall stand at last.

And in the silence past the stars then truth shall have her way,
    When swords are sheathed, and flags are furled, and all the shouting done,
And there shall be no drums to drown the voice that then shall say,
    'Kaiser of Germany, make answer for her son!'

Source: Margery Ruth Betts, *Remembering and Other Verses,* Sydney: Australasian Authors' Agency, 1917, pp. 21-22; *The School Paper for Grades VII and VIII,* No. 226, August 1918, p. 103.

BEATRICE VALE BEVAN

Beatrice Vale Bevan. Photographer unknown. State Library Victoria.

Beatrice Vale Bevan (who also wrote as Mrs Willett Bevan) came from a family distinguished by intellectual, legal, medical and artistic achievements. Born in St Kilda in 1874, Beatrice was the daughter of Rachel Vale (née Lennox) and William Mountford Kinsey Vale (1833–1895). She was educated at the Presbyterian Ladies College at Melbourne, and in 1901 married the Reverend Hopkin Llewelyn Willett Bevan. The marriage was a union of two highly cultured, devout and public-spirited immigrant families.

Beatrice's father William and his brother Richard were sons of John Vale, bookseller of London and his wife Elizabeth (née Taylor). The brothers arrived in Australia in 1853 with their parents and sisters and settled at Castlemaine, setting up as booksellers. Richard soon went to set up business in Beechworth. William moved to Ballarat, before journeying back to England where he married Rachel Lennox. Having returned to Australia, William and Rachel established a large family in which Beatrice was affectionately called 'Trissie'.

William entered politics as a Liberal representative of Ballarat, and occupied a succession of portfolios including Commissioner of Public Works, and Commissioner of Trade and Customs. He sold up his Ballarat business and moved to Melbourne before travelling to England, qualifying as a barrister in 1878 and returning to Australia to practise law (sharing an office with Alfred Deakin), and winning the seat of Fitzroy. He was appointed Attorney General in 1880-81, and his reforming and promotional activities throughout the later quarter of the nineteenth century included provision of such intellectual establishments as a Public Library, a Museum and a National Gallery. A puritanical Congregationalist who nonetheless believed politics should have nothing to do with religion, he supported the establishment of the Victorian Alliance for promotion of Temperance, and was a founder of the Working Men's College. He died of Bright's disease at Collingwood in 1895, survived by three of his five sons and four of his five daughters.

William and Rachel Vale supported their talented children's aims. One of their sons, William, followed his father's profession in the law, and the daughters, widely acknowledged as intellectually gifted and public-minded, followed other paths. Grace graduated in Medicine from Melbourne University in 1894 and had a distinguished professional life as a practitioner in Ballarat and Melbourne and as a medical educator in Victoria and New South Wales. A promoter of women's suffrage and working women's organisations, she was a member of the Victorian Medical Women's Society that established the Queen Victoria Hospital for Women and Babies. Her sister May Vale was an artist and enameller who studied first in Australia, then at the Royal School of Art in London and the Académie Julien in Paris; back in Australia, she studied at the National Gallery School with George Folingsby and Frederick McCubbin. Her work is widely represented in the State and regional galleries in Victoria and in the Art Gallery of New South Wales. Her sisters Faith and Elsie (who was also an artist) established a private school at Mayfield, while Beatrice was esteemed as a writer and, as the Adelaide *News* put it in 1928, 'an artist of considerable merit', who had studied at the Melbourne Art Gallery with her sister May.

In 1923, Beatrice wrote a brief biography of the South Australian poet Mrs C.T. (Caroline) Carleton (1811-1874). Carleton, like Beatrice, was accomplished in music and several languages, and was married to a clergyman. In later years, Beatrice was a strong supporter of the League of Nations.

Bevan was fondly remembered by Gawler citizens, the local newspaper, the *Bunyip* reporting in an obituary note that her educational abilities 'were of very high standard' and her life 'one of graciousness and deep sympathy in all suffering'.

§

Beatrice's husband, Hopkin Llewelyn Willett Bevan (called Rev. Willett Bevan, or the Rev Hopkin Bevan, to distinguish him from his father), was born in 1871, the eldest son of the Reverend Dr Llewelyn David Bevan, an internationally renowned Welsh preacher who had served as a Congregational minister, first in England and then at the Brick Presbyterian Church in New York: his American friends included Ulysses S. Grant, Ralph Waldo Emerson, Oliver Wendell Holmes, and Henry Wadsworth Longfellow.

In 1886, the Revered Doctor Bevan came with his family to Australia to take up the position of Principal of Parkin Congregational College in Adelaide. He and his wife Louisa had seven children, of whom Beatrice's husband was one, and an adopted daughter. After a short period in Adelaide, the Reverend Doctor Bevan accepted an appointment as Professor of the Victorian Congregational College in Melbourne. The sons of the family were already known in their English and Australian schools as 'the brainy, brawny Bevans'. Their mother, Louisa, was also an intellectual with scholarly and musical interests; she illustrated and published hymns, was an accomplished linguist who had learned Greek and Sanskrit at the age of sixty, and in Melbourne in 1890, instituted a cultural circle called Daughters of the Court—of which Beatrice Vale became a member and thereby met her future husband.

In 1920, two years after her husband's death, Louisa Bevan wrote and edited *The Life and Reminiscences of Llewelyn David Bevan*. By the time the Reverend Dr Bevan died, his sons had taken up prominent positions across Australia. David John Davies Bevan was a judge (later Supreme Court Judge) in the Northern Territory; Willett Bevan (Beatrice's husband) was a minister in the Adelaide suburb of Woodville; Louis Rhys Oxley Bevan was a Professor of International Law at the Imperial University of Tai-Yuan Fu and later Peking University; and Dr Sybil Bevan (in Adelaide) was on the way to becoming a leading public health official in New South Wales. Another son, Dr Penryn Vaughan Bevan, Professor of Physical Sciences at the University of London, had died in 1913.

Louisa Bevan died at the Bevans' Victorian country home, 'Pen Bryn' in Upper Beaconsfield, Victoria, in 1933.

§

Beatrice's husband had been educated at St Paul's School and the Merchant Taylor School in London, and Melbourne Grammar School and Melbourne University, from which he graduated B.A. in 1893 and M.A. in 1895 with first class honours in philology. He studied theology at the Victorian Congregational College and at Marburg in Germany and Mansfield College, Oxford, before taking charge of educational work for the London Missionary Society in Shanghai in 1903 where he served as Principal and Headmaster of Medhurst College. In Shanghai, Beatrice served as President of the Ladies Auxiliary of the London Missionary Society, and otherwise assisted her husband's ministry and teaching activities.

Beatrice and Willett Bevan's only son, Medhurst Llewelyn Willet Bevan, was born in Shanghai, and they left China when he contracted tuberculosis in 1913. They left that year for South Australia, where Willett's parents had moved in 1910. Willett accepted a call to Kilkenny Congregational Church, where he stayed until 1919 when he was appointed to the Church at Gawler. He remained there until his death in 1933.

The Bevans' son Medhurst, who completed high school at Gawler and studied Law at Adelaide University, graduated in the same class as poet and future Chief Justice John Jefferson Bray in 1930. He worked as a journalist and lawyer, and when he married in 1935, Beatrice moved back to Victoria to live with her siblings Elsie, Faith, William and May, along with Faith's family, in Ardoyne Street, Black Rock on Melbourne's eastern bayside, where she died in 1945.

If Beatrice or Willett maintained diaries in China, they are not publicly available, though Beatrice's later poems recall her time in Shanghai and Japan, as a poem, 'O Tsuto San', published in the Adelaide *Observer* in 1917 exemplifies.

From the foregoing, it's clear that Beatrice Vale Bevan's families on each side were complementary in respect to intellectual interests and attainments. Her poetry is of its period, which is to say heavily accented with 'improving' sentiments and sentimentality. She wrote graceful hymns and devotional verse, and at the same time had a fine sense of humour and enjoyed light verse. In a letter to the Adelaide *Register* in August 1915, in answer to a correspondent who attributed the proliferation of poor quality verse to current circumstances, she wrote,

> Some little time ago a correspondent in *The Register* commented upon the present 'outburst of trashy poetry' (or words to that effect), and laid the responsibility upon the war. Last week, when I came upon the verses which I enclose, it occurred to me that the magazine therein referred to might have something to do with the 'outburst' of which your correspondent speaks: —
>
> 'Rabbit O!'
>
> My line, you know, is 'Rabbit 0,'
> But 'biz' was rather slack,
> 'Twas hard to find the cash to buy
> My clothes, and get a snack.
>
> One day I busted sixpence on
> A 'first class magazine,'
> And read the cutest article
> That I have ever seen.
>
> It said that any chap who liked
> Might dollars easy earn
> By writing verses for the 'Mags'
> If they would only learn.
>
> The little tricks called 'poet trade'—
> A dictionary use—
> (The poets!) and consult at once
> A woman called 'the Muse.'
>
> 'Why here,' thinks I, 'is luck indeed—
> The very thing for' me'
> I'll leave off crying "Rabbit O!"
> And take to poetry.'

Well, lidy, when I asked a chap
Where I could find 'the Muse'
He said things—I won't soil your ears
By speaking his abuse!

The poets' dictionary then
I sought, but found it cost
Enough to feed me for a month—
The thing was quite a frost.

That magazine I burnt, I think;
The trick it played was low.
I wouldn't waste time writing verse—
Hey, 'Rabbit—rabbit, 0!'

Bevan contributed verses to metropolitan Adelaide newspapers and journals, among them the *Advertiser, Chronicle, Register, Observer, Port Augusta Despatch, The Journal* and the *Express* and *Telegraph*; her poems were also reprinted across a broad range of regional and interstate papers including the *Mount Barker Courier and Onkaparinga and Gumeracha Advertiser,* and the *Argus.*

The major poem reproduced for this collection, 'The Worn-Out Sentry', an artfully constructed though intensely 'improving' narrative subtitled 'A Vision', relates the events observed by a sentry at the end of his tether during a cold night: the 'stranger' who approaches is spared even though he refuses to answer to the soldier's 'Qui vive?' The sentry relates in stream-of-consciousness manner how he gives the stranger his coat and, as the dawn breaks, sees the sleeper bearing the lineaments and wounds of Christ. The poem alternates between initial suspenseful anticipation of the stranger's death at the hands of the sentry, and a peaceful resolution in the sentry's refusal to kill an unarmed fellow man. The setting and events generate a dream-like atmosphere in keeping with the unreality of the 'vision' and the wishful moral of the tale. Some of the shorter poems also attest to a profoundly religious conviction. The poem 'Passed—with honour' celebrates another unexceptional combatant's more ordinary 'vision' of duty, and the poem 'I wonder are there many (such / as she!)' is one of the most poignant post-War love and loss poems. In her letters to newspapers, Bevan repudiated the 'white feather crusade' conducted by anonymous persons against men who for reasons of their own did not enlist; her empathy shines through all her writing.

Other poems in Bevan's 1922 collection *Sketches in Verse and Prose* range from wartime topics to flowers, tapestry, friends (a series of 'Portraits'), and Christmas. Among martial themes are the poems 'Previously Reported Dead' (pp. 23-24), 'The Song of the Sandbags' (pp. 27-28) in which eloquent sandbags sing how they stop bullets meant for the soldiers, and 'Final Leave' (pp. 28-30), a galloping poem of a man taking leave of his horse so he can go and defend France and Belgium. A concluding 4-line prayer to the 'Lord of Empires' voices a wish that the Southern Cross keep the 'other Cross' always in sight, so we can 'live aright' (p. 45).

Publications:
Mrs Willett Bevan, *Sketches in Verse and Prose,* Adelaide: W.K. Thomas, n.d. [1922].
Mrs Willett Bevan, *Adam Lindsay Gordon* [a play], Sydney: Robert Dey, n.d. [1938].
The Unknown Warrior [Sequence from *The Unknown Warrior*]. Adelaide: Mrs Willett Bevan, 1942.

References
Niel Gunson, 'Bevan, Llewelyn David (1842–1918)', Australian Dictionary of Biography, National Centre of Biography, Australian National University, http://adb.anu.edu.au/biography/bevan-llewelyn-david-5228/text8799, published first in hardcopy 1979, accessed online 24 March 2018.
Dirk Van Dissel, 'Parkin, William (1801–1889)', Australian Dictionary of Biography, National Centre of Biography, Australian National University, http://adb.anu.edu.au/biography/parkin-william-4367/text7101, published first in hardcopy 1974, accessed online 16 January 2016.
Joy E. Parnaby, 'Vale, William Mountford Kinsey (1833–1895)', Australian Dictionary of Biography, National Centre of Biography, Australian National University, http://adb.anu.edu.au/biography/vale-william-mountford-kinsey-4770/text7931, published first in hardcopy 1976, accessed online 24 March 2018.
Hope and Fear: An Anthology of South Australian Women's Writing, 1894-1994, Anne Chittleborough, Annie Greet & Sue Hosking, eds, Adelaide: Centre for Research in the New Literatures in English, 1994, p. 7 [Brief account of Bevan's career].
'Grace Vale, 1960-1933, Doctor, Suffragist', Collingwood Notables. http://collingwoodhs.org.au/view/collingwood-notables/entry/175/ Accessed online 24 March 2018.

'William Mountford Kinsey Vale, 1833-1895, Bookseller, barrister, Member of Parliament, Protectionist', Collingwood Notables. http://collingwoodhs.org.au/view/collingwood-notables/entry/177/ accessed online 24 March 2018.

'May Vale, Portrait of the Artist's Father, William Mountford Kinsey Vale', https://www.artistsfootsteps.com/html/Vale_artistsfather.htm Accessed 24 March 2018.

'William Mountford Kinsey Vale Protectionist; Politician, Bookseller, Barrister', *Newsletter Friends of St Kilda Cemetery Inc.*, January 2017, p. 3.

'Church Intelligence. New Congregational College: Arrival of Rev. Dr Bevan'. *The Advertiser* (Adelaide), Monday 21 February 1910, p. 5.

'Chinese Problems. Religious and Social. Interview with Rev. H.L. Bevan', *Daily Herald* (Adelaide), Monday 18 August 1913, p. 3.

Mrs Willett Bevan (Beatrice Vale Bevan), 'O Tsuto San (From Songs of the East', *Observer,* Saturday 28 July 1917, p. 2.

'Rev. Dr Bevan Dead. A Remarkable Career'. *Register,* 20 July 1918, p. 7 [Obituary for the Reverend Dr Llewellyn David Bevan].

Mrs Willett Bevan (Beatrice Vale Bevan), 'Enlistment', *Register,* 18 May 1915, p. 11 [Bevan writes against anonymous 'white feather crusade' proponents].

Mrs Willett Bevan (Beatrice Vale Bevan), 'Trashy Poetry', *Register,* 6 August 1915, p. 3.

Argus, Wednesday 9 October 1918, p. 1 [Family notices: death notice of Rachel Vale of 50 Shaftesbury Parade, Northcote, on 6 October 1918].

'Mrs Bevan, Poetess Resident of Gawler. New Verses to be Published', *News* (Adelaide), Tuesday 11 September 1928, p. 11.

Bunyip, Friday 27 November 1931, p. 3 ['Social and Personal'; Llewellyn Bevan graduates LL.B.].

Advertiser, Monday 21 December 1931, p. 67 ['New Lawyers': Medhurst Llewelyn Willett Bevan admitted to Bar].

Chronicle (South Australia), Thursday 4 January 1934, p. 51 [Obituary of Rev. Hopkin Llewelyn Willett Bevan].

'In Memoriam. Rev H.L. Willett Bevan', *Bunyip* (Gawler), Friday 12 January 1934, p. 5.

'Beatrice Vale 1876-1945 Poet, missionary in China', Collingwood Notables, Collingwood Historical Society Inc, http://collingwoodhs.org.au/view/collingwood-notables/entry/311/ Accessed 7 April 2018.

Argus, 11 April 1945, p. 2 [Death notice of Beatrice Vale, widow of the late Rev. Willett Bevan, of Gawler, S.A., and Shanghai, China].

Argus, Friday 13 June 1947, p. 31 [Law Notices: Medhurst Llewelyn Willett Bevan granted probate of Beatrice's estate].

Beatrice Vale Bevan
Previously Reported Dead
From 'Country Etchings'

'Twas the time of Christmas lilies,
With the poppies all aglow,
And the corn was all aturning,
On the hillside, just below,
And I leaned against the sliprail,
And I laughed and tossed my head,
And I said I'd have my fling first or ever I was wed.

'Tis the time of Christmas lilies,
And the poppies come again,
And the corn is all aturning,
On the hill, as it was then;
But my heart is hurt to breaking,
Since I laughed, and tossed my head,
And said I have my fling first—or now my lad is dead!

'Twas the time of Christmas lilies,
But the drought had spoiled their bloom,
And the cattle, all were starving,
And the war had brought its gloom.
But I danced, and laughed, and flirted;
Oh, I laughed, and tamed my head;
But my lad, he up and 'listed, and now my lad is dead!

'Twas the time of Christmas lilies,
Oh, how white, and straight they stand!
And the poppies all ablooming,
And the harvest will be grand;
And, last night, I danced and flirted,
Yes, I laughed and tossed my head;
But my lad was slain in battle, and my heart with him is dead!

O, you white, white, Christmas lilies,
And you poppies rosy red.
Corn on hill-side golden turning,
Far away my lad lies dead!
Never will he come awhistling,
Pull a blade, or pluck a bloom,
Where he lies I cannot go to put sweet blosssoms on his tomb.

O my lilies, O my poppies,
O my golden-turning corn.
Does the wind, awhispering through you
In the glory of the morn
Softly breathe to you my secret?
Or the birds, while flying by,
Tell the news my heart is singing, that my brave lad did not die?

Source: *Register,* Saturday 5 February 1916, p. 4; *Observer* (South Australia) Saturday 12 February 1916, p. 4.

Beatrice Vale Bevan
Passed—with Honour!

'You! a dreamer with a vision!'
Cried his form, in great derision.
'Dreams won't pass exams, old chap!'
'Wars aren't fought upon a map,'
Said a master. 'Wake up, boy,
Such as you would take no Troy!'
But he slowly plodded on,
Made no dash—no prizes won.
'Why, the fellow never crams
When it's getting near exams!'
This the verdict of his class
When he got a simple 'pass.'
But that boy of dream and vision
Met his death with brave decision.
Cheered his comrades in the fight,
And his 'visions', gave them light.
One with sorrow's crown upon her,
Hears that he has 'passed-with honour!'

Source: *Fitzroy City Press,* Saturday 18 March 1916, p. 1.

Beatrice Vale Bevan
The Worn-Out Sentry: A Vision

Here in the darkness of the night I stand
And wait! For what? The shadows close at hand
Seem to grow denser, and my quickened ear
Catches the sound of someone creeping near.
Was that a shot which broke the stillness there?
My nerves are jangled! I, who once would dare
Face any terror clam and undismayed—
Leap to meet danger—stand here sore afraid.
God! How I tremble, head to foot am wet,
Shiver with cold, although I reek with sweat.
Fain would I be again in thickest fight,
I hate this waiting in the lonely night,
Waiting for—God knows what, not I.
Ah, who is this? 'Tis someone drawing nigh.
Halt, or I fire! The password! Who goes there?
If enemy, then say a final prayer.
No password? Then surrender, or I fire!
My God, I cannot. Gone, my power, desire—
I cannot slay. Then shoot me, man, have done—
And God forgive us both, for Christ, His Son!
Forgive me if I fail to do the right,
Neglecting duty at my post tonight.
Oh! Must I slay? 'Twere better he slay me—
But that would leave the post I'm guarding free—
Free for the enemy to enter in.
O God, direct me, keep me free from sin
'Gainst mine own honour, country, King, and Thee.
Come out from yonder darkness, man! I see,
Yet see not. Give the password, quick—
This waiting in the darkness makes me sick.
God, I *must* shoot! I cannot bear suspense!
I see the moving yonder by the fence—
Creep through the fence. Now nearer! Now, the word
Speak louder! Louder still! I have not heard.
Yes, I must shoot— my duty now is clear!

A child! Good God, what art thou doing here?
Fled from the enemy? Nigh slain by me
Here in the darkness where I could not see!
Well, I will guard thee, little one; lie here,
Wrapped in my coat, and know that I am near.
Sleep, little one! My strength hath come gain;
Maybe thy presence doth relieve the strain!
Sleep, and my terror fled, I watch will keep.
Wait! Say a prayer, child, ere thou fall'st asleep!

* * * *

From out the darkness of the clouds the moon
Hath crept. 'Tis three, and morning will be soon!
A strange child this, and yet what manly grace!
How wan and sad the moonlight shows his face,
More like a man's than child's! I notice now
Queer markings on the whiteness of his brow!
Who is this child whose form lies like a cross,
Who hath preserved me from disgrace and loss?
Whence hath he fled? And from what enemy?
As I lean closer, what is this I see
Upon the palms which lie so whitely there?
And are those brambles tangled in his hair?

Source: Mrs Willett Bevan, *Sketches in Verse,* Adelaide: W.K. Thomas & Co Print, 1922, pp. 22-23.

Beatrice Vale Bevan
[Untitled] 'Lord God of Empires, now we raise'

Lord God of Empires, now we raise
To Thee a song, of joy and praise;
We give Thee thanks for love and care,
For all Thy blessings everywhere.

Lord God of Empires, pain and woe
Into each life must come, we know;
To gain the joy must pain be borne,
To reach the rose we grasp the thorn.

Lord God of Empires, sun and rain
Are Thy good gifts, and joy and pain;
Our lives are fashioned on Thy plan
Who wiser art than wisest man.

Lord God of Empires Lord of, all,
Teach us this truth, that though we crawl
And drag through wastes of misery,
The path of anguish leads to Thee.

Lord God of Empires, give us peace!
From war's alarms grant us release!
While for Thy love and care we raise
This Empire Day our song of praise.

Source: *Register*, Thursday 24 May 1917, p.6.

Beatrice Vale Bevan
[Untitled] 'I wonder are there many'

> They deplored his loss. But so many had gone; so many had been deplored. Human nature is only capable of a certain amount of deploring while retaining its sanity.—William J. Locke.

I wonder are there many (such
As she!) deplore their loss too much?
All that she was and had she gave!
I planted violets on her grave,
And Jean, the French girl, wrote that she
Had planted to his memory
The woodland violets, where he lay.
The thought has come to me today
That he and Margaret, hand in hand,
Perhaps, are walking, in that land
Where, so they say, the heavenly flowers
Shed perfume through the blissful hours.

Those lovers! He who fought and died;
And she, who with brave patience tried
To fill her life with work to be
Comfort in others' misery.
To do her duty, live, and smile,
And keep her sanity, the while
Her heart was broken, and its pain
Proved for her strength too great a strain!

The war is over! There are blanks
In life! But you (returning thanks!)
Can pin upon the coat lapel
Of him who came from—yes—from hell—
The flower which grows beside your door
(Which Margaret but last winter wore),
Which means, 'The more I see of you
The more my heart to you is true.'
'The more I see, the more I love!'

And, he and Margaret, now above,
(Since heaven's above?) no loss deplore,
But love each other more and more!
Why say we 'dead?' 'Immortal dead!'
'Immortal living!' some have said,
When was this violet in my hand,
When summer scorched and dried the land?

Source: *Register*, Friday 20 June 1919, p. 9.

MARION BRAY

Marion Adeline Bray was the daughter of Emilia Selina Adeline Amelia Frederica Bray (née Sturt) and Captain Norman Alton Bray. Collateral descendants of the Bray family place Marion's date of birth around 1885. Marion had one brother named Norman, named after her father, a Lieutenant (later Adjutant) in the Omagh-based Royal Iniskillen Fusiliers, which had served in the Straits Settlements and Madras. Her father, who had risen from the rank of Lieutenant and Adjutant in 1879, to Captain, died in Burma on 5 April 1891, of sunstroke.

Marion Bray counted among her forebears Augusta Sturt, daughter of Henry Sturt (who joined the Royal Navy in 1813 and served as Captain in North America and the West Indies from 1843). She was also a niece of the explorer Captain Charles Sturt (1795-1869) and Charles's brother Evelyn Shirley Pitfield Sturt (1815-1885), sons of a judge in Bengal under the East India Company. Charles had arrived in New South Wales in 1827 and embarked on exploration the following year. Evelyn arrived in New South Wales in 1836, served as commissioner for crown lands but gave up his commission to establish a sheep and cattle station and overland sheep and cattle. In 1849, he accepted an appointment as Victoria's first Police Magistrate and Superintendent of Police, a position he held until 1878.

The Sturt women were highly conscious of their family's distinguished English and northern Irish connections: the Sturt family had lived in Dorset for generations and included many notable civil (including Parliamentary), military and naval figures in the male line. Marion's mother, who died in 1939 at the age of 82, lived for a time with Marion at Ivanhoe, as did Marion's aunt Charlotte Theresa Jane Sturt, who migrated to Australia from Dorsetshire in 1889 and died aged 88 in 1941 at Ivanhoe. At the time of her death, Charlotte was the sole surviving niece of Charles and Evelyn Sturt, and her obituaries also noted that she was a cousin of Lord Alington (Henry Gerard Sturt) and a kinswoman of Lord Napier of Merchiston.

Marion Bray was postmistress of the eastern Melbourne rural district of Rosanna, where she owned eight acres and leased another two hundred, on which, in 1914, she ran forty cattle. Marion acted as tutor: a history of the locality records that she and her mother lived diagonally across from the residence of W.C. Davies, his wife Eleanor and their daughter Yvonne ('Bonnie), whom Marion tutored as governess until Yvonne commenced school at 'Coerwull' (later Ivanhoe Grammar).

On Bray's sudden death at her home on 29 November 1947, her friends paid tribute to her in press notices.

As a poet, Bray contributed sparsely to the *Leader* and other newspapers during the War. Her early patriotic verse was highly conventional in its imperial and religious sentiment and archaic diction, as the poem called 'Peace', published in the *Leader* in November 1914 attests. Bray was given to coinages that read—and often rhyme—very awkwardly: a case of too much striving for poetical effect. By 1922, another poem, 'Wind o' the wild that bringeth', published in *Art and Letters: Hassell's Australian Miscellany,* indicates continued adherence to the tepid conventions of late Victorian language and form. Marion Miller Knowles, reviewing the poems contained in *Melba's Gift Book* in August 1915, wrote that 'Marion Bray's "Socks" is likely to have many a line of it inserted with soldiers' comforts. It is simple but effective'—a comment that aptly measures Bray's modest accomplishment.

References:

Bray Families, http://members.dodo.com.au/~nevmoya/bray%20families2-o/p157.htm Accessed 3 June 2016 [For details of dates for Norman Aiton (sic) Bray and Marion Adeline Bray].

'Henry Richard Sturt, Esq, Commander', Royal Naval Biography, https://en.wikisource.org/wiki/Royal_Naval_Biography/Sturt,_Henry_Richard, accessed online 15 April 2018.

'Sturt, Henry Charles (1795-1866), of Crichel House, Wimborne Minster, Dorset', The History of Parliament, http://www.historyofparliamentonline.org/volume/1820-1832/member/sturt-henry-1795-1866, accessed online 15 April 2018.

Army Lists—1839-1915—Hart's Army Lists—1894-1901—New annual army list, militia list and yeoman cavalry list—1895, http://digital.nls.uk/british-military-lists/archive/102695965 Accessed 15 April 2018 [for gazetting of Norman Alton Bray].

The Colonies and India and American Visitor; A Weekly Journal of General Information https://www.newspapers.com/newspage/35677629/ Accessed 15 April 2018. [for report on Saturday 2 May 1891, p. 17 concerning death from sunstroke, of Captain Norman Acton Bray, 2nd Battalion of Royal Inniskilling Fusiliers D.A.Q.M.G., at Edawgyi near the Jade Mines, Burma].

H. J. Gibbney, 'Sturt, Charles (1795–1869)' Australian Dictionary of Biography, National Centre of Biography, Australian National University, http://adb.anu.edu.au/biography/sturt-charles-2712/text3811, published first in hardcopy 1967, accessed online 4 June 2016.

Alan Gross, 'Sturt, Evelyn Pitfield Shirley (1816–1885)', Australian Dictionary of Biography, National Centre of Biography, Australian National University, http://adb.anu.edu.au/biography/sturt-evelyn-pitfield-shirley-4663/text7709, published first in hardcopy 1976, accessed online 4 June 2016.

Rosanna Views, http://www.wikinorthia.net.au/rosanna-views/ Accessed 3 January 2016.

Heidelberg News and Greensborough and Diamond Creek Chronicle, Saturday 11 July 1914, p. 3.

Age, Wednesday 1 November 1939, p. 1 [Family Notices: Funeral Notices relating to Adeline Bray].

Argus, Wednesday 12 February 1941, p. 4 [Death and Funeral notices relating to Charlotte T. J. Sturt].

Argus, Tuesday 2 December 1947, p. 9 [Death and Funeral Notices relating to Marion Bray].

Marion Miller Knowles, 'The Ladies' Page', *Advocate* (Melbourne), Saturday 28 August 1915, p. 33.

Marion Bray, 'Wind o' the wild that bringeth', *Art and Letters: Hassell's Australian Miscellany,* Edward A. Vidler, ed., Adelaide: Hassell, 1922, p. 47).

Marion Bray
Peace

Peace is not resting on slothful abandonhood,
    Under the iron walls painfully, raised.
Through the slow years with tears and warm life blood,
    Thy shelter a name the dead centuries praised.

While o'er thy barriers unanswered, unheeded,
    Drifted the cry where the helpless go down,
Withholding thine aid where most it is needed;
    This is not peace, though ye call it thine own.

That nation shall give its peace—coronation,
    To the war-weary world that uses aright,
Unmindful of blame of false adulation.
    Her glorious name and her God-given might.

Shall it be thou, little mother of nations?
    Encradled amid the rough billows of strife,
Restless and free as the ocean there surges,
    The blood of thy sons and the war-clouds are rife.

War through the earth spreads her dread conflagrations,
    Ah, who would have thee stand idle aside?
Daughter of fortune and mother of nations,
    Heaven be thy keeper and duty thy guide!

                        Rosanna, Vic.

Source: *Leader,* Saturday 14 November 1914, p. 52.

Marion Bray
Socks

Oh, soldier brave, I thought of you,
As to and fro my needles flew,
As stitch by stitch my knitting grew;
Of you and all who bear the brunt
Of modern warfare's dread affront.

'God bless my brothers at the Front,
In pride of race no fear have I
That heart should fail or courage fly;
I know that thousands greatly die
That other thousands nobly live.

Thy peace, oh Lord, Thy mercy give
To those who fall, to those who strive
That we in safety may abide.'
God keep thee, friend, whate'er betide
For whom this little task I plied.

                        Rosanna, Vic.

Source: Franklin Paterson, ed., *Melba's Gift Book of Australian Art and Literature*, Melbourne: George Robertson, 1915, p. 24.

MARY BRIGHT

Mary Charlotte Arnold Carwardine was born in 1869 at Sandhurst [Bendigo]. She was one of eleven children (and elder of two daughters) of Walter Henry Carwardine (1833-1923), and his wife Elizabeth Arnold née Thorpe (d. 1911, aged 70).

Three of Mary's siblings (John, Thomas, and Albert Augustus) died in infancy. The children who survived were, in order, Henry (Harry) Thorpe Carwardine, Hugh Wilcox Carwardine, Guy Carwardine, Mary Charlotte Arnold Carwardine, Rose Elizabeth Carwardine, Walter Henry Carwardine, James Arnold Carwardine ('Arnold'), and George Frederick Brunsdon Carwardine.

Mary's father had commenced business on the Dunolly goldfield as a merchant before establishing a soap and candle enterprise in Bendigo in 1868, and his eldest son Harry in time assisted him as manufacturer and traveller for the company. Guy Carwardine (1867-1943) married Minnie Lansell (1863-1954), a member of the prominent Sandhurst family of William Lansell. The Carwardine commercial enterprise prospered, and during the South African War, the family was generous in providing comforts for Victorian troops serving abroad, a practice they maintained during the First World War.

In 1866, Mary's father had been a founding member of St Paul's Church in Bendigo where, on 22 September 1891, Mary married Luther Edwin Goldsmith Bright, a commercial traveller who was the son of Alfred Bright and Sophia (née Jacobsen) Bright of Chapel Street, South Yarra. Mary and Luther moved to 27 Perth Street, Prahran, where they lived until 29 July the following year, when Luther died at their home at the age of 27. Less than three months later, Mary bore her only child, John (Jack) Goldsmith Bright, at her parents' house in Charleston Road, Bendigo on 24 October 1892.

Further tragedy dogged the Bright and Carwardine families in following years. On 8 February 1896, Luther's sister Nellie Sophia Bright died at the age of nine of tubercular meningitis at South Yarra. Several relatives were to die in the First World War, and another death occurred closer to home, when Mary's oldest brother Harry, who had become manager of the family business, was killed on Monday 9 October 1916, when a dog attacked him while he was riding his bicycle close to his home in Bendigo.

Several members of the Carwardine and Bright families enlisted in the AIF during the First World War. Mary's youngest brother George Frederick Brunsdon Carwardine, an accountant with the Colonial Bank at Benalla, enlisted on 31 November 1915, served with the 24th Battalion, and was killed in action at Villers-Bretonneux on 2 August 1916, aged 28. He had embarked from Australia in February of that year, a month after his brother James, who was ten years older, had embarked. James survived the War with the rank of Acting Sergeant, and died at Heidelberg, Victoria, in 1947.

Mary's son Jack, who had enlisted in the AIF on 22 June 1915 and been promoted to Lance Corporal, was killed in action on 8 December 1916. His cousin, Harry Carwardine's son Eric, who had enlisted on 13 January 1916 and served in the 6th Battalion in France, returned to Australia on 21 July the following year. Mary's nephew Reginald Jack Bright, who enlisted on 18 April 1916 and served as a driver in the 37th Battalion in France, was killed on 29 March 1918. Many other members of the Carwardine and Bright families who had enlisted were more fortunate.

A joint memorial notice on 18 December 1917, in the Melbourne *Argus,* for Mary's son Jack and his cousin George Carwardine, bears the stamp of Mary Bright's embrace of Indian religious thought. The quotation that concludes the notice is taken from the *Bhagavad Gita* (verse 27), where Krishna instructs Arjuna how to dispel grief and assures him of the immortality of the soul: 'Certain is death for the living, and certain is birth for the dead; therefore over the inevitable thou shouldst not grieve'. On the death of her brother Guy, in July 1942, the same consoling text she had caused to be added to the death notice of her son Jack appeared in the death notice in the *Argus.*

Mary's mother had died at her home in Charleston Road, Bendigo, in May 1911. Mary's father Walter died at the age of 90 in 1923 at the residence of his son Arnold at Caulfield.

Mary died at a private hospital in Bendigo on 6 September 1942, fifty years after the death of her husband, and her ashes were interred in his grave in St Kilda Cemetery.

§

Mary turned increasingly to Indian spirituality and the Christian religion in the years after her son's death. She joined a Liberal Catholic congregation to which she donated a monstrance in memory of her brother and her son. In September 2014, at the Liberal Catholic Church of St John the Beloved at Glen Iris in Victoria, Russell Cole, while cleaning the Monstrance, found an 'In memoriam' inscription on the base, for 'George Carwardine and Jack Bright, killed in France 1916. George Frederick Brunsdon Carwardine 28 killed at Villers-Bretonneux 2.8.1916. Reginald Jack Bright 21 killed at Doullens 29.3.1918. Presented by Mary Bright'.

Her poetry also reflects the intensification of thought. Her 1926 volume, *Poems to the Master,* published in India by the Theosophical Publishing House, contained a note of optimism that flowed through subsequent volumes *Open Sesame* (1940), *Palladium,* (1941) and *Sappho's Lyre* (1942). The first of these did not make overt reference to the First World War, nor did her later books specifically address the Second World War. All three volumes expressed gratitude for life and consolation for loss. Poems occasionally take the form of hymns to the 'Beloved', sometimes addressed as her 'Friend celestial' or 'Father-Mother'. Christ, the Buddha, Isis, the Great World Mother, and other message-bearers and gods are conflated in such a way as to suggest unity of all beings and redemption for humanity. Redolent at times of the language and shifting passions of Francis Thompson and other late-Victorian and early twentieth century English Catholic poets, Bright's language draws on the assurances of Christian, Theosophical and Indian texts.

Her 1940 collection, *Open Sesame*, is dedicated to Kitty Williams, her 'friend of many lives', and images of rebirth abound throughout the poems: flowers, trees, insects, and birds, along with poems addressed to the dawn and evening reinforce her belief in life after intense suffering and further, life beyond the terrestrial span. Several poems make overt reference to transcendental beliefs and religious lore. Her 'Ode to a Flower' intimates a previous existence in which she saw 'the Master's flower' in Elysium. Bright also invokes Sappho, as exemplar of the intensity of love, and her poem 'To Kitty' speaks of her friend as a sharer in a dream of such 'perfect love'. Bright's examples of other-worldly love include the soul's yearning for unity with God, and the love of God the Father for the Son. In a 'Hymn to the Beloved' in *Palladium* (pp. 49-50) she writes,

> What though my life seem dark with care?
> In deepest solitude, Most Fair,
> Beneath the bitter, angry tears,
> The pain, the woe, the sorry fears
> Thou hidest. 'Neath the smart, the sting
> Of hate and passion Thou dost cling
> With eager eyes to Thine own Son,
> With whom forever Thou art one.

An overarching theme, sometimes pointedly stated, of her last book, *Sappho's Lyre,* is thankfulness for the restoration of her will and capacity to write poetry, her chief consolation, in spite of what she calls, in a poem titled 'Eclipse' (dated '10.11.1919–40'), the 'awfulness, the hideousness' of 'this dark, sin-struck age':

> What sayest thou? My poetry lacks merit,
> Is foolishness, is idle, upstart pride?
>   If it were not for Poesy my spirit
>   Were lost in nothingness—my soul had died.
>
> . . . . .
>
> 'Twas my salvation. It would be pure madness
> If I, a Poet, ceased my song to sing.
>   If I sang not, my country, starved, to sadness
>   Would straightway fall—I should betray my King.

('The Poet Protests', *Sappho's Lyre*, p. 75)

It is this refusal to surrender to self-pity or to retreat from the world that makes Mary Bright's self-aware poetry unique. Rather than surrender to loss or dwell on political cause and effect, she endorses for the creative impulse that refuses madness. For resoluteness to win through dark times, and for the sheer number of reprises of the theme of salvation through poetry, Mary Bright's voice is unique in assertion of life through and beyond immense personal loss.

She continued to write and read her poetry to professional and other organisations until her death.

§

Mary Bright's poems with more direct reference to the War and its effects were contained in her 1938 collection, *The Song of the Happy Warrior*. The title overtly echoes Wordsworth's 1807 poem 'The Character of the Happy Warrior', written on the death of Lord Horatio Nelson, and enumerating the qualities of such an exemplar, 'skilful in self-knowledge', faithful and compassionate, who 'makes his moral being his prime care'.

Bright's book is structured in seven sections, whose reverential tone, vocabulary and orthography are established by the rousing opening dedication:

> O glorious Christ! Immortal
> Giver of light and truth!
> Accept the gift we offer,
> This song of endless youth
> And of the Happy Warrior
> Who fought so fearlessly
> That Thou o'er shame and evil
> Might'st have the victory!

The adoption of the collective pronoun, the identification of the Allied victory with Christ's triumph over evil, and the sense that the poems constitute an oblation, will all be reprised in the ensuing poems. Bright's visionary linking of Anzac, redeemed mankind, Australia's 'election' or manifest destiny, and Christ's sacrifice and millenarian reign make her collection a sort of gold standard against which other effusions on the significance of Australia's participation in World War One can be measured. Bright's section titles establish a liturgical framing for the entire collection: 'The Dreamer'; 'The Kiss of the Gods'; 'The Well-Beloved'; 'Motherland' (including three poems specifically addressed to England); 'Peace'; 'Australia Felix, and 'The New Race'.

The first 47 poems specifically concern Gallipoli, with a bonus 'Anzac Day Sermon 1919' (p. 48), a 'Credo' (p. 18), 'Dulce et Decorum' (p. 50), 'Joy Cometh in the Morning' (p. 33), 'The Judgment of Osiris' (p. 30) and 'The Young Gods' (p. 55). These poems dealing with the abstract lessons of the war are interspersed with poems like 'Blinded by a Shell' (p. 52) and 'Pozières' (p. 67), where realism and literalness replace Bright's characteristic urge to find transcendent qualities and import in every aspect of the Gallipoli campaign, the war in general, and the soldiers' demeanour.

Publications

Mary C.A. Bright, *Poems to the Master,* Chennai, India: Theosophical Publishing House, 1926.

Mary Bright, *The Song of the Happy Warrior,* Melbourne: Robertson and Mullens, 1938.

Mary Bright, *Open Sesame,* Melbourne: Stuart Taylor, 1940.

Mary Bright, *Palladium,* Melbourne: Stuart Taylor, 1941.

Mary Bright, *Sappho's Lyre,* Melbourne: Brown, Prior & Anderson, 1942.

References

Mary Bright, *The Song of the Happy Warrior,* Melbourne: Robertson and Mullens, 1938 (Dedication, p. 3).

Victorian Registrar of Births Deaths and Marriages, Registration No. 24844 birth of Mary Charlotte Arnold Carwardine.

'Carwardine Walter married Elizabeth Thorpe 1863'. Familytreecircle. http://www.familytreecircles.com/carwadine-walter-married-elizabeth-thorpe-1863-38732.html Accessed 14 April 2018.

'Jubilee of St Pauls. Story of its Progress', *Bendigonian,* Thursday 7 November 1918, p.8 [Walter Henry Carwardine is recorded as one of the ten-member building committee of St Paul's Church, Bendigo.]

Argus, Monday 10 March 1884, p. 5 [Report on Walter Henry Cawardine's award for soap manufacture, at the Calcutta International Exhibition, 1884].

Argus, 24 September 1891, p. 1; *Bendigo Advertiser,* Saturday 26 September 1891, p. 2; *Australasian,* Saturday 3 October 1891, p. 46 [Marriage of Luther Edwin Goldsmith of South Yarra and Mary Charlotte Arnold Carwardine of Bendigo].

Bendigo Independent, Friday 22 April 1892, p. 3 [Marriage of Guy Carwardine and Minnie Lansell on 21 April 1892].

Argus, Saturday 11 July 1942, p. 2 [Family Notices: Death of Guy Carwardine, aged 74 at Cohuna].

Bendigo Independent, Saturday 30 July 1892, p. 2; *Bendigo Advertiser,* Saturday 30 July, p. 4 [Death of Luther E.G. Bright].

Bendigo Advertiser, Saturday 5 November 1892, p. 7; *Bendigonian,* Saturday 5 November 1892, p. 46 [Notices of birth of Bright's son].

Argus, Monday 10 February 1896, p. 12 [Death of Nelly, youngest daughter of Alfred Goldsmith and Sophia Bright].

Argus, Monday 16 October 1916, p. 1 [Death of Harry T. Carwardine at Bendigo].

'Obituary, Harry Cawardine', *Bendigonian,* Thursday 12 October 1916, p. 26 [Report of death of Harry Cawardine, aged 52].

Argus, Saturday 6 January 1917, p. 1; *Bendigonian,* Thursday 11 January 1917, p. 7 [Report of death of John Bright in action].

'Australian Composers' and Writers' Association, Melbourne', *All About Books,* vol.9, no. 9, 13 September 1937, p. 146 [Mary Bright reads 'particularly strong' verses about the war at an Association meeting on 10 August].

Argus, Saturday 18 July 1942, p. 2 [Death notice of Guy Cawardine, at Cohuna, Victoria, on 10 July].

'Obituary. Mrs Mary Bright', *Age,* Thursday 10 September 1942, p. 3. [Other notices in *Argus,* Tuesday 8 September 1942, p. 2—death of Mary C.A. Bright, aged 72; Also *Argus,* Friday 11 September 1942, p. 1].

Mary Bright, 'The Song of the Cicadas', *The Adyar Theosophist,* vol. 51, September 1930, p. 375.

Australian Composers' and Writers' Association, Melbourne, *All About Books,* vol.9, no. 9, 13 September 1937, p. 146 [an instance of Mary Bright's reading from her verse at a meeting of the Association on 10 August 1937].

'Parish Happenings', *Harbinger* [newsletter of St John the Beloved church, Glen Iris], no. 52, September 2014, p.1. http://www.liberalcatholicchurch.org.au/Newsletters/vic/Vic14_3_Sep.pdf

William Wordsworth, 'Character of the Happy Warrior', *The Poetical Works of William Wordsworth,* Thomas Hutchinson & Ernest De Selincourt, eds, London: Oxford University Press, 1950, pp. 386-387. Wordsworth's poem continues to provoke single and multiple-authored collections (including a 1919 Tasmanian YMCA volume) of war-related verse bearing his poem's title. A recent example is Paul Barrett and Kerry B. Collison's *The Happy Warrior: An Anthology of Australian and New Zealand Military Poetry,* Hartwell, Victoria: Sid Harta Publishers, 2012.

Mary Bright
Blinded by a Shell

Up from the trench they bore him, caked in mud,
Smothered by slimy filth, his comrades' blood.
He dreamed of Melbourne, of a sunny lane
Bordered by wattles—he was home again.
A kookaburra laughed not far away—
He wondered would the blighters let him stay.
Sudden an anguished voice rang out, so clear—
"Blind! O, not blind, not blind! My dear, my dear!"
"Whom do they mean?" he murmured, "not,—not me?
Why, I can see quite plainly; that gum tree;
Those bluebells over there—and what is that?
A tiny mushroom! Yes, they knocked me flat.
I'm all right now!" He rose up in his bed,
Then fell back trembling. "I am blind!" he said.

Source: Mary Bright, *The Song of The Happy Warrior,* Sydney: Robertson & Mullen, 1938, p. 52.

Mary Bright
The Song of the Women

What, we afraid to send you forth to die!
And did you not, the men we cherished so,
Sons, husbands, fathers, give to fear the lie,
Then why should it be ours? There was no foe
Could steal your strength, your liberty, your fame,
Steal your great hearts, your love for us, your own—
Could we let grief and sorrow bring you shame—
Dark vultures brooding o'er a Monarch's throne,
Cast a great shadow on you, on your land?
That you had coward Women none shall say.
Rather, like Sparta's boy, each good right hand
We offered to some ravening beast of prey.
Courage triumphant banished all our fear.
'Twas soon forgotten—honour was too dear!

Source: Mary Bright, The Song of *The Happy Warrior,* Melbourne: Robertson and Mullens, 1938, p. 84.

Mary Bright
Pozières

We filled our bags with water
And with aching heart and brain
    Into the deadly trenches filed,
    To face the fight again,
The flies, the lice, the rats, the mud;
And every ugly name
    We could we called old Pozières,
    There where we earned our fame

We didn't find much glory
When we left our Austral home.
    We found more squalor and more dirt
    Than ever graced old Rome.
We couldn't speak the language
And we couldn't find our mates.
    They were all scattered far and wide
    Through death's untimely gates.

Many had gone. We who were left,
The remnant of our band,
    Were not too sorry when they called
    Us to the Better Land.
They tell us to some happy home
We shall again be sent.
    It may be—only time can tell—
    What! Sorry that we went?

We didn't want to die—for fame
Nor glory did we care.
    We had to go, our country called—
    We did but do our share.
We had to fight—for England,
For her honour, for her fame.
    We did the only thing we could,
    You would have done the same!

Source: Mary Bright, *The Song of the Happy Warrior,* Melbourne: Robert

Mary Bright
Credo

I believe in the spirit of Anzac,
    And may it forever abide,
Till it flows through the whole of Creation
    Like a terrible, wonderful tide.
Till it floods every soul with its beauty,
    Till it fills every heart with its song;
And that is the only true Credo
    For which an Australian need long.

I believe in the spirit of Anzac,
    The spirit which ever inspires
All those who are willing to suffer—
    The spirit which lighted the fires
That blazed on the hot sands of Egypt,
    France, Belgium, Gallipoli's heights.
The spirit of all who are ready
    To turn down their own little lights.

I believe in the spirit of Anzac,
    The spirit of Do and of Dare.
The spirit of him who is striving
    Himself with all others to share.
That is a creed worth defending,
    Worth living and dying for—aye,
A Creed no man need be ashamed of,
    A Creed for which all men might die!

Source: Mary Bright, *The Song of The Happy Warrior,* Melbourne: Robertson & Mullens, 1938, p. 18.

MURIEL BEVERLEY COLE

Muriel Beverley Cole was born at 'Westfield', Armadale Street, in Armadale, Victoria on 3 January 1888. She was the sole daughter and eldest of four children of Mary Blanche Cole (née Young, born 1863), formerly of Dundas Station, in the western Victorian district of Coleraine, and London-born John Francis Cole (born c. 1859), bank manager of the London Chartered Bank of Australia at Colac, Victoria. John and Mary had married on 9 February 1887 at Mary's mother's home at 338 High Street, Windsor.

Muriel's forebears had been exemplary go-getters. Her grandparents on the Young side were pioneer residents of Tasmania and Victoria. In 1825, her grandfather Thomas Young, with several siblings and his parents, William (1794-1865) and Rachel Young (1792-1866), emigrated from Scotland on the ship *City of Edinburgh* to Van Diemens Land, where, in the course of a visit, Governor Macquarie granted William five hundred acres of land.

In 1839, William, in partnership with fellow Tasmanian landowner Dr Adam Turnbull, was granted a lease of 36,840 acres at Mt Koroite and Dundas Stations in western Victoria, and the Young family, now numbering nine children, removed there in 1846.

Muriel's grandparents, Thomas Young and his wife Belinda (née Bunster), were married in Campbell Town in Tasmania in December 1848. Thomas had been born in Edinburgh in 1823, and his wife Belinda (née Bunster) in London in 1825. Like William and Rachel before them, Thomas and Belinda Young became parents of nine children, of whom Muriel was the seventh. She and her siblings were brought up in the expansive pastoral ambience of Dundas Station, which her father and his brother George would inherit on the death of the patriarch William.

When William died in 1875, Thomas and George Young ran Dundas, under the name T. and G. Young. At one time, the brothers found themselves in court, defending their overly-fastidious managerial style against the grievances of long-term employees, who were found by the court to have been underpaid. Thomas Young died in 1876, and the *Hamilton Spectator* newspaper reported his personal wealth at his death as £6250. The paper also noted Thomas's relationship with the then Lord Chief Clerk of Scotland, Lord George Young, his first cousin.

The Young family retained Dundas Station, which had changed from leasehold to freehold in 1873, into the twentieth century, and they acquired residential addresses in Melbourne; Thomas's widow, Belinda, died at the age of 97 in Malvern. The family also kept up contact with close relatives abroad: Muriel's sisters Ada Louisa and Alice Christie Young were sent to live with their uncle James Bynon and his wife between 1877 and 1882. (Bynon, a Vice-Admiral in the Chilean Navy, was married to Belinda Young's sister Jane Bunster.)

§

Muriel's father, John Francis Cole, came from quite another background, but one nevertheless closely associated with finance. Born in London about 1859, John Francis arrived in Australia at the age of twenty-one and embarked on what would be a distinguished career in banking. Employed from the outset at the City of Melbourne Bank, he successively worked as an accountant in branches of the London Chartered Bank in Sydney and Melbourne, and at the time of his marriage to Muriel, was manager of the Colac branch of the London Chartered Bank of Australia. At the peak of his career, he was a leading member of the Masonic order (Master of the Duke of Manchester Lodge), and had built up what his peers considered one of finest branch businesses in Victoria.

The year after his retirement, John Francis Cole died at Blackburn in 1923. Mary Blanche Cole, his widow died on 6 January 1963, aged 102, at the family home 'Tasma' at 32 Avoca Street in Elwood, and was buried beside her husband at Box Hill Cemetery.

§

Muriel's three brothers worked in banking, and the two oldest served in the Australian forces in World War One.

Victor (Sydney Thomas Victor Cole), born in Sydney on 6 December 1894, was first to enlist. He had been educated at Church of England Grammar Schools in Sydney and Melbourne, and worked in the Sunshine branch of the Bank of New South Wales from 1912 until he moved to the Flinders Street West branch on 17 March 1914 and then the Bourke Street Melbourne office on 6 August 1914. He enlisted in the AIF on 4 August 1915 and served in Egypt before transferring to the

Australian Flying Corps in 1917. Appointed First Lieutenant in number 3 Squadron AFC, he served in England until his return to Australia in 1919. His appointment ended on 14 January 1920.

Victor's older brother, Russell (Louis Vivian Francis Russell Cole, born in 1891), enlisted on 4 January 1917 and worked as a bank officer before joining the Australian Army Pay Corps. He embarked from Sydney on 30 April among a contingent of reinforcements for the Field Artillery Brigade, and served in England until war's end.

Muriel's youngest brother, Vernon (George Francis Vernon Cole, born in 1905), was employed by the Commonwealth Bank, of which he was an executive manager by 1928. It was his distinction to have registered in his own name the design of the Commonwealth Savings Bank moneybox in the shape of the bank's head office building in Sydney, and to have registered a map of Australia in his own name. In this respect, he followed in the vein of his forebears Thomas and George, attentive custodians of their personal financial interests.

After their sister Muriel's death in Mont Park Hospital, Macleod, Victoria in Melbourne on 3 August 1947 all three brothers continued to commemorate their sister, in annual newspaper notices.

§

Cole's poetry gives small hint of, let alone attention to, her family heritage, education, or her personal circumstances. Her monograph publication, *Australian Gum Leaves* was produced as a fundraiser for the Wounded Soldiers' Fund. Three editions appeared in 1915-1916. The individual poems in the volume were widely published in capital city and provincial newspapers. Melbourne *Table Talk* magazine reported on a patriotic fair held in Prahran in 1916 and included a short appraisal of the collection:

> *Australian Gum Leaves* is a little booklet of verse by Muriel Beverley Cole, launched upon the sea of publicity to gather something towards the Wounded Soldiers' Fund, to which all the proceeds go. The verse ranges from good to indifferent, and the metre at times halts, but it has the true ring, and the best is good indeed. It is a little paean of patriotism from first to last, and some of it deserves wide publicity. 'The Sigh of Anzac' has a good rhythm,

and the sentiment will echo in the hearts of Australasians. 'Oh! Southern Cross! In Australasian skies, symbolic of our young land's sacrifice', is the opening, and later it is described as Anzac Cross. 'Christmas Hymn' is beautiful, and will surely form the earnest prayer of one and all. Again, 'Ora et Labora' voices the inmost thoughts of Australian women, probably of the women of all countries whose men are fighting. 'Louvain' expresses a beautiful thought, also 'Love Conquers Death.' 'Oh, England' gives voice to a widespread feeling, while 'Oh! Come on, Australia!' has the right rousing ring for a rallying call. There are other verses, but these are the best, any one of which is worth the sixpence asked for the entire booklet. On the cover is a memorial wreath of gum-leaves and blossom, on which appear the names Anzac, Dardanelles, Gallipoli, Lone Pine, Sari Bair, Achi Baba, and Cape Helles. (p. 27)

I include the poem 'Oh! Come on Australia' as a prime instance of the sort of effusion that Barry Humphries called innocent Austral verse (in his collection of the same title).

Publications
Muriel Beverley Cole, *The Appeal of the Rose Sellers.* Melbourne: Shovelton and Storey, 1915 [poem on single sheet published for Belgian Relief Fund].
Muriel Beverley Cole, *Australian Gum Leaves,* Melbourne: Shovelton and Storey, 1915 [16 page pamphlet; two further editions appeared in 1916].
Muriel Beverley Cole, *After the War,* Melbourne: Specialty Press, 1917.

References:
Birth Certificate of Muriel Beverley Cole, no. 366/148 (Victorian Registry of Births Deaths and Marriage, Births in the District of Armadale in the Colony of Victoria).
The Telegraph, St Kilda, Prahran and South Yarra Guardian, Saturday 14 January 1888, p. 5 [Family Notices: records birth of a daughter to wife of John Francis Cole, at Armadale, on 3 January 1888].
From Edinburgh to Hobart Town: The Young and Murray Families, http://www.cocker.id.au/murray/young_family.php Accessed 3 March 2018 [for information about ancestry and extended family of Thomas and George Young].
'Mr Thomas Young', *Hamilton Spectator,* Saturday 28 October 1876, p. 3 [Obituary].

'Our Letter Home', *Hamilton Spectator,* Tuesday 23 January 1877, p. 2 [Thomas Young's will proven and personal estate valued at £6250].

'Mount Koroite Homestead Complex', http://vhd.heritagecouncil.vic.gov.au/places/23420. Accessed 24 April 2018 [Heritage listing of property originally owned by William Young].

'About People', *Age,* Thursday 18 January 1923 [Obituary of John Francis Cole].

Argus, Friday 25 February 1887, p. 1 [Family notices: Marriage of John Francis Cole, son of Lewis Cole of Windsor, to Mary Blanche Young, son of late Thomas Young of Dundas, Coleraine, at the bride's mother's house by Rev. Charles Strong].

Hamilton Spectator, Saturday 26 February 1887, p. 2 [Family notices: Marriage of John Francis Cole and Mary Blanche Young, youngest daughter of the late Thomas Young].

Australasian, Saturday 5 March 1887, p. 3 [Family notices, marriage of John Francis Cole and Mary Blanche Young].

The Young Family: From Edinburgh to Hobart Town: The Young and Murray Families, http://www.cocker.id.au/murray/young_family.php Accessed 23 April 2018 [details of Muriel Young's ancestry].

'Cole, Sydney Thomas V. (1894–1968)', People Australia, National Centre of Biography, Australian National University, http://peopleaustralia.anu.edu.au/biography/cole-sydney-thomas-v-23514/text32539, accessed 5 March 2018.

'Sydney Thomas Victor Cole', Anzacs Online. http://anzacsonline.net.au/2011/11/cole-sydney-thomas-victor/ [Includes a photograph of Sydney Thomas Victor Cole in AFC uniform]. Accessed 5 March 2018.

'Cole, Sydney Thomas Victor', Pictorial WW1 Honour Roll of Victorians, http://ww1vic.gravesecrets.net/co.htmlCole, Accessed 23 April 2018 [War record and photograph of Lt Sydney Thomas Victor Cole, 3rd Squadron AFC].

WWI Pictorial Roll of Honour of Victorians. http://ww1vic.gravesecrets.net/ Accessed 5 March 2018 [War record of Sydney Thomas Victor Cole].

'Getting Ahead of the Savings Bank', in 'Puffs, Pars, & Personals', *Freeman's Journal,* Thursday 20 December 1928, p. 15 [concerning Vernon Cole's registration of the Commonwealth Bank money-box, and a map of New South Wales, in his own name].

Melbourne Table Talk, Thursday 6 April 1916, p. 27 [Report on Prahran fundraising fair, and notice of *Australian Gum Leaves*].

Argus, Monday 4 August 1947, p. 9 [Funeral notice of Muriel Beverley Cole, by brothers Vernon, Russell and Sydney, and sisters in law Bebe [sic] and Wyn].

Argus, Tuesday 3 August 1948, p. 2 [Family notices: memorial notice of Muriel Beverley Cole by brothers and sister-in-law Bebe].

Argus, Friday 4 August 1950, p. 16 [Family Notices: memorial to Muriel Beverley Cole by bothers and sister-in-law Bebe].

Muriel Beverley Cole
The Allied Dead

Hail to the dead who nobly died.
Whatever their race, whichever their side,
So long as they stood by the light within,
However they, lost they were bound to win.
For each must answer at God's own call,
And by his answer alone, can fall.
Whether 'tis German or Turk or French
Or Russian, dying to save his trench,
God is General over us all;
He's raising an army—for peace instead
Of war—the Host of the Allied Dead.

Source: Muriel Beverley Cole, *Australian Gum Leaves*, Melbourne: Shovelton and Storey, 1916, np [p. 4].

Gippsland Independent, Buln Buln, Warragul Berwick, Poowong and Jeetho Advocate, Friday 22 September 1916, p. 6.
Dunmunkle Standard, Friday 22 September 1916, p. 5.
Evelyn Observer and Bourke East Record, Friday 22 September 1916, p. 5.
Gisborne Gazette, Friday 22 September 1916, p. 5.
Camperdown Chronicle, Saturday 23 September 1916, p. 6
Maldon News, Tuesday 26 September 1916, p. 4.
Euroa Gazette, Tuesday 26 September 1916, p. 1.
Bewick Shire News and Pakenham and Cranbourne Gazette, Wednesday 27 September 1916, p. 4.
Malvern Courier and Caulfield Mirror, Friday 29 September 1916, p. 3.
South Eastern Times (South Australia), Friday 6 October 1916, p. 5.
Gundagai Independent and Pastoral, Agricultural and Mining Advocate, Thursday 23 October 1916, p. 7.
Beverley Times (Western Australia), Saturday 6 January 1917, p. 1.
Laverton Mercury (Western Australia), Saturday 10 February 1917.

Muriel Beverley Cole
In Memory. 63rd Regimental Ball

This time last June
Our hearts were free from care,
Our flying feet kept tune
And music thrilled the air.
This time last June,
With hearts so light and gay,
We never guessed how soon
Life's Joy would pass away.
This time last June
Our dreams were wondrous fair;
But this time last June,
Who thought of Sari Bair?

        June 26th, 1915

Source: Muriel Beverley Cole, *Australian Gum Leaves,* Melbourne: Shovelton and Storey, 1916, n.p. [p. 8].

Muriel Beverley Cole
Oh! Come on Australia!

Oh! Come on Australia!
They rush to meet the foe,
Not driven into battle,
Australia's heroes go.
On! Come on Australia!
Advance Australia fair,
To live up to her motto:
Australia must be there.
On! Come on Australia!
To far Gallipoli;
There's no such word as failure
With such a battle cry.
On! Come on Australia!
We coo-ey back reply:
We're coming on Australia,
To do and dare-or die.
On! Come on Australia!
'Twill echo down the years,
When war is but a memory
of sacrifice and tears.

Source: *Gippsland Times,* Monday 23 July 1917, p. 4.

Muriel Beverley Cole
The Sign of Anzac

Oh, Southern Cross, in Australasian skies,
Symbolic of our young land's sacrifice,
Shine on our way, and keep our faith still pure,
And give us strength, our sorrow to endure.

Oh, Southern Cross—how like that other one,
Whereon was crucified God's only Son,
How many only sons have died that we
Might still call ours the Land of Liberty.

Dear Southern Cross! Their love of thee and home
Was intermingled, till it grew as one;
And when strange stars oft woo'ed them with bright eyes,
Thine, brighter still, looked down from memory's skies.

Than Anzac Cross, what fitter name could be
To mark our loss and keep their memory
Each time we saw thee in our Southern skies—
A monument of stars to their great sacrifice.

What, tho' they sleep in foreign, unnamed graves,
Who died for home and thee;
Their fame, emblazoned on the "Anzac Cross,"
Shall live eternally.

22/2/16.

Source: *Argus*, Wednesday 23 February 1916, p. 7; subsequently reprinted in the following:

Cobram Courier, Thursday 7 September 1916, p. 7.
Evelyn Observer and Bourke East Record, Friday 8 September 1916, p. 5.
Dunmunkle Standard, Friday 8 September 1916, p. 5.

Gippsland Independent, Buln Buln,Warragul Berwick, Poowong and Jeetho Advocate, Friday 8 September 1916, p. 5.
Camperdown Chronicle, Saturday 9 September 1916, p. 6.
Euroa Gazette, 12 Tuesday 12 September 1916, p. 1.
Maldon News, Tuesday 12 September 1916, p. 4.
Malvern Courier and Caulfield Mirror, Friday 15 September 1916, p. 3.
Camberwell Citizen, Friday 22 September 1916, p. 3.
South Eastern Times (South Australia), Friday 22 September 1922, p. 6.
Gundagai Independent and Pastoral, Agricultural and Mining Advocate, Thursday 12 October 1916, p. 7.
Beverley Times (Western Australia), Saturday 23 December 1916, p. 1
Laverton Mercury (Western Australia), Saturday 27 January 1917, p. 3.

Muriel Beverley Cole
The Journey's End

I've watched them come for two long years,
    The happy ones returning;
And smiles have had to conquer tears
    That in my eyes were burning;
For as I bid them Welcome Home
    At the journey's end,
I wonder when my turn will come
    To welcome home a Friend?

But still they come, so still I go;
    And sometimes I pretend
And look for one among them who
    Reminds me of a friend.
Then, smiling, put my sweetest flowers
    Into his hands—Oh, Friend!
He little knows for whom he stands
    At the journey's end.

Source: Muriel Beverley Cole, *After the War,* Melbourne: Specialty Press, 1917, n.p. [11pp.].

[This attractively got up pamphlet is dedicated 'To Our returning Brave'. A poem on page 10 ('Kitchener's Men') asks if Kitchener still has the men whom he urged to enlist in his thoughts. Kitchener is supposed to reply that God gave him his choice, and 'I chose, by the Power of Love, / To lead you to vanquish the Foe.']

Muriel Beverley Cole
1918

I hear the mourning of a broken People
        Whose hearts beat high with hope four years ago,
Whose flower of youth and chivalry went forth
        With heads triumphant held to meet their foe.

They heard the children singing as they passed
        Thro' flower-strewn streets, where women's blessings fell
Upon the heads of warriors who turned
        To smile once more on those who wished them well.

Ah, Glory! Flower that springs from War's red seed.
        Men follow gladly when thy call they heed;
But, oh, the desolation in thy train!
        The hearts that break—the eyes that watch—in vain!

Oh, God of Love, in pity steep our hearts!
        Teach us to build, not break; to heal, not kill;
To gather up the fragments of the world
        And bind them closer still.

I hear the mourning of a Broken Nation
        That, had Fate turned the scales by just a breath,
Might well have been Our Own—the desolation,
        The bitterness—more bitter far than Death!

Source: Muriel Beverley Cole, *After the War,* Melbourne: Specialty Press, 1917, n.p. [p.14].

MARTHA COXHEAD

Photo credit: J. Ward Symons Studio, Footscray, 1916.
Courtesy of Maxwell Coxhead

Martha Alderson Coxhead (1864–1947) was the daughter of Thomas Alderson, born in Hurworth, Durham in 1822, and Elizabeth Mary Alderson (née Dann, 1834-1912). Her father was the joint owner of a vineyard that produced communion wine, at Bet Bet, a district that included Dunolly and Tarnagulla but is now part of the Central Goldfields Shire.

Martha's parents married at Bet Bet in 1861, and they had six children, of whom Martha was the second. She had an older brother, Edgar, and four younger siblings: Mary, Thomas, Susan and William. While some members of the family moved elsewhere, Thomas and Elizabeth remained in the district, Thomas dying at Dunolly in February 1906, and Elizabeth in 1912; both are buried in the Dunolly Cemetery.

Martha married Sandhurst-born George Robert Coxhead (1856-1943) in 1883. His father ('old George'), born in Godalming in Surrey in 1824 or 1825, had married Ann Arnold (born around 1831) in 1854 before migrating to Australia the following year on the emigrant ship, *Shand*. Family sources report that George the elder worked in forestry at Dunolly and elsewhere. Ann died at Footscray in 1899 and old George followed in July 1907.

§

Martha and George Coxhead had two daughters and seven sons. Harold Arnold, their first child, born in 1884, died at the age of three. The following children were Annie Victoria Mary (1885-1937, who married Arthur John Tomkins in 1911), Ivan Dann (1887-1931), Eric James Major (1890-1928), Edwin [Ted] Thomas George (1892-1950), Alan Robert Gad (born 1895), Roger Alderson (1897-1960), Ronald Septimus Hungerford (1900-1934), Lawrence Joseph Louis ('Lou', born 1902), and Amy Alma ('Alma', born 1905, who married Keith Charles White in 1936).

The family lived in the Footscray and Williamstown districts; Martha and George's residence appears on the Victorian Electoral Roll for the years 1903 to 1921 as Melbourne Ports, then Maribyrnong from 1922 to 1943 (the year in which George died at Footscray). Martha's son Ivan ran a boot shop at Footscray, and all the family were active in community, church and charitable activities. Alan Coxhead was involved in sporting (tennis and other) clubs and organisations. Martha was an accomplished organist, but in her later years was confined to a wicker wheel chair and could use only one arm, the result, so her descendants suspect, of a stroke.

Martha died on 13 July 1947 at her daughter Amy's house at Williamstown, where the Williamstown Church of Christ pastor, J. E. Searle led the funeral service. The burial took place at the Footscray cemetery, where Martha's father-in-law and husband were buried—and where the poet John Shaw Neilson had been buried in a grander civic ceremony in 1942.

The death notice for Martha in the *Williamstown Chronicle* referred to her extant family as a daughter and five sons; the *Argus* listed their names as Eric, Edwin, Alan, Roger, Louis and Alma.

§

According to family sources, three Coxhead brothers migrated to Australia in the nineteenth century; one (George) settling in Sydney, another in Melbourne, and the third in New Zealand. In World War One, five men with the name Coxhead, three of them brothers, served in the New Zealand Army: Rifleman Cyril Henderson Coxhead; Lance-Corporal Edward Frederick Coxhead; and Rifleman Norman Soward Coxhead. The Anzac bond was doubtless more than an abstraction to Martha's family.

Though the date of publication of Martha's book, *Lost, a Continent!: Heroes of Anzac and Verses,* is usually given as 1917, it was listed by the *Argus* newspaper as available for sale at Cole's Book Arcade in October 1916.

Coxhead's topical verse shows a sense of appropriate poetic style for handling public occasions. Tennyson, John Greenleaf Whittier, Henry Newbolt, Rudyard Kipling and other public-spirited poets, along with the Rossettis, Francis Thompson and other poets of spiritual or religious sentiment, shape the tone of Coxhead's wartime poems.

Barry Humphries included the title poem of Coxhead's volume, along with 'To the Kaiser', 'It's a long way from dear Australia', 'Toll the bell mournfully' (a lament for Edward VII), and four poems relating to children, as instances of what he considered Martha Coxhead's unwittingly hilarious verse, in *The Barry Humphries Book of Innocent Austral Verse.* This did her no great service. Impelled by a sustained humanitarian impulse, Coxhead aimed high, and, if, as the *Age* reviewer of 14 October 1916 observed, 'her sentiments are often trite, and her vocabulary is largely conventional, her work reveals a healthy sympathetic mind, together with a fine patriotism and an ability to depict the simple virtues in a pleasant, attractive way'. On 18 November 1916, the Ballarat *Courier* newspaper was more appreciative, noting that in Coxhead's foreword to her book, 'she lays no claim to any serious pretensions as a poet but this does not limit her many beautiful expressions in sympathetic verse. At the same time, there is more of the consolation of religion displayed here than the hopefulness of an optimistic spirit'. The *Courier* also remarked that most of the work was written in 'purely lyric or ballad metre, and makes easy reading. Several hymns are worthy of inclusion in any form of religious worship, while throughout there is evidence of a thoroughly patriotic spirit'.

The reviewers' comments were judicious, and they can as easily be applied to much of the wartime poetry of the period, and to much of the popular verse that preceded Coxhead's appearance in print. Instances of unconsciously bathetic verse occur in the output of many canonical poets from Wordsworth to the present. Coxhead's 'innocent' verse is in good company alongside the lyrics of William Blake's *Songs of Innocence* and, perhaps most obviously, much of the patriotic verse, including hymns and national anthems, of Coxhead's Australian and British contemporaries.

I include Coxhead's poem 'The Friend of the Wounded' in the present volume as a signal example of 'vision' poems based on reports of supernatural phenomena experienced by servicemen on World War 1 battlefields. In similar vein, Beatrice Vale Bevan's poem, 'The Worn-Out Sentry: a Vision', which I also include in this anthology, is another contribution to the genre. (Myra Morris's 1918 collection *England and Other Verses* contains a poem, 'Expiation', in which a benighted and dying soldier is imagined stumbling upon a stone and wooden crucifix by the roadside. As his strength departs, the soldier becomes aware that the figure of the Christus speaks to him and that he will die shriven of 'mortal sin'. I have omitted that poem: one can have too much of a good thing.)

Dreams and visions, whether spiritual or psychological in nature, are far from rare in the poetry of male wartime poets as well. Wilfred Owen's 'Strange Meeting' is a famous instance. The Australian soldier-poet Leon Gellert included more than one vision or dream poem in his 1917 volume *Songs of a Campaign,* a collection rich in old-fashioned 'poetical' jargon and references to various afterlife experiences. Do I let Coxhead off lightly? I hope so. I think her imagination and her convictions much underestimated.

Among her non-poetry writing is an account of the 'haunted castle' at Maribyrnong.

Publication
Lost a Continent!: Heroes of Anzac and Other Verses, Melbourne: Modern Printing, 1917.

References

Martha Alderson Coxhead. Find a Grave http://www.findagrave.com/cgi-bin/fg.cgi?page=gr&GRid=125143958 Accessed 7 June 2016.

'Ruths, Kealys, Clancys, Lyalls, etc', Rootsweb, https://wc.rootsweb.ancestry.com/cgi-bin/igm.cgi?op=GET&db=marycotter&id=I95327571' Accessed 7 June 2018 [information about George Robert Coxhead 1856-1943].

Jan Bassett, *As We Wave you Goodbye: Australian Women and War*. Melbourne: Oxford University Press, 1998.

Thomas Alderson (1822-1906), https://www.wikitree.com/wiki/Alderson-233 Accessed 7 June 2018.

Elisabeth Janson et al., 'Pioneer Families in Victoria'. http://mepnab.netau.net/c/c30.html Accessed 7 January 2016.

Argus, Saturday 14 October 1916, p. 4 [Notice of publication of *Lost, a Continent! Heroes of Anzac and Verses*].

Age, Wednesday 12 May 1943, p. 6 [Death notices: Death of George Robert Coxhead on 11 May 1943].

Williamstown Chronicle, Friday 18 July 1947, p. 2 ['Obituary: Mrs M. Coxhead'].

Argus, Monday 14 July 1947, p. 18 [Family Notices: Death of Martha Coxhead].

Age, Saturday 14 October 1916, p. 4 [Review of *Lost! A Continent: Heroes of Anzac and Other Verse*].

Courier (Ballarat), Saturday 18 November 1916, p. 4 [Review of *Lost! A Continent: Heroes of Anzac and Other Verse*].

Barry Humphries, *The Barry Humphries Book of Innocent Austral Verse*, Melbourne: Sun Books, 1968.

Leon Gellert, *Songs of a Campaign,* Sydney: Angus & Robertson, 1917: 'The Moving of the Shades' (p. 7); 'The Trumpets of Heaven; (p. 21); 'Dreams of France' (p. 37); 'War!' (p. 65); 'Fever' (pp. 88-90); The House Delirious' (pp. 91-96); and 'The Soul Forsaken' (pp.115-116).

John Coxhead, private communication, 31 March 1918; Maxwell Coxhead, private communication (email), 1 April 2018.

Robert Cameron, ATL Docs 101814_Information on NZ WW1 soldiers. https://robertcameron.files.wordpress.com/2014/08/atl-docs-010814.xls Accessed 2 April 2018.

Martha (Mrs G.R.) Coxhead
The Friend of the Wounded

While the whole world is travailing in its night of fiercest pain,
And the sun looks down on trenches filled with wounded and with slain;
While the hearts of men are dumbly asking what is yet to be,
Comes a story, strange and wondrous, full of untold mystery.

After many a hot engagement, 'mid the rain of shot and shell,
Walks a form in whitest raiment, busy tending those who fell—
Seen at Sissons and the Argonne, seen at noon or break of day,
Heeding not the hovering danger, calmly moving on his way.

Snipers sniped and shot fell round him, scathless, onward, still he trod,
Bending o'er the helpless sufferers on the pitiless damp sod—
Till the story gathered credence, men were telling what they saw
Of the brave, heroic stranger—speaking softly, and with awe.

I who laughed and told them sure their nerves were getting weak,
When of such unheard of nonsense they so credulous could speak;
Said, for my part, were I wounded and in danger of my life,
All the help that I expected would be from a German knife!

Next day things were getting lively; big guns roared from dusk to dawn,
Calmed and lessened down at nightfall, and began again at morn.
Word was sent to take the trenches, full two hundred yards or more;
Not a man held back or wavered, though our lads fell by the score.

I was wounded—badly wounded in both legs, as down I fell;
Fearful pains and faintness seized me, like unto the pains of hell;
Yet dared not move a muscle, for but fifty yards away
Were the Germans, scant their mercy shown to foes who helpless lay!

Then the soft enshrouding nightfall wrapped me in its quiet fold;
Soon I heard a footfall nearing, and with anxious fears untold,
Waited, listening, watching, wondering, with each sense alert and keen;
Was it friend or foe advancing with such firm and upright mien?

Little guessed my heart the sequel; little dreamed till one in white,
With a soft and healing presence, stole so gently on my sight;
Then again the rifles started with their deadly, deathly rain;
And across his noble features came a saddened look of pain.

Yet He stood with arms extended; faint His words came with a moan,
Nothing plainly could I gather save the words, 'If thou had'st known',
And the ending of the sentence, as He gazed towards the skies,
Were the words, they seemed familiar, 'Now they're hidden from thine eyes'.

Then He stopped, and, oh, so gently gathered me up on His breast;
Me, a Hercules in stature! stricken sore, by pain distressed.
Anguish must have caused a faintness, for I woke beside a stream;
And I thought, as I awakened, that 'twas but a fevered dream.

Sheltered in a cave which kept me from the battle's awful sounds;
While above me bent the Stranger binding up my bleeding wounds:
Wounds which gave me untold suffering, such as ne'er I'd known before,
Yet such happiness o'erflowed me, fear of pain and death was o'er!

Oh, the gentle hands that touched me! oh, that tender, pitying gaze!
All my being bowed before Him in a wondering sweet amaze!
And I felt a mighty cleansing in my nature then was wrought
By the touch of One who soothed me with a love beyond all thought.

And I felt renewed and freshened, like unto a little child;
While above me bent that Stranger and my every fear beguiled.
Tending, soothing, calming, cheering: thus He did His vigil keep,
Till my stricken body yielded to the mystery of sleep.

When I woke, an eager longing filled my heart unto its core,
And I yearned to love and serve Him with a zeal ne'er felt before.
Looking up I saw Him standing, and His hands were clasped in prayer;
Then I saw those hands were wounded—blood was slowly trickling there.

And I cried aloud in sorrow; 'twas to me a bitter thing
That those gentle hands which blessed me should of suffering feel the sting.
'You are wounded, oh, my comrade!' pitifully then I said,
For to me it seemed more dreadful than the wounds which war had made.

But He answered, very gently, "'Tis a wound of long ago,
But of late again I feel it: sorrow makes these drops to flow.'

'Twas with pain again I noted that His feet were wounded too;
then I marvelled in amazement that this Friend I never knew
Loved and comforted and tended in compassion pure and sweet,—
Yet I did not recognise Him till I saw His hands and feet!

Oh, I knew Him! then I knew Him whom I'd put aside in youth
In the rush of life's hot fever I had spurned His love and truth.
And I longed to thank and bless Him, but as yet my lips were dumb;
Not a syllable I uttered, not a single word would come!

Swift He came and stood beside me with a sweet and pitying eye;
And He bade me, oh, so gently, by those placid waters lie.
'Stay and rest until the morrow, I have work which you can do;
Rest awhile, and in the morning I will come again for you'.

So He went, my tender comrade; weak I lie in fiercest pain;
But the thought of Him is blessed, and I know He'll come again;
He has promised, and I trust Him; thought of Him has banished sorrow;
So I bear my pain and weakness, for I know He'll come tomorrow,

Stay and ponder, oh my reader; list to words the Master said
Ere He went unto His Father from the dark abode of dread:
'Of the Day no man may know it, when on earth I am made known;
In the day ye least expect it, lo, the Son of Man may come!'

Source: Mrs G.R. [Martha] Coxhead, *Lost a Continent!: Heroes of Anzac and Other Verses,* Melbourne: Modern Printing, 1917, pp. 28–32. [Mrs G.R.] Martha

Martha Coxhead
Belgium

The blood of nations is poured out like water,
    And millions are gathering in battle array;
While Belgium, the scene of such carnage and slaughter,
    For honour and country is fighting today.

Our hearts, they are thrilling with pride in the nation
    That is facing a foe of such prowess and power;
Who, scorned by dishonour to avoid her spoliation,
    And fail in her bond lest the war clouds should lower!

Though the hearths and the homes of this people are wasted,
    Their lifeblood is shed, and their cities are burned;
Though their hope as a nation for years may be blasted,
    The blot of dishonour indignant they've spurned!

No quarrel had she with the foes who have wronged her;
    In this conflict, courageous, a martyr she's stood,
While the untrammelled hordes of the Germans have thronged her,
    And steeped their foul hands in her innocent blood!

Might may seem to be right, but, as God's in His heaven,
    He will surely avenge her wrongs speedily now;
And His vengeance will fall upon those who have striven
    To trample her down and her cities o'erthrow!

Oh Belgium! Brave Belgium! How mournful thy story;
    Thy homes devastated, thy hearthstones lie cold,
But with eyes, flashing pride, men shall sing to thy glory,
    And thy honour and valour through time shall be told!

Source: Mrs G.R. [Martha] Coxhead, *Lost a Continent! Heroes of Anzac and Other Verses*, Melbourne: Modern Printing Company, 1917, pp. 92-93.

VIOLET B. CRAMER

Violet Bertha Cramer was born on 17 May 1879, at 'Rosstrevor', 84 Bay Street, Brighton, where her parents had moved after their marriage. She was the second daughter of William George Cramer and Emily Louisa (née Duncan), who had been married at William's residence at Pentridge in 1874 by the Rev. H.S. Cramer, Baptist Minister and brother of the groom. William and the Rev. H.S. Cramer were sons of Charles Augustus Cramer, who had migrated to Australia from Newry in Ireland. Emily Louisa was the eldest daughter of George Oliphant Duncan Esq., Inspector-General of Penal Establishments in Victoria.

Cramer's older sister, Constance Mabel Cramer (born at Brighton in 1876), became a registered nurse. Cramer excelled in music and began a teaching career by the turn of the century. The Melbourne *Argus* reported on Monday 2 November 1896 (p. 5) that she was successful in the senior division for pianoforte examinations of the London Trinity College of Music held at Melbourne. She also held certificates from the Association Board of the Royal Academy and London College of Music. She advertised for pupils of pianoforte in 1901, at her home in Middle Crescent and in private homes and in schools. There followed more than half a century of teaching the piano, travelling further outside Melbourne.

In 1908, the Geelong *Advertiser* newspaper reported her performance of a piano solo at a Geelong High School concert. By 1910, she had moved to Horsham, where she taught pianoforte, organ and theory, from her home in Andrew Street and then Baillie Street. She also travelled in the Wimmera district, to teach and to examine students, and every summer until the 1950s, she advertised the commencement of tuition at Horsham, and provided the local paper with news of her pupils' successes in examinations held by Melbourne University's music department. So, for example, in December 1924, the *Horsham Times* reported a concert at which her pupils played 30 items. In 1927, the paper reported that all eight of Cramer's students sent for university examination had passed. In 1952, the *Horsham Times* reported on the success of four of her students in university practical examinations. At her death in 1968, Cramer's music students and friends raised money for a commemorative window in her local church, in appreciation of her life and work.

Violet's sister Constance joined the Australian Army Nursing Service on 5 May 1915 and served in England and France during World War One. She returned to Australia on 12 April 1919, but moved abroad and lived for twenty years in South Africa, until she again returned, to live with Violet from 1946 until her death in 1963.

§

Cramer's patriotic verse coincided with the outbreak of the War and reflected signal events. Late in December 1914, her poem 'The Cry of Belgium' recounted the sufferings of Belgian women and children, and noted,

> We have never known the anguish of the battlefield, and bloodshed,
> We can only hear their echo, dimly sounding o'er the main;
> And while brave men give their lives for us, we rest in peace and plenty,
> And take our round of pleasure, little recking of their pain.

At this stage of the War, Cramer urged prayer for the unfortunate population of Belgium and implied that (presumably male) Australians should do more than enjoy their easeful life. In subsequent years, her pro-conscription tone became more pronounced as she hymned the heroic British and Australian dead. She donated proceeds of the sale of her *Memories of the Great War* to the Red Cross.

At war's end, Cramer continued to write poetry, chiefly of a lyrical cast, reflecting an intense enjoyment of the natural beauty of her region. The diction and vocabulary often remained old-fashioned. Thus 'Two Pictures' (1926), concerning a mountain prospect, exclaims 'Green trees and verdure clothed each sloping side / In raiment meet'. She also wrote Anzac commemorative poems that drew on religious vocabulary.

Publications

Memories of the Great War. Horsham: Wimmera Star Print. n.d. [1916]
    [Advertised for sale in *Argus*, Friday 21 July 1916, p. 5].
Stray Thoughts. Horsham: Horsham Times, 1921.

References

Australasian, Saturday 7 March 1874, p. 1 [Family notices: Marriage of William George Cramer and Emily Louisa Duncan at Pentridge].

Australasian, Saturday 24 May 1879, p. 25 [Family Notices: birth of Violet Bertha at Rosstrevor, Brighton on 17 May 1874].

'Professional'. *Brighton Southern Cross,* Saturday 9 March 1901, p. 2 [Cramer advertises for pupils].
'Miss L. Duncan's Class', *Geelong Advertiser,* Tuesday 2 June 1908, p. 6 [Violet Cramer's solo at a Geelong High School Concert].
'No Holiday', *Horsham Times,* Tuesday 14 June 1910, p. 4 [Violet Cramer advertises herself as teacher of the pianoforte, organ and theory, at one guinea per quarter at Baillie Street, Horsham].
Horsham Times, Friday 27 January 1911, p. 5 [Violet Cramer resumes teaching pianoforte, organ and theory].
'Miss Violet Cramer', *West Wimmera Mail,* 12 June 1914 [Cramer advertises her travels to Natimuk to provide musical tuition]. http://www.swvic.org/goroke/wwm1914.htm
Horsham Times, Friday 28 January 1916, p. 4 [Cramer advises resumption of tuition at Baillie Street].
Violet Cramer, 'The Cry of Belgium', *Horsham Times,* 29 December 1914, p. 5.
'Students' Recital'. *Horsham Times,* Friday 19 December 1924, p. 6.
Violet Cramer, 'Anzac Day, 1925', *Horsham Times,* Friday 1 May 1925, p. 5.
'Music Tuition', *Horsham Times,* Friday 4 February 1927, p. 4 [Violet Cramer advises she will resume tuition].
'Two Pictures', *Horsham Times,* Tuesday 2 March 1926, p. 5.
'Piano Students' Success', *Horsham Times,* Friday 4 November 1927, p. 4 [All of Cramer's students pass examinations].
'Miss Violet Cramer, 5 Andrew Street, Teacher of Music', *Horsham Times,* Tuesday 28 June 1932, p. 1 ['Vacancies for Pupils'].
Music Examinations. *Horsham Times,* Friday 26 October 1934, p. 4 [Miss Eunice Stone passes university pianoforte Grade 4].
Miss Violet Cramer, Teacher of Music. *Horsham Times,* Tuesday 22 October 1935, p. 1.
'Personal', *Horsham Times,* Friday 8 March 1946, p. 2 [Cramer's sister returns from South Africa to make her home at Horsham].
'Four Pianoforte Students Pass', *Horsham Times,* Friday 31 October 1952, p. 2 ['Four Pianoforte Students Pass'].

Violet B. Cramer
The Lusitania

You call yourselves men! Aye, cultured men!
        Give us the savage, then, wild and free.
We are glad to fight with an honest foe,
        And will dare to death over land and sea.

You think we are craven because we fight
        Keeping the rules of the game we play,
But we'll fight to the finish, so beware—
        The day may come when we shall repay.

Thunder of cannon and bayonet's gleam
        We look for in strife with any foe,
But poisonous gas and burning stream!
        Do you think a Briton would stoop so low?

Would you have us fight with your own vile tools?
        If we've no choice we must do the same;
But we don't sink boats with civilian crews.
        We leave that to you. 'Tis the coward's game.

You have stirred us up with that last foul blow.
        Oh! if we women were only men!
Vengeance we claim for the innocent drowned.
        Oh for an arm with the strength of ten!

You made it high holiday in your land;
        Joyed in the women and children slain.
But the ocean will not suffice
        To wash from your hands their crimson stain.

                        May, 1915

Source: Violet B. Cramer. *Memories of the Great War.* Horsham: Wimmera Star Print, n.d. [1916], p. 6.

Violet B. Cramer
Death of Miss Cavell

She had sinned a deadly sin,
    And they wrote her down a spy.
Sheltering British and Belgian men,
    Aiding the fugitives home again.
She had nursed sick Germans. True—
    What then?
    'Twas time that she should die

A saint in a nurse's garb!
    Through pathway of thorn and flam,
Tending the suffering, friend or foe,
    As the White Christ did long years ago;
Threading in footsteps that shine an glow,
    Leaving a martyr's name.

Cowards and cads that you are;
    Where is your Kultur to-day?
Blinded by arrogance, pride and greed,
    You see no light in a noble deed.
Your only right is a brutish creed
    Teaching to fight and slay.

Will you hang your heads in shame
    When you stand before God's throne?
'Have you been merciful, just, and true?
    Where are the lives I require of you?'
You cannot bluster as now you do
    When all your deeds are known.

    Aye, hang your heads; humble you low as the dust,
    But answer your Maker's demands you must.

        October, 1915

Source: Violet B. Cramer. *Memories of the Great War*. Horsham: Wimmera Star Print, n.d. [1916], p. 10.

Violet B. Cramer
Fight! Be Men!

A call for help! And our brave boys
Rose, thrust aside their play.
'Ready!' they cried, and forth they marched
To fight. Why did you stay?

They squared their shoulders to the task
Tho noblest man can find,
To fight, or die, in Freedom's cause—
How were you left behind?

None can recall the strong, free souls
That trod the paths of fame.
Are you the riff-raff that are left?
The blind, the halt, the lame?

Some will return with glory, but
God bless the men who fell.
What are you doing for your land?
Are you a ne'er-do-well?

All cannot go: but you who have
No ties to bind you here—
You lose the greatest chance in life—
Why don't you volunteer?

Perhaps you fear you may be shot,
And suffer hardships, too.
Then stay at home and save your skin
What is the worth of you?

So heroes suffer for the weak;
Men die, while cravens fear,
Oh! seekers after wealth and ease,
Is it you do not care?

June, 1915.

Source: Violet B. Cramer, *Memories of the Great War,* Horsham: Wimmera Star Print, 1916, p. 7.

Violet B. Cramer
In Memoriam J.C.T.

Tread softly; it is holy ground.
The dark pines wave o'erhead,
The stars look down with shining eyes
Upon the quiet dead.
The night breeze stirs the grass that waves
And ripples like the sea,
And he lies sleeping a t our feet—
It is Gallipoli.

We hear no more of battle's roar,
No shot and shell that blind.
War came and broke this land's repose,
But only left behind
Green mounds upon the grassy slope,
White crosses gainst the sky,
To mark the last long resting place
Where sons and brothers lie.

When the grey dawn was in the sky,
And cliffs loomed steep ahead;
Over a still and shiny sea
The boat like swallows sped.
A year ago, and he was there,
Eager and strong and gay,
Heedless of shots, that rained around—
Quiet he lies to-day.

Few were the men who reached that shore,
But 'Follow me!' his cry.
They charged the heights, they won a name
Which now can never die.
But one by one they fell at last
Beneath that rain of lead;
They laid the leader with his men,
Where sleep the peaceful dead.

A year ago but those we loved
Have journeyed far and wide;
From out this bourne of time and place
To the dim other side.
They did the work they came to do,
And earned the rest they keep.
Pray God we each fulfil our task
Ere we, too, fall asleep.

    April, 1916.
    Baillie Street.

Source: Violet B. Cramer, *Horsham Times* (Victoria), Tuesday 18 April 1916, p.6, and *Memories of the Great War,* Horsham: Wimmera Star Print, 1916, p. 12.

Violet B. Cramer
The Conquest of Jerusalem

Into the mystic Holy Land,
We marched with a measured tread;
Khaki figures, and some were gay,
Some grave—for the hot and dusty way
Seemed peopled with seers long dead.

Zion, City of Mighty Kings,
We fought out our way to thee;
Colours floated against the sky,
A gleaming symbol of purpose high—
The flag of a nation free.

Strife and warfare we left without,
And peacefully entered in;
Not for the greed of gain we came,
But our hearts were lit with holy flame,
To give back tho prize we'd win.

Scattered abroad, an alien race,
The children of Zion stand;
Banished from home, an ancient sin
Has been your curse; but now come in,
Come back to the Father-land ,

Land of strangers you made your home,
Yet dwelt there apart, alone.
Now the price is paid, and these fair lands,
God-given before, through British hands
He gives to you back—your own.

Driven from sea to rolling sea,
Hunted and held at bay;
Hounded by heathen — and, with shame
We say it, by some who bear the name
Of the Christ you cast away.

Take at our hands your long-lost land,
And greet us as brothers true;
Come from the North and South, a far,
From East and West—your guiding star
Hangs here in the sky for you.

Source: Violet B. Cramer, *Stray Thoughts,* Horsham: Horsham Times, 1922, pp. 7-8.

Violet B. Cramer
Surrender or German Warships

'Good-morrow to you, stately ships
And whither are you bound?
That sail across the ocean blue
In silence so profound.
Perchance you search for treasure isles
Across the distant main;
To load your holds with gems and gold
Then swift return again.'

'Nay, stay us not, we are not bent
On pleasure or on gold;
We have stern duty to perform
And straight the course we hold.'

'Oh are you on the warpath then
With guns that point so true,
To humble kings and bid them bow
Their haughty heads to you?
To wrest the sceptre from their grasp,
And trample on their crown,
To float your colors on their towers,
And haul their ensign down?'

'Nay, we are not for war and strife
The victory has been won;
We on a peaceful mission sail
Towards the west'ring sun.'

'Ah, then ye trade with merchandise
Across the ocean foam,
Or haply carry pioneers
To countries far from home,
Where savage men will learn your worth,
Hear wisdom from your store,
Learn laws of righteousness and peace
To them unknown before.'

Nay, we have only hands aboard
To man our warships true,
No pioneers for distant land
Can aid the work we do.'

'Good-morrow then, ye stately ships
That steal so swiftly by,
We cannot guess your purpose, nor
The goal to which you fly.
Just two and twenty mystery ships,
Come, tell us where you trend .
What is that flag upon your mast?
And are you foe or friend?

'Alas! we are the German Fleet!
Our course is well-nigh run;
We go to give our vessels up
Before the set of sun.

We are that mighty German Fleet
Whose doom is sealed, Alack!
We go to visit Britain, and
Will not be coming back.

Source: Source: Violet B. Cramer, *Stray Thoughts,* Horsham: Horsham Star, 1921, pp. 8-9.

ENID DERHAM

Photograph by Alice Mills, of Enid Derham, Honorary Secretary of Women Workers of the Second Infantry Brigade. *Punch* magazine, 31 May 1917, p. 20. National Library of Australia.

Enid Derham, a classical scholar and lecturer in English at Melbourne University, was born at Weinberg Road, Hawthorn, on 24 March 1882, the eldest daughter of Bristol-born solicitor Thomas Plumley Derham Jr (1844-1932) and his wife Ellen Hyde (née Hodgson, 1858-1932).

Enid's father's parents had migrated to Australia in 1856. Thomas Plumley Derham the elder (1816-1867), a Southampton auctioneer, arrived in Victoria in 1856, with his wife Sarah Ann Derham (née Watts, born 1820) along with the first of their eventual ten children. He established a mercantile concern at Sandhurst (Bendigo), operating as an auctioneer and draper until he became insolvent at the end of 1865. The business was sequestered, to recommence trading in June 1866 as Derham and Son, under the management of the founder's oldest son, Francis. When Thomas, the founder, died in March 1867, and his oldest son Francis in 1869, Frederick, the third oldest son, took on responsibility for the family, and commenced an illustrious career in brokerage, importing and manufacturing on his own account.

A younger son named Thomas, born in 1849, studied law, and on 13 May 1880 at Wesley Church in Melbourne married Ellen Hyde, youngest daughter of the merchant and importer Richard Hodgson. In February the following year, the couple suffered the loss of their first child, a stillborn male. In that year also, the Derham matriarch, Sarah Derham died aged sixty, at Hawthorn, where Enid's family set up home.

Enid Derham, the future poet, was the first living child of the marriage. Her younger siblings were Una (1883-1955), Francis ('Frank', 1885-1957), Alfred (1891-1962), and Margaret Ruth (1894-1961).

Enid's father and elder relatives were notable members of Melbourne's professional elite. At his death in 1932, her father was one of the oldest practising solicitors in Melbourne, having eventually turned the firm of which he was originally partner into a father and son business, Derham and Derham. Enid's eldest Derham aunt, Sara (1846-1917) was the organiser and secretary of the conservative Australian National Women's League, founded in 1904 to promote monarchy and the British Empire, support free trade, and to resist socialism, through appeal to women voters. The League was allied with the interests of the Victorian Employer's Federation, of which Enid's uncle Frederick Thomas was President. Frederick made his fortune in wheat milling and biscuit manufacturing (through partnership with Thomas Ariell and later Thomas Swallow), as well as preserved fruit in country centres, and Queensland sugar planting and refineries for production of treacle and golden syrup. A Member of the Legislative Council and former Postmaster General in Victoria and, in 1903, Federal Senate candidate, Frederick Derham opposed compulsory arbitration and other evils including the proposed transcontinental railway and the commencement of work on a National Capital outside Victoria.

Enid grew up in a family in which Imperial and nativist patriotism combined with philanthropic and charitable support for churches, schools and kindergartens. Her wartime patriotic output is of a piece with her pre-War domestic and institutional inculcation though she could still surprise, as in certain lyric poems speaking of loneliness and yearning.

She first attended Hessle College in Camberwell, a private school run by its founder, Miss Ada Gresham B.A., before proceeding to the Presbyterian Ladies College, which her younger sisters also attended. The school maintained the classical English tradition, and Enid's performance won her a scholarship to Ormond College at Melbourne University. She commenced in 1900, gaining a B.A. degree in classical philology under Professor T.G. Tucker in 1903, and the award of a scholarship to complete her MA, in which she again received first-class honours.

Enid's brothers Frank and Alfred attended Scotch College before proceeding to university. Frank studied Law and joined his father's firm in 1906. Alfred began medical studies but had not completed his studies when the War broke out. Both enlisted and had distinguished military careers. Francis served in the Field Artillery in France, where he became a Lieutenant Colonel and was awarded the Distinguished Service Order and the Croix de Guerre. After the War, he continued to work in the family firm, which in 1929 became Moule, Hamilton and Derham. At the same time, he remained attached to the army, being promoted Colonel in 1930 and commanding artillery and infantry brigades; he was also a leading organiser in the clandestine right wing organisation, the 'White Army', in the 1930s.

Alfred served at Gallipoli, where he was wounded and awarded the Military Cross, and then in France until March 1916 when he was permitted to return to Australia to complete his medical degree. He continued to serve in the Australian Army Medical Corps, commanding field ambulances in the Militia in the1930s, while running a medical practice and specialising in children's diseases. In 1940, he went to Singapore as Assistant Director of Medicine, but was interned at Changi along with his son, Thomas, when the Japanese invaded.

§

Enid Derham tutored in English at Trinity and Ormond Colleges and lectured at Castlemaine and elsewhere in the State for the University Extension Board and the Workers Educational Association on a wide range of topics from Shakespeare to Women in Literature, and Australian Literature. She was among the first Australian poets to promote the poetry of Emily Dickinson.

In 1912, she published a lyrical collection, *The Mountain Road and Other Verses,* poems reprinted from the *Trident, Lone Hand, Book* Lover,

Australian Onlooker, and *Heart of the Rose*, and dedicated to her parents. In her 1922 Introduction to the *Study of Australian Literature,* Zora Cross remarked on the book's evidence of Derham's love of the bush as being 'very deeply marked'. This is so, but the poems speak of solitude, and longing for a loved person variously apostrophised as 'Ada', a dark female companion, 'Laura', and 'She for whom I died', among other female figures.

In 1912, Derham also arranged the staging of 'Empire', a theatre work expressly designed to raise funds for the Victoria League, and which Derham called 'a morality play for children'. The *Leader* newspaper called the latter work 'a masque of Empire', following its performance at the Princess Theatre on Friday 24 May. The *Argus* newspaper called the work 'a miniature history of the British Empire', which packed 'a plain, but not unimportant lesson, that "the law of England is to love and serve"'. The Melbourne *Herald* referred to *Empire* as a 'morality play, with Imperialistic ideals'. The Melbourne *Age* review noted the allegorical figures (Britannia and the Dominions, Peace, Discovery and so on) as 'abstractions', and commented on the Kiplingesque and John Davidsonian influences. Like the *Argus*, it pointed up the moral lesson, that 'Britannia's mission and her ultimate destiny is to hold sway not by means of war, but by pursuance of justice and the arts of peace'. The characters and singers of the first performance included Vera Deakin, daughter of the former Prime Minister. The playscript (with music by Miss Ewart) was published as *Empire,* for school performances. The following lines voiced by 'Britannia' give some hint of the work's poetic style:

> Is Empire mine? Then welcome be my fate,
> Something within me murmurs to be great,
> To gaze abroad where'er the sun may shine,
> To see Earth's people and to know them mine;
> My hand shall bless them and my hand shall smite—

Derham became a foundation member of both the Lyceum Club and the Classical Association of Victoria. Shortly before the War, she spent six months at Oxford, studying Anglo-Saxon and Old English before returning to tutor at Trinity and Ormond. She lectured in English at the University of Western Australia in 1921, and in 1922 became the first woman to be appointed lecturer in English at the University of Melbourne. In May 1912, she had stated at a meeting of graduates that women should be eligible for the Senate of the university, and she was appointed to the University Council. In May 1918, she was active, with other women academics, in working for establishment of a women's hostel for the University. She became a senior lecturer in 1924, and took leave to study again at Oxford in 1927, before resuming work at Melbourne. In 1938, she was briefly promoted to Acting Professor.

Derham was a member of the Catalysts group of women graduates of the Presbyterian Ladies College. Founded in 1898 and emerging in 1910 as a private club in Melbourne, whose members met each month to share a meal and a paper, the Catalysts constituted a diverse range of talented women from the start, and came to include Australia's first women lawyers, doctors and other professionals, such as Jessie Webb (appointed Professor of History at Melbourne University in 1910, at the age of 29), pioneer motor racer Kathleen Braithwaite, novelist Joan Lindsay, composer Margaret Sutherland, and artist Ethel Spowers. Anne Longmire, historian of the club, recalled that Derham was conservative in her views, but her best friend was Elizabeth Lothian, a Fabian who mixed in the society of H.G. Wells, Annie Besant and other English Fabians.

Derham frequently spoke on literary topics at the Lyceum Club to Catalyst members and others. She was elected President of the Lyceum in July 1917.

Derham's war work took the form of fundraising talks as well as membership of a servicemen's Comforts Depot organisation (of which she was secretary) at The Block in Melbourne. (A fashionable shopping precinct to this date, the Block, an arcade modelled on Milan's Galleria Vittorio Emanuele II, connects Collins Street, Little Collins Street and Elizabeth Street, is promoted as 'one of the finest examples of a 19th-century shopping arcade on the planet'). She also addressed public meetings in Rutherglen and elsewhere to urge women to support enlistment.

Derham's published poetry, like her scholarly publications, was relatively small in volume. She wrote several texts for students of English, and contributed poems to literary journals including the Melbourne *Spinner* in the 1920s and later, but her sole collection after the 1912 and 1918 volumes and the facetious poem *How the Animals Came to Australia* was the posthumous *Poems* (1958). Some of her wartime periodical verse continued to speak of loneliness and yearning, as in her poem 'Music', published in the *Bookman* and republished in the *Adelaide Register* in 1915:

When the flute rejoices,
When the violins
Mourn with human voices
Immemorial sins

I am hearing only
Wastes of melody,
Where my spirit lonely
Wanders seeking thee.

Reminiscent of her admired poets, including Emily Dickinson, the poem's epigrammatic compression and short, tombstone lines set the emotion at a cool distance. Like her poems touching on wartime themes, it marks a stylistic step away from the quasi-Decadent lushness of her earlier 'Mountain Road' verse, and to my mind, has some commonality with the prosodic modes of her contemporaries, HD and Lesbia Harford. Imelda Parker, who wrote the entry on Derham for the *Australian Dictionary of Biography,* remarked in 1981 that while Derham's reputation was that of a minor lyric poet, her 'later poems, especially, reveal an intensity of emotion, even passion, quite unsuspected by those who knew her well'. I think the intensity, the result of the compression and conciseness of her language, distinguishes much of her early work as well.

§

Derham died of a cerebral haemorrhage at her home in Kew on 13 November 1941. In 1943, a prize was instituted by subscription at Melbourne University to perpetuate her memory. The award was open to the candidate who completed a four-year degree with honours in English Language or Literature and who showed the greatest appreciation of poetry.

Publications
The Mountain Road and Other Verses, Melbourne: Osbaldstone, 1912.
Empire: A Morality Play for Children, Melbourne: Victoria League of Victoria, 1912.
How the Animals Came to Australia: An Uncensored Account, Melbourne: The Author, 1930.
Poems, Melbourne: Melbourne University Press, 1958.

References

Imelda Palmer, 'Derham, Enid (1882–1941), Australian Dictionary of Biography, National Centre of Biography, Australian National University, http://adb.anu.edu.au/biography/derham-enid-5960/text10169, published first in hardcopy 1981, accessed online 12 February 2016.

Argus, Tuesday 14 December 1865, p. 2 [Advertisements: Sequestration of estate of Thomas Plumley Derham, draper]; also reported in *Herald*, Tuesday 16 June 1865, p. 4 [Advertisements].

Bendigo Advertiser, Monday 18 June 1866, p. 3 [Advertisements: Public notice of change of name of Thomas Plumley Derham's business to Derham and Son].

Age, Tuesday 26 March 1867, p. 4 [Family Notices: Death of Thomas Plumley Derham, auctioneer aged fifty, at Sandhurst on 24 March 1867].

Illustrated Australian News for Home Readers, Monday 22 February 1869, p. 54 [Family Notices: Death of Francis Plumley Derham, at Richmond, aged 29].

Argus, Monday 17 May 1880, p. 1 [Family Notices: Marriage of Thomas Plumley Derham, solicitor, Melbourne, to Ellen Hyde, younger daughter of Richard Hodgson, merchant, Melbourne, on 13 May 1880].

Illustrated Australian News, Saturday 12 March 1881, p. 62 [Family Notices. Notice of Thomas Plumley Derham's wife's stillborn son.]

Argus, Saturday 23 April 1881, p. 1 [Family Notices: Death at Hawthorn of Sarah Derham, widow of Thomas Plumley Derham, formerly of Sandhurst, on 22 April].

The Australasian Sketcher with Pen and Pencil, Saturday 2 April 1882 p. 126 [Family notices: birth of Enid Derham on 24 March 1882].

Argus, Saturday 13 June 1896, p. 1 [Family Notices: Death of 'Thomas Plumley, second son of Thomas Plumley Derham, aged 9' on 12 June 1896].

'Weddings. Green-Derham', *Table Talk*, 22 March 1906 [Wedding of Una Derham; Enid attending as bridesmaid].

'Derham-Bowden', *Australasian*, 16 October 1909, p. 47 [Wedding of Ruth Derham].

'Obituary. Mr T.P. Derham', *Argus*, Friday 28 October 1932, p. 6 [Summary of career of Enid's father]. Jeffrey Grey, 'Derham, Alfred Plumley (1891–1962)', Australian Dictionary of Biography, National Centre of Biography, Australian National University, http://adb.anu.edu.au/biography/derham-alfred-plumley-9985/text17635, published first in hardcopy 1993, accessed online 15 February 2016.

'Biographies'. Australian Women's National League (1904-1944), https://trove.nla.gov.au/people/598652?c=people Accessed 6 May 2018.

Michael Cathcart, *Defending the National Tuckshop: Australia's Secret Army Intrigue of 1931*, Melbourne: McPhee Gribble/Penguin, 1988, pp. 45, 56, 57, 69 [Francis Derham's membership of White Army leadership].

'The Catalysts', Hindsight, ABC Radio National. 11 September 2011. http://www.abc.net.au/radionational/programs/hindsight/the-catalysts/3591324

'Presbyterian Ladies College. Miss Derham on Australian Literature. An Anticipation', *Leader* (Melbourne), Saturday 25 November 1911, p. 47.

'Summary', *Penshurst Free Press*, Friday 24 May 1912, p. 1 [Enid Derham calls for women to be eligible for membership of University Senate].

'Women and Literature', *Weekly Times*, Saturday 27 May 1922, p. 10 [Derham lectures at the Women's Political Association'].

Enid Derham, *The Mountain Road and Other Verses*, Melbourne: Osboldstone & Co. Pty.Ltd. Printers, 1912: 'To a Friend, on Her Arrival in England', pp. 28-30; 'Psyche', pp. 34-35; 'Lost', p. 39; 'The Companion', p. 43; 'Service', p. 50; 'To Laura, Reading', p. 51.

Zora Cross, *An Introduction to the Study of Australian Literature*, Sydney: Teachers' College Press and Angus & Robertson, 1922, p. 70.

'Empire Day: A Morality Play', *Weekly Times*, Saturday 18 May 1912, p. 33 [for précis of Derham's 'Empire' and her description of he work].

'Miss Derham's Morality Play', *Age*, Tuesday 21 May 1912, p. 7 [Review including remarks on 'eloquence' and the 'moral'].

'Empire Pageant: Miss Derham's Morality Play', *Age*, Saturday 25 May 1912, p. 13.

'Empire', *Argus*, Wednesday 15 May 1912, p. 12 [Summary of the 'lesson' of Derham's theatre-piece 'Empire'].

'A Masque of Empire', *Leader*, Saturday 18 May 1912, p. 47.

'University Extension Board Miss Enid Derham. "Women and Literature"'. *Mount Alexander Mail*, 24 August 1912, p. 3 [Lecture at Mechanics' Hall, Castlemaine].

'Comforts Depot', *Preston Leader*, Saturday 23 September 1916, p. 2; 'Brigade Depot Opened', *Weekly Times*, Saturday 30 September 1916, p. 9.

'Women's Monster Meeting. Women's Duty in the Recruitment Campaign', *Rutherglen Sun and Chiltern Valley Advertiser*, Friday 2 March 1917, p. 2 [Derham's rural rallying of women's support for enlistment; meeting addressed by Mrs Harrison Moore and Miss Enid Derham].

'Melbourne Notes', *Punch*, Wednesday 29 May 1918, p. 7 [Derham, Dr Georgina Sweet, Miss S.J. Williams and others report on developments of a women's hostel at Melbourne University].

'Lecturer for University. Miss Derham Selected', Herald, Tuesday 7 September 1920, p. 5. [Reference to Derham's 'morality play', *The Mountain Road*].

'The Block', What's On: Melbourne Landmarks, https://whatson.melbourne.vic.gov.au/Placestogo/MelbourneLandmarks/Historic/Pages/6062.aspx Accessed 10 March 2018.

'Women Graduates Red Cross Aid Committee', *Punch*, Thursday 12 October 1916, p. 30 [Derham delivers lecture on an Elizabethan subject in aid of Red Cross at the Lyceum].

'National Council of Women. Midday Talks to Factory Girls', *Age,* Saturday 24 February 1917, p. 18.

'Women Workers of Second Infantry Brigade'. *Punch*, Thursday 31 May 1917, p. 20 [Photo of Derham and other committee members included].

'Goldsmith Comedies Discussed', *Weekly Times,* Saturday 9 March 1918, p. 8 [Talk to Repertory Theatre Club].

'General Notes', *Weekly Times*, Saturday 21 July 1917, p. 10 [Derham elected President of the Lyceum Club; Lady Spencer and Mrs M.M. Phillips Vice-presidents].

'University Council', *Argus,* Tuesday 17 January 1922, p. 7.

'The Australian Novel. "Flowering Stage" Reached', *Age*. Friday 5 May 1933, p. 7 [report on lecture].

Advocate, Thursday 27 November 1941, p. 11 [Miss Enid Derham obituary].

The Enid Derham Prize (1943). University of Melbourne. UTR6.72–Lesser Awards. The University of Melbourne. http://www.unimelb.edu.au/unisec/utr/utr6072.html Accessed 15 February 2016.

Anne Longmire, *The Catalysts: Change and Continuity 1910-2010*, Burwood [Melbourne]: The Catalysts, 2011.

Enid Derham, 'Music', *Register,* Saturday 27 March 1915, p. 4.

Enid Derham
Gallipoli 1917

Night falls dark on the hills where they lie alone,
    The dead who died in vain on a desolate shore,
Far from the land they loved, far, far from their own,
    The ranges and cities and streams that they will see no more.

Dawn comes over the hills and the graves of the slain,
    And a dewbright gleam from the least little leaf is shed,
And Honour and Youth and Valour shine out again,
    And Love, and the great triumphant souls of the dead.

Source: Enid Derham, *Poems*, Melbourne: Melbourne University Press, 1958, p. 16.

Enid Derham
The Return

Now they come back to the winds and the stars they know,
>   Now the ship lifts to the lilt of the Southern foam,
From the fields of Troy, from the desert sands and the snow,
>   Wounded and blind, they have set their faces home.

But who are those among them that no man sees?
>   Whose are the feet that pace the deck unheard?
When the ship draws in and into the shouting quays,
>   Is there no word for those shining ranks, no word?

There's a prayer breathed low and a tear that's inly shed,
>   And a light in the soul that the coming years shall prove;
You too return, O beloved, O gallant dead,
>   Ye too return—there is no death in love.

Source: Enid Derham, *Poems*, Melbourne: Melbourne University Press, 1958, p.16.

'E' (MARY E. FULLERTON)

Miss Fullerton, photo by Marietta Studio, Melbourne, *Australasian*, Friday 3 July 1925, p. 14. State Library Victoria.

Mary Eliza Fullerton was the second surviving child of the seven children of Robert Fullerton and Eliza Leathers, who were married in Victoria in 1863. She was born at Glenmaggie in Gippsland, on 14 May 1868. Her mother's parents were Jonathan Leathers and Eliza (née Smith). Her father had migrated from Belfast with his sister at age twenty to seek his luck on the Victorian goldfields, where he met his future wife, who had migrated from Sussex at age fourteen.

On a small farm at Glenmaggie in Gippsland, the Fullerton family lived in a bark hut built by their father. Fullerton's mother educated her at home until a schoolhouse opened at Glenmaggie. Fullerton attended the school from age seven to thirteen, and became an avid reader and memoriser of English poetry and the Bible. Her favourite poets were Milton, Burns, Shelley and Byron, and she also read the essays of Hazlitt, Lamb and Macaulay. After leaving school, she continued to educate herself while she lived and worked on her parents' farm until she was twenty-five. Although she grew up in a strict Presbyterian family, she came to reject orthodox religion in favour of what she called 'a certain vagueness'.

Fullerton published her first poem at twelve in a regional newspaper (the *Trafalgar Journal*). She had read Australian poets Adam Lindsay Gordon and Henry Lawson, whom she called 'a Homer, a Chaucer in moleskins', and she was enthusiastic about the Sydney *Bulletin*. In 1893, determined to make her way as a fulltime writer after successes in the Melbourne *Argus* and other papers, she moved to Prahran. By 1894, she had achieved publication in the *Australian Town and Country Journal*—and in the *Bulletin*, where her poems would appear for the next fifty years.

Fullerton's closest sister Lydia (born a year after her) and her eldest sister Annie had married and left home when Fullerton went to Prahran, and her parents and three younger sisters joined Fullerton when she moved from Prahran to Hawthorn. Will, the only son of the family, stayed on the farm.

Fullerton's father died in 1901, and her mother nineteen years later. From 1904, Fullerton was engaged in Victorian radical political and literary circles, and she regularly contributed to Vida Goldstein's suffragist paper, *Woman's Sphere*, which ran an article in 1904 on Miles Franklin, who later became one of Fullerton's lifelong correspondents. Fullerton's first book, *Moods and Melodies: Sonnets and Lyrics,* was published in 1908, and from 1909, she worked as a journalist on Goldstein's second paper, *Woman Voter,* the organ of the Women's Political Association. In 1911, Fullerton became Acting President of the Association when Goldstein travelled to England to help the cause 'at the heart of the action'.

By that time, Fullerton had already met fellow activist and office-bearer Mabel Singleton, whose family came from England's industrial west country. Mabel Singleton was ten years younger than Fullerton, and when she married Robert Singleton, in a Registry Office in London in October 1904, Mabel Jupp was twenty-seven and Singleton sixty-three. Robert had retired as chief accountant of Victorian Railways in 1900, and was believed to have amassed a large fortune from discovery in the 1860s of the gold reef that started the Royal Standard mine at Wood's Point—a fortune that enabled him to purchase a mansion ('Haverbrack') in Glenferrie Road, 'the most aristocratic part' of Malvern where he and his first wife, Sabina Embling established a family. Singleton had served the Victorian government since his commencement as a field assistant in the Department of Lands and Works in 1858, and risen from draughtsman in the engineering accountants branch to accountant before that section was merged with the accountants' branch of the Railways service. His first wife Sabina, whom he had married in 1871, died in 1887 at the age of thirty-four after bearing six children.

In 1898, Singleton had given evidence in England at a suit before the Privy Council in connection with construction of a railway line, and on return to Victoria had retired from government service. He was resident again in London before his marriage to Mabel, who found that life as chatelaine of a mansion in Malvern did not accord with her political inclinations. She had met Vida Goldstein by 1908, and by 1911 was chair of the committee supporting Goldstein's bid for election to Parliament. For his part, Singleton wanted no more children and was furious when Mabel became pregnant and bore a son, on 14 January 1911. Singleton acknowledged the child, named Denis Gordon Singleton, as his own, but he effectively banished Mabel from his home. Fullerton, who welcomed the infant's arrival, made several journeys from the city to visit Mabel and Denis at the Singletons' country house 'Muyanato' at Mount Dandenong. At the same time, she wrote angry poems about Mabel's husband.

In June 1912, Fullerton, Mabel and Denis travelled to England. Mabel's husband made a new will, appointing his oldest son as executor and settling real estate and personal property on him, and cash amounts on two other surviving children from his first marriage. He allowed Mabel two hundred pounds for herself and 800 pounds for Denis's education. (In later years, Denis told Sylvia Martin, Fullerton's biographer, that his father was a 'brute'.)

Fullerton's trip to England was relatively brief, and on her return to Australia, she became prominent as an anti-conscription speaker and as a writer in the *Woman Voter* and in [Samuel] Ross's *Monthly Magazine of Protest, Personality and Progress*. Fullerton's poems, sometimes signed 'M.E.F.' and at times in full, appear with those of several Australian and overseas poets in *Ross's Monthly* magazine, which also featured anti-war writings by Ross, Sinclaire, Frederick T. Macartney, John Le Gay Brereton, Adela Pankhurst and (in translation) Karl Liebknecht. The *Woman Voter* reported Fullerton's public addresses, such as her July 1917 Melbourne speech on the topic, 'Australia an Island of Voluntarism in a Sea of Conscription'.

§

Evidence of Fullerton's efficacy as public speaker is contained in private as well as public records. One of the latter occurs in the wartime reflections of Tom Purcell, a Yarraville railway employee, who from 1881 until his death in 1920 kept a diary in which he noted minutiae concerning his daily activities—religious devotions, household accounts, activities, friendships, and correspondence. During the War, he included the names of neighbours and associates killed or maimed in the conflict, his fears for his enlisted sons George and Leo, the replacement of facts by euphemisms and lies in official announcements, and his growing disillusion with the press and the government. He also attended meetings on the Yarra Bank and elsewhere, where political speakers canvassed the inequality of sacrifice and the decline of working-class living conditions, and voiced opposition to compulsory conscription. As historian John Lack writes, Purcell

> heard Adela Pankhurst speak at a street meeting in Middle Footscray on 20 April [1917], and next evening he heard Senate candidate Vida Goldstein demand civil, legal and wage equality for the sexes, and denounce 'the new cult of National Service [which] meant industrial conscription and the loss of all that has been gained by arbitration, wages boards and unionism'.
>
> A week later on Sunday 29 April, Tom was at the Yarra bank where 'Miss Vida Goldstein and Miss Pankhurst [,] Fullerton etc Fleming, Lynch etc etc' spoke. And the following week (6 May) he was again at a 'Great gathering on the Yarra Bank' to hear Goldstein and Pankhurst. Tom's enthusiasm outlasted the election. On Sunday 13 May he attended a 'women's peace meeting' that was addressed by Mrs Singleton, Miss Fullerton, Miss John[s], and Rev Frederick Sinclaire, whose denunciation of the exploiters of the poor affected him strongly.

(In the event, Tom Purcell's sons' war experiences confirmed Tom's misgivings. Both young men were wounded in France and invalided home, George in 1917 and Leo to England in 1918 with a gunshot wound, before being returned to Australia in 1919.)

§

Fullerton's 1921 volume of poems, *The Breaking Furrow*, bears the dedication 'To My Friend Mabel Singleton'. In the following year, Fullerton left Australia to live for the remainder of her life with Singleton, first at the garden city of Letchworth, then at Maresfield in East Sussex, and finally London. She died on

23 February 1946, and legal notices in Australia recorded her address as 'Late of "Sandbank", Budletts, Uckfield, Sussex'. Her executrices were Sophia Smyth Fullerton and Isabel Fullerton (both of 'Arden', 24 Evansdale Road, Hawthorn), and Emily Fullerton of 31 Ocean Street, Bondi in New South Wales.

Mabel Singleton's son Denis Gordon Singleton, whose early years were spent in the care of the two women, was a Mosquito pilot in the RAF in World War Two. He achieved the rank of Wing Commander and was awarded a military OBE. He retained affectionate memories of the two maternal presences in his early life, and died in October 2008 at the age of 97.

§

Fullerton's first collection of poems, *Moods and Melodies,* published in Melbourne in 1908, was issued under her own name though she published individual works under pseudonyms that included 'E. Alpenstock', 'Robert Gray', 'Turner O. Linger', and 'Gordon Manners'. She published her mature work chiefly under the pen-name 'E'. Her biographer, Sylvia Martin, speculated that Fullerton may have initially adopted the pen name out of conviction that her gender and lack of tertiary education gravitated against recognition of her work, but by the 1920s, her authorship of the novels published under her own name—*Two Women* (1923), *The People of the Timber Belt* (1925) and *A Juno of the Bush* (1930)— had made her something of a celebrity. In 1925, the *Australasian* spoke of her recognition in 'artistic circles in Great Britain', especially after publication of the second of these novels, noting that her earlier (1923) autobiographical novel, *Clare, Margaret*, had shared a £250 prize offered by the publisher, Philpots.

Fullerton's friend and colleague Miles Franklin (Stella Maria Sarah Miles Franklin, 1879-1954) also employed pen-names ('An Old Bachelor' and 'Vernacular', but chiefly 'Brent of Bin Bin'), but Franklin's identity became known early in her literary career. On Fullerton's death, Franklin arranged publication of Fullerton's last two poetry collections, *Moles Do So Little with their Privacy* and *The Wonder and the Apple,* both of which bore the attribution 'E' at Fullerton's insistence; the latter title bore Fullerton's dedication to 'The four Australian generations of my family'.

The poems in Fullerton's first collection of verse foreshadowed her concern with woman's love and independence. *Moods and Melodies* contained 39 sonnets and nine lyrical verses, whose language and themes reflected her religious upbringing and focus on doomed hero-figures, from a range of kindred, sometimes outcast spirits including Eve, Hagar,

Judas, and Joan of Arc. Poems on love also advance the sense of fated desire and action, as in her poem 'From the Star World': 'You and I must have met / In a star-world long ago; the thrill is with me yet, / I worshipped and loved you so'. Also present is her insistence on the desire and striving for reform of relationships, in poems like 'The Attributes', 'Talent and Genius', and 'The Reformer'.

In subsequent years, Fullerton's poetry confirms her adaptation of nationalist mythology to emphasise woman-oriented identity. Her poems, polemical writing and fiction, as well as her 1921 memoir *Bark House Days,* memorialise pioneering (in every sense) women, and portray the land and native flora as possessing sensuous female correspondences. Spring, rain, the bushland, youth, 'violets of joy' and what she called, in a poem of 1903 ('In the Night-Watches'), the 'soft luxurious warmth' of solitude, hold subtle significance of female desire. The world of men is correspondingly portrayed as mechanistic, gadget-obsessed (as in her poem 'Gadgets'), and unthinkingly or otherwise cruel to women (in her poem 'Puppets'). By contrast, her poems dwelling on the effects of war (exemplified in the poems reprinted here) are characteristically focused on women's pain rather than legendary aspects of mythic Australian male heroism.

References

Sally O'Neill, 'Fullerton, Mary Eliza (1868–1946)', Australian Dictionary of Biography, National Centre of Biography, Australian National University, http://adb.anu.edu.au/biography/fullerton-mary-eliza-6258/text10779, published first in hardcopy 1981, accessed online 7 February 2016.

Janice N. Brownfoot, 'Goldstein, Vida Jane (1869–1949)', Australian Dictionary of Biography, National Centre of Biography, Australian National University, http://adb.anu.edu.au/biography/goldstein-vida-jane-6418/text10975, published first in hardcopy 1983 and online version subsequently amended, accessed online 28 May 2016.

AustLit: The Resource for Australian Literature, 'Fullerton, Mary E.' http://www.austlit.edu.ezproxy.une.edu.au/run?ex=gGuidedSearch&type=simple&generalSearchString=fullerton%2C+mary&searchWhere=author Accessed 14 March 2006 [for Fullerton's religious upbringing].

'Haverbrack', *Local History News. Malvern Historical Society Inc. Newsletter* no. 20, August-September 2009, p. 2.

'Mr. Robert Singleton. Death Announced', *Argus*, Tuesday 24 February 1914, p. 9.

Argus, Monday 28 June 1929, p. 1 [Death of 'Ella, wife of late Robert Fullerton of Glenmaggie, aged 68 years'].

Sylvia Martin, *Passionate friends: Mary Fullerton, Mabel Singleton & Miles Franklin*, London: Onlywomen Press, 2001.

Sylvia Martin, Becoming-Violet: Mary Fullerton's Poetry and Lesbian Desire. Journal of the Association for the Study of Australian Literature, [S.l.], p. 99-104, Feb. 2013. ISSN 1833-6027. Available at: <https://openjournals.library.sydney.edu.au/index.php/JASAL/article/view/9514/9404>. Date accessed: 09 mar. 2018.

'Women's Peace Army at Guild Hall', *Woman Voter*, Thursday 19 July 1917, p. 1 [Fullerton's speech on 'voluntarism'].

John Lack, 'The great madness of 1914-1918: families at war on Melbourne's eastern and western fronts', La Trobe Journal, No. 96, September 2015 [p. 78] https://www.slv.vic.gov.au/sites/default/files/La-Trobe-Journal-96-John-Lack.pdf, accessed 15 May 2018.

Joy Damousi, 'Ross, Robert Samuel (1873–1931)' Australian Dictionary of Biography, National Centre of Biography, Australian National University, http://adb.anu.edu.au/biography/ross-robert-samuel-8274/text14497, published first in hardcopy 1988, accessed online 5 February 2016.

'Mary Fullerton—The Mysterious "E". She Wrote for Labour', *Tribune* (Sydney), Friday 24 May 1946, p. 4.

Argus, Wednesday 1 May 1946, p. 19 [Probate notification relating to Fullerton's estate].

Telegraph Announcements, Tuesday 9 February 2008 ['Death of W/Cmdr Denis Gordon Singleton OBE on 20 October 2008']. http://announcements.telegraph.co.uk/deaths/87947/singleton. Accessed 1 February 2016.

Mary Fullerton, 'In the Night-Watches', *Bulletin,* 6 June 1903, p. 12.

Mary Fullerton ('E'), 'Gadgets' and 'Puppets', in *The Penguin Book of Australian Women Poets*, ed. Susan Hampton and Kate Llewellyn, Ringwood: Penguin, 1986, pp. 28-29.

Publications
Poetry
Moods and Melodies: Sonnets and Lyrics, Melbourne: Lothian, 1908.
The Breaking Furrow, Melbourne: Sydney J. Endacott, 1921.
Moles Do So Little With Their Privacy, Sydney: Angus and Robertson, 1942.
The Wonder and the Apple, Sydney: Angus and Robertson, 1946.

Novels (the first three under her own name)
Two Women: Clare, Margaret, by Two Anonymous Writers, London: Philpot, 1923 [Clare is attributed to Fullerton].
The People of the Timber Belt, London: Philpot, 1925.
A Juno of the Bush, London: Heath Cranton, 1930.
Rufus Sterne: A Novel, Edinburgh: William Blackwood, 1932 [Written under pseudonym Robert Gray].
Murders at the Crab Apple Café, London: Herbert Jenkins, 1933 [written under pseudonym Gordon Manners].

Memoirs
Bark House Days, Melbourne: Sydney J. Endacott, 1921.
The Australian Bush, London: J.M. Dent, 1928.

Mary Fullerton
The Targets

All over the world the women
    In travail by day and night;
Are bringing to life the targets
    For the day when the monarchs fight.

All over the world the women
    Think they are rearing men,
So they and the failing fathers
    Shall live in their youth again.

In many a cot the woman,
    With the babe on her shelt'ring breast,
Is nursing his limbs for battle
    A-crooning her son to rest.

All over the world the women
    Give service and love and life;
While over the world the tyrants
    Are brewing the brew of strife.

All over the world the women
    Are yielding their sons to-day
For well is the lesson taught them
    That the woman must obey.

And the sons of the women fettered
    Alone in the right to give,
Are slaves of the ancient system,
    And shall be while they live.

And the fathers toil and suffer
    For the day when the world runs red:
Feeding their sons for targets,
    With a hard won bitter bread.

Oh, women, the wide world over,
    Oh, fathers, who father men,
Shall yet the word awake you
    That's won by the flaming pen.

By the soul that knows the value
    Of the sons your patience breeds:
That tyrants themselves are mortal,
    And mortal the tyrants' creeds.

Shall never the word awake you,
    Spoke by the seer's stern mouth;
So the rulers shall seek for targets
    And find them nor north nor south.

Shall never the vision wake you,
    Sprung living within the soul;
Ye sons of the sacred masses,
    The pieces that make the whole.

Oh, not till the hour ye take it
    That light to your spirits dim;
Will the tyrant lose his targets
    And the world be quit of him.

Till the mothers, sons and fathers,
    Rise up as a single soul:
Crying, "You are not master,
    We will not render toll.

The breed of the slave is perished,
    The race of the gods begun,
We say it each sire and mother,
    We say it each sacred son.

We toil for the home and nation,
    We live for the joyful earth;
Not the red recurring harvest,
    And the terrible aftermath.

Soul is too great for target,
      The life for a tyrant's pawn;
No more is the unit only
      A parcel of muscle and brawn.

All over the world the toilers
      Have travailed the god to birth;
And we who died for the despot
      Shall live for the fruitful earth.

For the lamp in the soul is lighted,
      And the clarion loudly rings:
"No more be the patient people
      The targets of bloody kings."

Source: The *Woman Voter*, Monday 5 October 1914, p. 2.

Mary Fullerton
The Gippslander

Oh, for the smell of the fern roots,
    As I broke them through with the plough;
I close my eyes and I fancy
    I'm back on the old flat now.
I'm turning the furrows even.
    In the slant of the setting sun,
In the paddock down by the river,
    Where the fern roots twist and run.

Where the young scrub sprouts for ever,
    And the flapping bark falls down
From the long, lean tree trunks loosened,
    Curling, and crisp and brown.
I fancy the fire of tussocks
    Tangy and sweet still burns
On the rugged fallow spaces,
    With the litter of scrub and ferns.

Oh, the blue smoke rolling upward
    In the chilly evening air,
Goes drifting down the river,
    To sleep in the shadows there.
And oh, for the sigh of Dobbin,
    When called by the early star,
With a slap on his back, the traces
    I loose from the swingle bar.

And along the narrow pathway
    Where the tussocks switch the knee;
Dobbin and I go homeward.
    Each to his well-earned "tea."
There in the kitchen window
    Mother has set the light,
And the table is waiting ready,
    And the room is warm and bright.

Somehow the work has tired me
    As it never used to do;
There's a weakness running through me,
    And an ache in my body, too;
So after supper's over
    Lord, I've had dreams again,
Dozed while I mused, till fancy
    Was fact in my weary brain.

I'm Private Jones in England,
    Far, far from the old home track;
With a shrapnel wound, in the shoulder
    And a bullet hole through my back.
Still, I'm not so sure I'm wanting
    Just yet to be home once more,
Till I've seen right through to the finish
    The job I enlisted for.

Source: *Weekly Times Annual* (Victoria), Thursday 4 November 1915, p. 41.

Mary Fullerton ('E')
Next Door

The waves of European conflict surge
    Against our shores, the striving millions fight,
But greater far calamity to him—
    The rabbit man's grey pony died last night.

About the town, men read the posted names
    Of those who strive no more for wrong or right;
And women weep: but what is that to him—
    The rabbit man's grey pony died last night.

The widow in his street is sore bereft,
    Her son is fallen, gone her spirit's light,
The European wave has reached her heart—
    The parson came and brought the news last night.

At last he finds community of grief,
    His home-bound-heart can comprehend her plight:
He knows the widow, and he knew her son:
    The rabbit man whose pony died last night.

Source: E (Mary Eliza Fullerton), 'Next Door', in *Birth: A Little Journal of Australian Poetry,* vol. 2, no. 24, November 1918, p. 4.

Mary E. Fullerton
War Time

Young John, the postman, day by day,
In sunshine or in rain,
Comes down our road with words of doom
In envelopes of pain.

What cares he as he wings along
At his mechanic part,
How many times his hand lets fall
The knocker on a heart?

He whistles merry scraps of song,
Whate'er his bag contain—
Of words of death, of words of doom
In envelopes of pain.

Source: Mary E. Fullerton, *The Breaking Furrow,* Melbourne: Commonwealth of Australia & Sydney J. Endacott, 1921, p. 29.

Mary Fullerton
A Man's a Sliding Mood

Ardent in love and cold in charity,
Loud in the market, timid in debate:
Scornful of foe unbuckled in the dust,
At whimper of a child compassionate,

A man's a sliding mood from hour to hour,
Rage, and a singing forest of bright birds,
Laughter with lovely friends, and loneliness,
Woe with her heavy horn of unspoke words.

What is he then with his conflicting moods,
Or is there in a deeper dwelling place
Some stilly shaping thing that bides and broods?

Source: *The New Oxford Book of Australian Verse*, ed Les Murray, South Melbourne: Oxford University Press, 1996, p. 86.

LESBIA HARFORD

Lesbia Venner Harford (née Keogh) was born at the Melbourne suburb of Brighton on 9 April 1891. Her mother, Helen Beatrice Keogh (née Moore), was related to the Earl of Drogheda, and her father, Edmund Joseph Keogh (son of Edmond Keogh of St Kilda) was a wealthy financial agent. Helen and Edmund Joseph were married at St Brigid's church, Fitzroy on 7 July 1890. Lesbia, their first child, was born with a congenital heart illness that would restrict her entire life. When Edmund Keogh's real estate business failed around the turn of the century, he moved to Western Australia to try to rebuild his finances. He worked for a time as a boundary rider and farmer, recording his occupation as camel driver, and Helen as his wife and next of kin, when he enlisted as a Private in 1917 in Western Australia. He served with the Imperial Camel Corps and the 14th Light Horse Regiment in Egypt, and returned to Australia in 1919. He later moved to Victoria, but never resumed life with his wife. He died in October 1945 in the Alfred Hospital as a result of injuries sustained when he was struck by a car in St Kilda Road.

To support herself and her children—Lesbia, Estelle (born 1892), Esmond (born 1895), and Gerald ('Jelly', born 1898)—Helen Keogh first found genteel jobs, took in boarders and begged relief from her relatives. She served as Superintendent of St Margaret's 'Trained Nurses Home' in St Kilda Road from at least 1912 until 1924, when she moved with her staff to Richmond. She died aged 81 in September 1951.

Lesbia Harford was educated at the Brigidine convent school, 'Clifton', in Melbourne, and the Loreto convent school 'Mary's Mount', at Ballarat. She abandoned her family's Catholicism, and by 1915 had joined the former Unitarian minister and socialist Frederick Sinclaire's Free Religious Fellowship, a left-wing group that espoused a Shavian, non-Marxist socialism. (Some other radical thinkers attracted by Sinclaire's ideas and activities included the playwright Louis Esson, poets Bernard O'Dowd, Frank Wilmot, and Marie E. Pitt, and the writers Vance Palmer and Nettie Higgins—later Palmer). Harford advocated free love, and maintained attachments to both men and women, including Katie Lush, a philosophy tutor at Ormonde College, at the University of Melbourne.

Harford enrolled in Law in 1912, and paid her way by teaching art in schools. She graduated LL.B. in 1916, in the same class as Robert Gordon Menzies, and was one of the very few Melbourne students to oppose Australia's participation in the War. Her interest in social issues led to her working in clothing and textile factories, and she was elected state vice-President of the Federated Clothing and Allied Trades Union. With her brother, Esmond Venner 'Bill' Keogh, she joined the Industrial Workers of the World (the 'Wobblies'), and she formed a friendship with Norman Jeffrey and became the lover of the Marxist scholar and fellow activist Guido Baracchi (1887-1975). Guido had studied abroad and returned to Australia in 1914, becoming a prominent anti-war campaigner and founder of the Australian Labor College. A member of the International Industrial Workers (after the name change brought about by censorship), he edited the organisation's journal, *International Solidarity* from 1917. Jeffrey and Baracchi became founding members of the Communist Party of Australia, which Lesbia never joined.

Lesbia went to Sydney in 1918 and lived with IIW friends engaged in a campaign for release of the Sydney Twelve (members of the organisation charged with treason, sedition, arson and forgery). When in good health, she coached university students and briefly worked as a maid in a Fairfax family. On 23 November 1920, she married Patrick John O'Flaghertie Fingal ('Pat') Harford, a fellow IIW member and a clicker (cutter of leather for shoe and boot uppers) in his father's Fitzroy boot factory. Pat and Lesbia returned to live at Lesbia's mother's boarding house, and Lesbia tried to complete her legal qualifications. Patrick worked with the émigré Scottish stained-glass designer and painter William Frater at Brooks Robinson and Co. Ltd., manufacturers of stained glass. Under the influence of Frater, who promoted post-Impressionist principles and practices in art, Pat became a modernist painter. He and Lesbia had no children, and were estranged in the final years of Lesbia's life; she wrote of Pat's alcoholism and also of his tenderness.

Harford completed her law articles in 1926, and in July 1927, she died of heart and lung failure at St Vincents Hospital in Melbourne. Attributions of the cause of her lifelong fragile health variously refer to her early heart problem and rheumatic fever to tuberculosis.

§

Lesbia's brother Esmond considered himself a Unitarian, and he was enrolled in agricultural science at Melbourne University when war broke out. Enlisting in the AIF on 13 November 1914, he was posted to the 3rd

Light Horse Field Ambulance. He returned to Australia briefly in 1915, disowning his pacifist principles. Posted again in 1916, he served on the Western Front. At War's end, he had been awarded the Military Medal and the Distinguished Conduct Medal. After the War, he reconnected with his radical friends, spent a year working on a soldier settler's farm with his alcoholic father, and took up medical studies at the University of Melbourne, completing final examinations one month after Lesbia died. His medical research career into viruses and cancer was outstanding, but he accepted no honours, and destroyed his papers. In May 1970 (the year of his death), he joined in a huge Anti-Vietnam Moratorium March in Melbourne.

Lesbia's younger brother Gerald Basil Venner Keogh enlisted in March 1917 at the age of eighteen years and seven months, embarked on 9 November 1917, and served in the 11th Australian Field Artillery Brigade from November 1917 until June 1918, before joining the Australian Flying Corps.

Lesbia's younger sister Estelle Venner Keogh (later Wilkins) trained at the Alfred Hospital, served at the Base Hospital in Glenroy, and volunteered to join Queen Alexandra's Imperial Nursing Service Reserve. She received the Royal Red Cross Medal First Class from the King at Buckingham Palace in January 1918 for her work in France. In Launceston in April 1918, she married Lieutenant George Wilkins MC, whom she had met during the voyage to Australia when he was being invalided home. Wilkins also served in World War II and died in Borneo in 1945. Estelle died in Sydney in 1966.

§

Much of Harford's poetry presents an engaging blend of realism and idealism, characterised by her immersion in the details of working-class experience, her practical involvement in social campaigns, the shared affections of what she called 'the lowly' (in her poem 'The Troop-ship'), and the beauty of 'enduring love'. Her poems have the lapidary polish of memorable epigrams. Her poem 'To Leslie' is exemplary in this respect. Her most recent editor, Dennis Oliver remarks 'I do consider Lesbia Harford's "Ours was a friendship in secret, my dear" the finest Australian poem of World War 1.'

Harford was first published in the Melbourne Literary Club journal *Birth* and the Club's annual in 1921. She showed poems to friends or enclosed them in letters, and she sang some of poems to tunes of her own composition. She remarked that she was in no hurry to publish.

In 1927, Percival Serle included three of her poems on memory and pain in *An Australasian Anthology*, and Nettie Palmer quoted four of Harford's poems in a review of the anthology, but Harford's poems were not collected until 1941 when Nettie Palmer edited an edition with Commonwealth Literary Fund assistance. Her notebooks, said to have been destroyed in a fire when her father's shack was burnt down, are in fact preserved in three folders in the Marjorie Pizer Papers in the Mitchell Library in Sydney. Harford's grave is in Kew cemetery. Her father died in September 1945, her mother in September 1951.

References

Lesbia Harford, *The Poems of Lesbia Harford,* with Foreword by Nettie Palmer, Melbourne: Melbourne University Press, 1941.

Lesbia Harford, *The Poems of Lesbia Harford,* ed Drusilla Modjeska and Marjorie Pizer, Sydney: Sirius/Angus & Robertson, 1985

Lesbia Harford, *Collected Poems*, ed Oliver Dennis, Crawley (Perth): UWAP, 2014.

Lesley Lamb, 'Harford, Lesbia Venner (1891–1927)', Australian Dictionary of Biography, National Centre of Biography, Australian National University, http://adb.anu.edu.au/biography/harford-lesbia-venner-6562/text11285, published first in hardcopy 1983, accessed online 25 January 2016.

Robin Gollan, 'Baracchi, Guido Carlo Luigi (1887–1975)', Australian Dictionary of Biography, National Centre of Biography, Australian National University, http://adb.anu.edu.au/biography/baracchi-guido-carlo-luigi-9422/text16563, published first in hardcopy 1993, accessed online 25 January 2016.

'Lesbia Harford'. Wikipedia. https://en.wikipedia.org/wiki/Lesbia_Harford accessed 26 January 2016.

'Social Notes', *Australasian*, Saturday, 23 March 1918, p. 37 [Return of Sister Estelle Keogh to Melbourne].

Lyndsay Gardiner and Geoffrey Serle, 'Keogh, Esmond Venner (Bill) (1895–1970)', Australian Dictionary of Biography, National Centre of Biography, Australian National University, http://adb.anu.edu.au/biography/keogh-esmond-venner-bill-10724/text19003, published first in hardcopy 2000, accessed online 26 January 2016.

'Estelle Venner Keogh–Staff Nurse, RRC, QAIMNSR', Discovering Anzacs, National Archives of Australia and New Zealand, http://www.discoveringanzacs.naa.gov.au/browse/person/901044. Accessed online 5 Nettie Palmer. 'Lovely Lyrics', *The Advocate* (Melbourne), Thursday 13 November 1941, p. 11.

Gerald Basil Venner Keogh. Australia Remembers. http://australiaremembers.net.au/anzacstories/anzac/?aid=159967#book5/page4-5. Accessed 8 February 2018.

Argus, Saturday 28 June 1890, p. 5 [Marriage of Edmond Joseph Keogh and Helen Beatrice Moore on 11 June 1890].

Argus, 10 September 1898. [Birth notice for Gerald Basil Venner Keogh].

Argus, 30 March 1916, p. 5 [University of Melbourne. 'Supplementary Annual Examinations, March 1916'. Fourth Year Law results].

New South Wales Registrar of Births Deaths and Marriages. Marriage of Gerald Basil Venner Keogh to Beatrice Elizabeth Gray, 1936 [No. 5817/1936].

Argus, Monday 15 October 1945 [Death of Edmund Joseph Keogh].

Argus, Thursday 20 September 1951 [Death of Helen Beatrice Keogh].

New South Wales Registrar of Births Deaths and Marriages. Death of Gerald Basil Venner Keogh, 1962 (No. 34538/1962).

Jeff Sparrow, 'Render it barely', Sydney Review of Books, http://www.sydneyreviewofbooks.com/collected-poems-lesbia-harford/ accessed 26 January 2016 [review of *Collected Poems: Lesbia Harford*, ed. Oliver Dennis].

Publications.

Lesbia Harford, *Collected Poems: Lesbia Harford,* Oliver Dennis, ed., Crawley (WA): UWA Publishing, 2014.

Lesbia Harford, *The poems of Lesbia Harford,* Drusilla Modjeska and Marjorie Pizer eds, North Ryde: Sirius, 1985.

Lesbia Harford, 'Flowering Plum', 'Lovers Parted' and 'Tree Wisdom', in Percival Serle, Frank Wilmot and Robert H. Croll, eds, *An Australasian Anthology (Australian and New Zealand Poems)*, London: W. Collins Sons & Co. Ltd., 1927, pp. 273-274.

Lesbia Harford
The Troop-ships

Up the river in the sun,
we rowed slowly.
Oftentimes the willow boughs
Screened us wholly.
Ours were all the tiny joys
That bless the lowly.

Mighty ships upon the seas
Outward bore you.
Battles dim and agony
Lay before you.
I half wished our willows spread
Their branches o'er you.

Source: *Collected Poems: Lesbia Harford,* Dennis Oliver, ed., Crawley (WA): UWAP, 2014, p. 16.

Lesbia Harford
['The people have drunk the wine of peace']

The people have drunk the wine of peace
In the streets of town.
They smile as they drift with hearts at rest
Uphill and down.

The people have drunk the wine of peace,
They are mad with joy.
Never again need they lie and fear
Death for a boy.

1918

Source: *The Poems of Lesbia Harford,* Drusilla Modjeska and Marjorie Pizer, eds, Sydney: Sirius, 1985, p. 103.

Lesbia Harford
['Ours was a friendship in secret, my dear']

Ours was a friendship in secret, my dear,
Stolen from fate.
I must be secret still, show myself calm
Early and late.

'Isn't it sad he was killed', I must hear
With a smooth face.
'Yes, it is sad.'—O my darling, my own,
My heart of grace.

Source: *Collected Poems: Lesbia Harford,* Dennis Oliver, ed., Crawley (WA): UWAP, 2014, p. 30.

Lesbia Harford
To Leslie

Across the sea
Come homeward ships
With freight of boys.

And still must we
Forgo the joys
Of meeting lips.

Source: *Source: Collected Poems:* Lesbia Harford, Dennis Oliver, ed., Crawley (WA): UWAP, 2014, p. 35.

GERTRUDE HART

Photograph of Gertrude Hart (1920/30) by Esther Paterson (1892-1971). State Library Victoria.

Gertrude Hart (who wrote also as E. Gertrude Hart, Ethel Gertrude Hart, E.G.H., and T.L.O.A) 1873–1965, was born in Williamstown, Victoria, and grew up in Stawell. Her parents, Mary (née Dilks, daughter of a merchant or chemist) and the Reverend Richard Hart (1818-1908), Wesleyan minister and steel manufacturer, were married at Leith, Greenock on 2 December 1851, and sailed for Hobart the following year, arriving in January 1853. Their first daughter was born and died at sea. The couple moved to Geelong, where the Rev. Hart was installed as a minister. Their surviving eight children were Mary Ruth, Richard Henry, Thomas Frederick, William Arthur, Flora Hannah Sarah, Mary Jane, Annie Alice and Gertrude. Gertrude's mother was 43 and her father 55 when Gertrude was born on 1 June 1873.

Gertrude published her first story at age fourteen, and by the turn of the century had published several books for children and young adults. The title page of her 1890 children's story, *Wanted—A Servant*, lists Gertrude as co-author of *The Man Next Door*, by T.L.O.A.—presumably 'Two Ladies of Australia', in token of the pseudonym A.L.O.E. ('A Lady of England') that had been employed by the popular nineteenth-century girls' writer Charlotte Maria Tucker (1821-1893).

With her sister Annie Alice Hart (1869–1966), a prolific short story writer, Gertrude wrote three children's books, all published by W. B. Horner in London: *Under One Roof* (1900), *The Man Next Door* (1900) and *At the Bend of the Creek* (1902). Writing as E. Gertrude Hart, she wrote two romances for girls, *Clouds that Pass* and *Nora's Night of Terror* before the First World War. The periodical *Graphic of Australia* reported in 1918 that Hart was living in Ivanhoe and launching out in a more ambitious direction with a novel entitled *The Laughter Lady*. The book, subtitled 'A Story for Children of Different Ages', was already in print. Like her sister, she contributed short fiction for adults to the *Australasian* newspaper, as well as the *Argus* and the Sydney *Bulletin*. Hart also wrote lyrics for several songs, including 'The Call of the Sea', with music by Bene Gibson Smyth and 'I Know the Roses', with music by George Sutton.

In 1930 and 1931, she ran a circulating library in Sandringham and, with Bernard Cronin, founded the Old Derelicts' Club to improve conditions for struggling authors and artists. (The Melbourne Society of Australian Authors grew out of this Club, with Cronin as first president from 1928-1934; the organisation wound up two years later, when, as Cronin said, it was becoming 'infiltrated by politics'.) The 1922 anthology *The Little Track and Other Verses* gives some flavour of the company she kept and the tone of their verse: Bernard Cronin and Cecil Doyle each contributed three poems, Hart four, Capel Boake (Doris Boake Kerr) five, and Myra Morris six. The moods are introspective and celebratory and chiefly related to the seasons, dreams, and rural sights. Three of Capel Boake's poems dwelt on memories of lost friends.

After the War, Hart published poetry sporadically, chiefly in the *Australasian*, and occasionally in the *Argus* and the Sydney *Bulletin*. Her poem, 'Armistice Day' is the most outstanding of those relating to the War.

The Australian electoral roll records Hart's successive changes of address through her adult life, from Corio, Newtown, Healesville, Ivanhoe, and Brighton, to Box Hill. Her address at the time of her death was listed as Ferny Creek, and she was buried at the Ferntree Gully Cemetery.

Publications

Poetry

Clouds That Pass, London: S.W. Partridge, 1898.
The Little Track and Other Verses, Melbourne: Robertson & Mullens, 1922. [An anthology, no editor indicated, containing poems by Bernard Cronin, Capel Boake, Cecil Doyle, Gertrude Hart, and Myra Morris. Hart contributed 'The Old Bush Track', pp. 10-11, 'Spring, The Laggard', pp. 15-16, 'Tide Way', p.21, and 'The Undertone', p. 32].

Fiction

Wanted—A Servant: An Australian Story, London: John Bateman, 1890 [picture book for children, illustrated by Ben Taplin].
The Man Next Door, London: W.B. Horner & Son, n.d. [189?]
[as E.G.H.] *Nora's Night of Terror,* London, W.B. Horner & Son, 1898.
[with Annie A. Hart], *At the Bend of the Creek: A Story of Australia*, London: S.W. Partridge, 1902 [young adult fiction].
The Dream Girl, Melbourne: George Robertson, 1912; New York: Doubleday, 1913.
The Laughter Lady: A Story for Children of Different Ages, Melbourne: The Melbourne Publishing Company, 1914 [children's fiction].
Chubby. London: Hutchinson & Co, n.d. [1937] [children's fiction].
Chubby and Pip. London and Melbourne: Hutchinson & Co., 1940 [children's fiction].

References

Weekly Times (Melbourne), Saturday 7 June 1873, p. 8 [Family Notices: Gertrude's birth on 1 on 1 June 1873 at Wesleyan Parsonage, Williamstown].
Bernice May [Zora Cross], 'Writer and Librarian: A Long-Distance Talk with Gertrude Hart', *Bulletin*, 21 November 1930, p. 2.
John Arnold, John Hay et al., *The Bibliography of Australian Literature:* F-J, St Lucia: University of Queensland Press, 2004, p. 367.
'Mainly About People', *Graphic of Australia*, Thursday 5 December 1918, p. 6 [Hart embarking on a novel].
Sally O'Neill, 'Cronin, Bernard Charles (1884–1968)', Australian Dictionary of Biography, National Centre of Biography, Australian National University, http://adb.anu.edu.au/biography/cronin-bernard-charles-5826/text9893, published first in hardcopy 1981, accessed online 2 February 2016.
Victorian Public Records (probate site). Probate of Gertrude Hart, spinster Ferny Creek, granted March 1965. Information courtesy of Stephanie Sharkey, email, 5 March 2019.

Gertrude Hart
We Must Do More

We must do more; we have grown slack in dreaming.
       While fruitful seasons smiled on our land—
While peace unruffled lulled us in its seeming,
          And that we wished for came into our hand.
              We have grown slack—now ask we pardon, Lord!

Too long we slept, and heeded not the warning.
       Mutter of thunder, and the thick, oppressive air;
sudden it broke, a piteous red dawning,
          And war had come—and war was everywhere!
              We are still slack—pardon our slackness, Lord!

We rest in safety; safety they are buying
       Who smile as death comes near them, giving life
For us who yet are passively denying
          Men who are needed in the mortal strife.
              We are still slack—wake us from slackness, Lord!

We must do more; the world is full of weeping
       And plain unspeakable and hideous unrest.
Shall it be said of us that we were sleeping,
          While others gave their dearest and their best?
              For this, our sinful slackness—oh, forgive, our God!

Afar they beckon; not for deathless glory—
       Not for a blazing record on life's endless scroll—
Not for yet one name in thrilling story—
          Or writ upon the world's great Honour roll.
              They call for help!—to deafened ears, oh God!

We must do more; there must be no false stilling
       Of our cleat duty while we glibly say,
'God bless those far ones, brave, and strong, and willing,
          Who light our cause through weary night and day.'
              We must send men; and quickly, quickly—
              Then we can truly pray—Send peace, oh God!

Source: *Argus* (Melbourne), Saturday 2 January 1915, p. 8; *Clarence and Richmond Examiner* (Grafton, NSW), Saturday 9 January 1916, p.2; *Shepparton News,* Monday 11 January 1915, p. 3; *Spectator and Methodist Chronicle* (Melbourne), Friday 18 June 1915, p. 878.

Gertrude Hart
April and After

This is the garden you loved so well.
    (April moods of an April day),
This the path where your footsteps fell,
    And the glimpse near the bend, of foam white bay.
The old shy, grace, is it vision or dream?
    Flitting form and eyes of grey,
A puzzled frown or sunny gleam,
    April moods on an April day.
        Eh! But the world grows old and grey!

For a chill crept round us like a blight
    (April rain on an April day),
And you seemed half hid from my longing sight
    While I kissed your lips, as a lover may.
'Twas a devil's doubt I had harboured long.
    And I flung it at you with a sneer,
While sudden thrilled a bird's wild song
    From the tall, white gum-tree swaying near,
        April rain on an April day—
        Fear or contempt in your eyes of grey?

The heavy drops fell thick and blent
    (April showers on an April day),
Drenched the roses and stole their scent,
    Blurring the glimpse of foam-white bay.
You turned and left me without a word,
    And you smiled a frozen, mocking smile.
All that was evil gathered and stilled
    My deep resentment, and your guile...?
        April showers on an April day—
        Eh! But it's all so far away

'Twas the blasting breath of my unjust doubt
        April mists over foam-white bay);
Lovers' ways are past finding out—
        Something of you I killed that day!
            Eh, But life is cold and grey!

Roar of cannon and scream of shell
        (April glamour is far away),
Life moves on to a tolling knell,
        And the love in your, eyes is gone for aye.
Had I but trusted—comes clearer light
        Where death lurks waiting for its prey.
Yet you steal to me in the fevered night,
        As if you have never been away.
Cool, little hands that touch my brow
        Soothing an evergrowing pain—
Something. is dimming from my sight—
        Would I might see you smile again,
            April gold of an April day.
            Eh! but the mists creep wan and grey!

Only last night I was full of life
        Only I fancy l see your face—
Only you've come, and, it seems I can sleep.
        Here—with the old, shy, wistful grace—
Death clears vision, and wants are few
        If, when I wake, there are flowers—and you!
            April gold of an April day.
            Eh! But the gold outshines the grey!

Source: *Australasian*, Saturday 5 May 1917, p. 40.

Gertrude Hart
Armistice Day

Two minutes—while the city holds its breath:
    Hushed in a pulsing silence quick with pride
And tender thought of those who gave their best
    To the great nation for whose sake they died!
Two minutes—while the thronging feet are still,
    And quiet broods, with sheltering, outspread wing:
And heads are bowed, and there are healing tears
    For hearts that quiver with remembering.
So much we give them who gave all for us—
    A pause in life: a grief that knows no shame.
Two minutes' silence—and a throb of pain
    At thought of some well-loved and honoured name!

Source: *Bulletin,* 11 November 1926, p. 10.

CAPEL BOAKE (DORIS BOAKE KERR)

Miss Doris Kerr, Melbourne *Table Talk*, Thursday 5 July 1917, p. 26.
State Library Victoria.

Doris Boake Kerr was born on 29 August 1889 at Summer Hill in Sydney, elder daughter of Adelaide Eva Kerr (née Boake) and Gregory Augustine Kerr, civil servant. Her maternal grandfather, Barcroft Capel Boake (1838-1921), had migrated to Australia in the 1850s and set up as a professional photographer, first in Melbourne, then Sydney. He was the father of the poet Barcroft Boake (1866-1892, surveyor, boundary rider, author of the famous ballad 'Where the Dead Men Lie'), whose death by suicide was frequently referred to in reviews of Doris's poetry and prose. In a 1917 review of Doris's first novel, for instance, Doris's mother, Adelaide was recalled as 'one of the three pretty misses Boake of a generation past, her brother being the unfortunate young poet, the late Barcroft Boake'.

Doris moved to Melbourne with her family in 1893 when her father (whose misshapen foot was eventually amputated) lost his position with the New South Wales Railways Department. Her father failing to hold down regular employment, Doris's mother supported the family by working for a professional photographer, and the family settled at Caulfield, where Doris lived until her death. Her father died in 1933, and her mother in August 1944. Doris predeceased her mother by two months.

Kerr attended a State school but considered that she educated herself at the Prahran Public Library. She left home early and worked first as a shop assistant, then typist, then librarian, experiences reflected in those of Helen Somerset, heroine of her 1917 novel *Painted Clay*. Kerr had adopted the pen name 'Capel Boake' before the War, and the name appeared with her first story in the *Australasian* in January 1916. By the time *Painted Clay* appeared, her identity was well-known in Melbourne. She wrote three further novels, the third of which, like *The Selected Poems of Capel Boake,* was published posthumously. With Bernard Cronin and Gertrude Hart, she was a founding member of the Society of Australian Authors, and by the early 1940s, she was working as secretary to the Australian book collector and literary patron J.K. Moir, credit manager at Payne's Bon Marché store in Melbourne's Bourke Street. In 1939, she received a small grant from the Commonwealth Literary Fund to support the writing of her novel *The Twig is Bent*, which appeared after her death.

When Kerr died suddenly of a cerebral haemorrhage on 5 June 1944 at home, her friend and fellow poet and novelist Myra Morris wrote to Moir, paying tribute to Kerr's qualities: 'I feel that I would like to write to you as we talked about you a lot yesterday — Doris and I. And I know how much this awful thing will mean to you ... There'll never be anyone else like Doris—so generous, so full of understanding, with so rare a mind ... I've lost my best friend—and you've lost an irreplaceable co-worker and friend'. In 1949, Morris wrote the forward to a fine limited edition of Kerr's poetry.

Kerr's poetic output was slender, but it evidences a discerning ear for dialogue and a gift for confident versification in lyrical and ballad forms. She contributed five poems to the 1922 anthology *The Little Track and Other Verses* that also contained poems by her friend and literary collaborator Bernard Cronin. Three of the five poems ('The Little Track', 'Forgetfulness', and 'Stitchin' Seams') have particular poignancy relating to lost friends.

Publications

Painted Clay, Melbourne: Australasian Authors Agency, 1917; London: Virago, 1986.

[With Bernard Cronin, under the joint name Stephen Grey], *Kangaroo Rhymes.* Melbourne: Smithson Bros, 1922 [Rhymes for children].

The Little Track and Other Verses, Melbourne: Robertson & Mullens, 1922, pp. 17-18. [An anthology, with no editor indicated, containing poems by Bernard Cronin, Capel Boake, Cecil Doyle, Gertrude Hart, and Myra Morris].

The Romany Mark, Sydney: New South Wales Bookstall Co., 1923.

The Dark Thread, London: Hutchinson, 1936.

The Twig is Bent, Sydney: Sydney: Angus & Robertson, 1946. [Serialised in the *Western Mail,* 1 December 1949-16 March 1950].

The Selected Poems of Capel Boake, Ferntree Gully: John Kirtley, 1949.

References

'Painted Clay' [review], *West Gippsland Gazette* (Warragul), Tuesday 10 July 1917, p. 6 [Reference to Adelaide Kerr's sisters and brother].

Age, Wednesday 17 May 1933, p.1 {Death notice of Gregory Augustine Kerr, at 'Kuringai', Keeron Street, Caulfield].

Age, Tuesday 6 June 1944, p. 5 [Death Notice of Doris Boake Kerr (Capel Boake) at 'Kuringai', Keeron Street, Caulfield].

Age, Tuesday 1 August 1944, p. 5 [Death Notice of Adelaide Eva Kerr, at 'Applegarth', Kent Avenue, Croydon].

John Arnold, 'An Extraordinary Man: John Kinmont Moir', *The La Trobe Journal*, nos. 47 & 48, 1991, pp. 100-106, esp. 102, on Doris Kerr's friendship with Moir. http://www3.slv.vic.gov.au/latrobejournal/issue/latrobe-47-48/t1-g-t9.html Accessed 24 February 2016.

John Arnold, 'Kerr, Doris Boake (1889–1944)', Australian Dictionary of Biography, National Centre of Biography, Australian National University, http://adb.anu.edu.au/biography/kerr-doris-boake-10728/text19011, published first in hardcopy 2000, accessed online 10 February 2016.

Gavin De Lacy, 'Three Neglected Women Writers of the 1930s: Jean Campbell, "Capel Boake", and "Georgia Rivers"', *The La Trobe Journal*, No. 83, May 2009, pp. 26-37, esp. pp. 35-36. http://www3.slv.vic.gov.au/latrobejournal/issue/latrobe-83/t1-g-t4.html

Capel Boake (Doris Boake Kerr)
Stitchin' Seams

I sit close ter the winder pane, an' stitch away at seams;
The winder glass is cracked an' broke, but still the sunlight gleams.
Across the sill, an' on my cheek its golden glory streams.
I hate it cos it makes me think, when I am stitchin' seams.

I must not think, I will not think, for that's a silly game;
The other girls they laugh an' joke—I used ter do the same.
But now I stitch an' stitch an' stitch, and bright the needle gleams;
I've got no time fer silly thoughts when I am stitchin' seams;

One day the soldiers all passed by home comin' from the war.
I loved ter see the soldiers once, but that was long before
They called ter me ter see them pass, an' laughed an' cheered an' cried—
I couldn't see the seams that day no matter how I tried.

Gawd! Work the tr'adle fast again, the thoughts, is comin' quicker;
I almost thought o' 'im agin—Oh, Gawd! they're crowdin' thicker.
Fast, fast the treadle flies, and faster; bright the needle gleams.
Thank Gawd the thoughts is gone agin—for I am stitchin' seams.

The seams I've done, the seams I've stitched, they're mountin' up so high:
I sometimes think, if I don't stop, they'll almost touch the sky,
For all day long I stitch an' stitch an' keep on stitchin' seams.
An' when at last the day is done, I stitch them in my dreams.

Me life is changed—Oh, Gawd! it's queer, I don't know what it means!
I only know that Bill is dead, an' I am stitchin' seams.

Source: *Australasian*, Saturday 31 May 1919, p. 43 and *The Little Track and Other Verses*, Melbourne: Robertson & Mullens, 1922, pp. 17-18.

Capel Boake (Doris Boake Kerr)
Anzac Day 1927

The scarlet poppy burns again,
   The tender grasses wave,
The bitter almond sheds her leaves
   On many a nameless grave.
The earth has healed her wound again
   Where Turk and Christian met,
And stark across an alien sky
   The cross of Christ is set.

From north and south and east and west
   With eager eyes aflame
With heads erect and laughing lips
   The young Crusaders came.
The waves still wash the rocky coast,
   The evening shadows creep
Where through the dim receding years
   They tread the halls of sleep.

Oh, sacred land, Gallipoli!
   Home of our youthful dead;
How friendly is the springing grass
   That shields each narrow bed!
The toiling peasant turns to pray,
   Calling on his God,
And little children laugh and play
   Where once their footsteps trod.

Mourn not for them, nor wish them back;
   Life cannot harm them now;
The kiss of death has touched each cheek
   And pressed each icy brow.
Yet, on this day when first they died,
   Turn back the troubled years;
Pause in the press of life awhile;
   Give them again—our tears.

Source: *Selected Poems of Capel Boake With an Introduction by Myra Morris.* Ferntree Gully: John T. Kirtley, nd, ns [p. 24].

MARION MILLER KNOWLES

Marion Miller Knowles, M.B.E. National Library of Australia.
Call number(s) PIC Box PIC/7627 #PIC/7627/1-2

Marion Miller Knowles, eldest child of Irish immigrants Anne Maria Miller (née Bowen) and storekeeper James Miller, was born on 8 August 1865, at Woods Point on the Goulburn River in Victoria. Her three sisters, Helena Bridget ('Daisy'), Margaret and Sophie, and her brother James would appear in different guise as child characters in her later fiction.

The population of Woods Point (named for the initial storekeeper Henry Wood, who had set up a store to supply local gold miners) was on the increase by virtue of its proximity to the gold diggings around the Morning Stars Reef, but the population declined from its height of thirty thousand by the time Marion Miller attended a local state school as a pupil-teacher in 1878. Educated earlier at home, she enjoyed poetry and soon began to write, continuing through periods when she was separated from her family and friends while relief teaching, which she began in 1886. She served in schools in Melbourne and in several country and remote one-teacher schools, until appointed junior assistant teacher at Box Hill in 1893. Her earliest themes, which continued to occupy much of her poetry, were love of nature and family. Her prose sketches, which she also commenced writing early, were predominantly concerned with rural characters and incidents of country life.

From 1893, while employed at Box Hill, Marion began to submit verse for publication in Victorian papers, and received encouragement from James Watterston, editor of the *Australasian*, who published her poems under her pen name 'John Desmond'. In 1896, she published her first novel, *Barbara Halliday,* and two years later, her first collection of verse, *Songs from the Hills*. Both books were subsequently reprinted three times. In 1900, a collection of prose sketches, *Shamrock and Wattle Bloom,* was published, followed by a hiatus in book publication that coincided with her marriage and the end of her official connection with the Victorian Education Department.

On 19 September 1901, at St Patricks Cathedral in Melbourne, Marion Miller married Joseph Knowles, the senior valuer of Melbourne City and widowed father of five children by his first wife, Henrietta ('Hetta') Keighran. Marion's and Joseph's daughter died in infancy. Their two sons, Adrian Florance and William ('Willie') Bowen, born in 1903 and 1905 respectively, lived to maturity, but the marriage did not endure. Joseph and Marion obtained a legal separation, and while he lived, Joseph paid Marion a small allowance for childrearing. After his death at the age of sixty on 18 June 1918, several Catholic organisations arranged a 'grand benefit concert' for Marion in Melbourne on 9 December 1918.

Knowles's stepchildren were by that time considerably older than her own. Joseph Knowles and Henrietta Keighran had married in 1882, and their children were Winifred (born 1883), Henry (1885), Ida Lee (1888), Pauline Anderson (1891) and Leon Noel (1894). By 1918, Pauline and Leon were already with the armed services: Leon had served in the Royal Australian Navy from 17 May 1915 until 11 October 1916, and thereafter with the Royal Navy as an artificer on a submarine. Pauline, giving her address as Auburn, Victoria, and her father's address as 'Town Hall, Melbourne', had enlisted on 13 September 1917, and served from November that year as a staff nurse with the Allied Forces in Mesopotamia. Relations between Marion and at least some of the older children appear to have been cordial and cooperative. Pauline in particular worked with Marion in money-raising activities for the French Relief Fund from 1914, and for numerous other charities until Pauline went abroad. Marion continued to work for War-related charities, especially those that assisted Catholic servicemen and women and their families.

§

Knowles became a notable public figure in the Catholic community from 1899, when she initiated a regular women's column in the *Advocate* newspaper. Earlier, she had advocated a Catholic book library. From 1900, under the name 'Aunt Patsy', she contributed a 'Children's Corner' to the same paper; both features would expand considerably under her editorial authority. Following her separation from her husband, her friend, Joseph Winter, the 'resolutely' ideological Irish nationalist *Advocate* manager, appointed Knowles to a regular staff position, a role she occupied even after Winter's death in 1915. The position enabled Knowles to work from her home, where she employed a housekeeper, an arrangement that, as her biographer Cecily Close recorded, Knowles was to maintain for the rest of her life.

Knowles's other Catholic social activities in the early years of her marriage included membership of the committee for St Joseph's Home for Destitute Children in Surrey Hills and, from 1913, presidency of the Catholic Women's Club, of which she, along with her friend Mary Anne Broderick, was a founder. In 1917, at a presentation to Knowles, who was named 'the Queen of Charity' by the St Joseph's community at Malvern, the General Secretary of the Catholic Federation, T.J. O'Brien, praised her for inaugurating and establishing the women's club 'in the face of much discouragement and some opposition'. In 1913, she further helped establish a Catholic Women's Club Hostel and a social club for single Catholics. During the War, she used her association with the paper to appeal for and organise dispatch of comfort parcels to Catholic soldiers and, in 1919, she chaired the committee that arranged the soldiers' welcome home.

§

While she continued to publish poetry with general appeal, such as those collected in the 1911 *Fronds from the Blacks' Spur*, commercially released by George Robertson, Knowles wrote prolifically for the *Advocate* and other Catholic publications (including the Dublin *Irish Catholic* newspaper). Some of her serial stories were published in book form or booklets by Pellegrini and other publishers, but Knowles also self-published several gift books of poems—a practice that increased later in her career, when the appeal of her rural romances and their celebration of Catholic values waned. As early as September 1917, Knowles had avowed to a large audience of friends and well-wishers during a presentation thanking her for her work on behalf of women and children, that 'her principal endeavour had always been that her pen should write no word that was not of the purest and highest'.

Several of Knowles's wartime poems praising individual heroes occasionally rose beyond idealisation of such virtues as the poems enumerated. She made a point of praising Catholic Irish and Australian soldiers who died in the conflict, and whose stories appeared in the news, but a 'A Tribute to Campbell Peter' is an unusually heartfelt lament for a young Presbyterian fellow teacher who died of wounds received at the Gallipoli landing. The poem appeared in the *Advocate* and in the Victorian *Education Gazette* in August 1915.

While several of her novels achieved commercial publication and distribution in the 1920s, Knowles increasingly turned to self-publishing after her severance from the *Advocate* newspaper in 1927. The newspaper arranged a testimonial committee, which raised 334 pounds, the deposit on a house at Kew, where Knowles spent the rest of her life. In 1931, she received a Commonwealth Literary Fund pension of ten shillings per week, and in 1935, a committee of friends contributed to publication of her *Selected Poems* (1935), reissued in two volumes in 1937 as *The Harp of the Hills* and *Lyrics of Wind and Wave*. In the following year, she was appointed M.B.E.

In her final years, Knowles's eyesight failed and she ceased to be active in literary affairs. She continued to work for charitable causes, helping to raise money until ill health prevented her. In 1940, she ceased active outdoor fundraising and instead arranged matters from her home, where she collected gifts for sale on behalf of St Joseph's Home at Surrey Hills. She died at Camberwell on 16 September 1949, and was buried in Brighton cemetery.

Publications

Poetry

Songs from the Hills, Melbourne: Melville, Mullen and Slade, 1898.
Fronds from the Blacks' Spur, Melbourne: George Robertson, 1911.
Roses on the Window Sill, Melbourne: Varleys, 1913.
A Christmas Bouquet, Melbourne: The Author, 1914.
Songs from the Land of the Wattle, Melbourne: The Author, 1916.
Shamrock Sprays, Melbourne: Advocate Press, 1916.
Songs from the Heart, Melbourne: The Author, 1917.
Christmas Bells, Melbourne: The Author, 1919.
Love, Luck and Lavender: Original Poems, Melbourne: The Author, 1919.
Ferns and Fancies, Malvern: The Author, 1923.
Selected Poems, Melbourne: Arrow, 1935.
The Harp of the Hills, Melbourne: Arrow Books, 1935.
Lyrics of Wind and Wave, Melbourne: Arrow, 1937.

Novels

Barbara Halliday: A Story of the Hill Country of Victoria, Melbourne: George Robertson, 1896. [Republished 1913 as *A Child of the Ranges*].
Corinne of Corrall's Bluff, Melbourne: W.P. Linehan, 1912.
The Little Doctor: An Australian Story, Melbourne: Varleys, 1919.
The House of the Garden of Roses, Melbourne: J.F. Bracken, 1922.
Meg of 'Minadong', Melbourne: E.A. Vidler, 1926.
Pretty Nan Hartigan, Melbourne: Pellegrini, 1928.
Pierce O'Grady's Daughter: An Australian Story, Melbourne: Pellegrini, 1928.

Short stories

Shamrock and Wattle Bloom: A Series of Short Tales and Sketches, Melbourne: Edgerton and Moore, 1900.

References

Cecily Close, 'Knowles, Marion (1865–1949)', Australian Dictionary of Biography, National Centre of Biography, Australian National University, http://adb.anu.edu.au/biography/knowles-marion-6988/text12147, published first in hardcopy 1983, accessed online 26 May 2016.
Argus, Tuesday 18 April 1882, p. 1 [Marriage notice of Joseph Knowles, son of William Knowles of Bedale, Yorkshire, and Henrietta, fourth daughter of late Thomas Keighran of Doodle Cooma Station, Riverina; the marriage occurring at Saints Peter and Paul Church, Emerald Hill on 17 April 1882].
Argus, Monday 19 July 1920, p. 1 [Death notice of Elizabeth Keighran, the aunt of Winifred, Pauline and Leon Knowles and Ida Ward, on 18 July].

John Desmond [Marion Miller Knowles], 'The Land of Childish Dreams' [poem], *Australasian,* Saturday 20 May 1893, p. 43.

Geoffrey Serle, 'Winter, Joseph (1844–1915)', Australian Dictionary of Biography, National Centre of Biography, Australian National University, http://adb.anu.edu.au/biography/winter-joseph-4958/text8153, published first in hardcopy 1976, accessed online 27 May 2016.

Advocate, Saturday 8 September 1917, p. 17 [Report on social evening and presentation by friends to Marion Miller Knowles as 'the Queen of Charity'].

'Wattle Day Appeal', *Argus,* Saturday 31 August 1940, p. 2 [Knowles collects donations from home, for Wattle Day Appeal].

Argus, Saturday 18 January 1946, p. 1; *Argus,* Saturday 15 January 1949, p. 12 [Death notice of Helena Bridget Miller, and Memorial notice for Daisy Helena B. Miller, both inserted by Marion Miller Knowles].

'The Final Call. Mary Broderick', *Record* (Emerald Hill), Saturday 1 March 1947, p. 2 [Account of career of Mary Anne Broderick, charity organiser and co-founder of the Catholic Women's Club and Catholic Women's Hostel].

Campbell McDiarmid Peter, The AIF Project, UNSW Canberra. https://www.aif.adfa.edu.au/showPerson?pid=239261 accessed 27 May 2016. The Great War Forum, accessed 27 May 2016.

'In Memoriam Service. Late Campbell Peter', *Cobden Times and Heytesbury Advertiser,* Wednesday 19 May 1915, p. 2.

Marion Miller Knowles
A Tribute to the Memory of Campbell Peter

Honourably he died,
    Doing his 'little bit';
None stand his grave beside,
    And yet, because of it,
The world is nobler far,
    And liberty more great;
More clear is Honour's star,
    Less mean, ignoble Fate.

Honourably he died,
    From wounds dealt by the foe;
On justice he relied,
    Be thou like him—and go!
Go where thy kindred fell,
    They friends were wounded sore;
With pride our bosoms swell,
    Though they return no more!

The shirker knows not shame,
    While safe is purse and home;
One day his face will flame
    When nobler men come home!
The laggard knows not pride,
    While volunteers march on—
But, O for joy denied,
    When self-respect is gone.

Source: *Advocate,* Saturday 17 July 1915, p. 33.

Campbell McDairmod Peter of Cobden, Victoria, enlisted in the AIF on 18 August 1914, aged 20. He served in the 8th Battalion and held the rank of Company Quartermaster Sergeant when he received a gunshot wound to his shoulder at the Gallipoli landing. He died at Heliopolis on 6 May 1915 and was buried in Cairo. The Australian War Memorial holds a photograph of Peter (Number P06504.002): https://www.awm.gov.au/people/P10256987/

The *Cobden Times and Heytesbury Advertiser* carried a report of the commemorative service held for Peter in the Cobden Presbyterian Church on Sunday 16 May 1915.

Marion Miller Knowles
His Mother

Oh, many a coloured streamer flew
    From the crowded deck and shore,
As the grand old boat swung out to sea
    That may come back no more!

Her decks were lines with gallant men—
    I saw but my brave son;
I had three sons a year ago,—
    To-day I have but one!

For Michael lies in Anzac ground,
    And John at Ginchy fell;
My youngest and my best-loved, now,
    Hath bidden me farewell.

I watched him till the last hand-wave
    To aching sight was lost;
I was but one where many wept—
    Who gave at fearful cost.

How slowly throbbed my heavy heart!
    How dreary seemed the day!
And, yet, the sound of singing came,
    All bravely from the bay!

They went with many a ringing cheer
    To fill their hearts with pride;
They heard no sobbing undertones
    Float outward with the tide.

And yet—and yet—perhaps there stood
    Some with dim eyes and grave,
Who sent again a backward look
    Across the trackless wave!

O son of mine, so dear—so dear!
Your fond eyes I shall see
Come life, come death, while memory keeps
Its faithful tryst with me!

Source: Marion Miller Knowles, 'His Mother', *Songs from the Land of the Wattle,* Malvern: H. Mullin, 1916, p. 38.

Marion Miller Knowles
O Wondrous Love!

(In Memoriam Father John Gwynne, S.J., Chaplain
of Irish Guards, '15, known as 'The Brave Little Priest.)

O wondrous love the love of Christ inspired!
O wondrous strength, whose sweet zeal never tired!
O glorious selflessness that sought no end
Save that which spent itself for foe and friend!

'Brave little priest,' thy soul's heroic mould,
By no man's measure either bought or sold,
Shines out a sun, dispelling doubt and dread,—
For Christ, thy Lord, moved with thee thro' the dead!

Thy hand was guided by His holy touch,
Thy pity glowed—because he pitied much;
Men marked thy deeds of generous tenderness,
Nor knew thy love for Christ brought Christ to bless!

O saving truth that calms a world o'erwrought,
O certain hope that stills a world's mad thought—
This life unstained, of priestly chivalry,
Lit, gracious God, by heavenly Light from Thee!

Source: Marion Miller Knowles, 'O Wondrous Love!', *Songs from the Land of the Wattle,* Malvern: H. Mullin, 1916, p. 27.

Marion Miller Knowles
'Jack'

I read your name in the list to-day,
You fell with your lads, in the thick of the fray;
'Killed in action' was all that they told
Of your brave young soul and your heart of gold!
The world wheeled round me, the sun grew black;
Was it for this that we parted, Jack?

I read your name in the list, with tears,—
So short a space seemed our lovelit years
So long the time since you whispered, Jack,
'Heart of my heart, I will soon be back!'
Your name, your name's in the list to-day—
To-morrow, maybe, I can weep and pray.

Shall I envy those who are 'next of kin'?
Who closed their hearts lest I entered in!
Nay, proud in my grief, I shall stand apart;
Shall I prove less brave than you were, sweetheart?
Alone in my anguish, I'm nearest still
To the grave where you lie, at the foot of the hill.

And oft in my dreams I shall seek the spot
Where they say you sleep—though I find you not;
I shall kiss the rough cross that some kindly hand
Hath raised to the brave, in an alien land;
And the pitying angels may bring you back,
Because my heart broke for your brave heart, Jack.

Source: Marion Miller Knowles, 'Jack', *Songs from the Land of the Wattle,* Malvern: H. Mullin, 1916, p. 33.

Marion Miller Knowles
Father Finn (Sedd-El-Bahr)
(When the right hand was shattered, he gave absolution with the left.)

He saw them fall—the men he loved,
        Their life-blood dyed the sod;
Were some among them living still
        Who craved for peace with God?

He pushed aside restraining hands,
        He flung all safeguards down;
Into the rain of death he ran,
        And won his martyr's crown!

Struck by the swift-descending hail,
        He fell, yet rose again—
The word of blessing on his lips
        That bought eternal gain.

The holy hand he raised on high,
        Was shattered as it told
The might of Jesus' tender Love
        Where Heaven's joys unfold.

But shattered limb and stricken form,
        And suffering deep and dire,
Quenched not that soul's heroic will,
        Quenched not its saintly fire!

To dying comrades, yearning still,
        His left hand gave the Sign
That set the seal on deathless words,
        On promises Divine.

O victory o'er sin and strife!
        O wondrous deed of love!
O golden ray of Light that streamed
        From thrones of Light above!

How poor the laurel wreaths they weave,
    Who worship earth's renown?—
This priest of God hath grander fame,
    He won the martyr's crown!

And long as human hearts can feel
    To noblest hearts akin,
The memory shall be evergreen,
    Of deathless Father Finn.

Source: Marion Miller Knowles, *Songs from the Heart: Christmas Flowers of Verse,* Melbourne: The Author, 1917, pp. 42-43.

PHYLLIS LEWIS

Lieutenant Raymond Lade and Phyllis Lewis, 20 April 1920.
Photograph by David Livingston Muntz, Glenferrie Road, Malvern.
Courtesy of Penny Lade.

Phyllis Cardin Lewis (born 12 July 1894, Elsternwick) was the daughter of James Bannatyne Lewis and Edith Augusta Lewis (née Haynes) of Armadale, Victoria. Phyllis's father, James Lewis, was the third son of twelve children of gold rush immigrant John Lewis and his wife Mary.

Through feckless living and ill-judged speculation, Phyllis's grandfather John Lewis had lost a fortune won by quartz reef mining. His sons were withdrawn from Scotch College, and his family was dispersed, and his wife separated from him by the time he died.

Phyllis's father's career was quite otherwise. He graduated from university as a civil engineer and worked successively for David Munro and Co. (the largest engineering contractor in the State), then as director of the Daylesford School of Mines, engineer with the Melbourne and

Metropolitan Board of Works, and bridge-builder in northern Tasmania. He married Victorian-born Edith Haynes in 1888, while working for David Munro and Co. Their children were first educated in Tasmania until Edith and the children returned to Melbourne in 1909; James joined them soon after. The Lewises rented a capacious house, which they named 'Remo', at Kooyong Road in Armadale, where they employed two maids, a washerwoman-charlady and two gardeners. More than sixty years later, Brian Lewis's books *Sunday at Kooyong Road* and *Our War* recounted the family's early days in that well-to-do suburb.

Phyllis's brothers were educated early in Launceston before completing high school at Wesley College in Melbourne. On the outbreak of the War, Keith, aged twenty-three, had already followed his father's career as a mining engineer and was working in Tasmania. He held a commission in the Melbourne University Rifles and offered to join the AIF Engineers, but, impatient of delay, joined the infantry in January 1915 and went to the Dardanelles. Athol Hugh Remo Lewis, twenty-one, was in his second-last year of a law course at Melbourne University, and he enlisted in February 1916 and served as a Lieutenant in the 3rd Division Artillery, before returning to Australia in March 1919. Ralph Haynes Lewis, twenty, was studying his final year of geology at the Working Men's College with the aim of enrolment in engineering at the university. Phyllis, aged nineteen, was in her first year of an Arts degree at Melbourne University, and Owen, Dux of Wesley College in 1913, was eighteen and studying first year engineering at the University. Ronnie, seventeen, was still at school, as were the youngest brothers, Neil (twelve years old) and Brian (almost eight).

Because wartime provisions forbade the export of gold, James's consulting work declined. He gave up his city office, tried to join the Australian Mining Corps, but failed the medical examination, and spent the War at his home.

Phyllis distinguished herself at Melbourne University, gaining final honours in her Arts degree, with an Exhibition [scholarship] in Greek I and II, Honours Latin I and II, Chemistry I, Comparative Philology I, English Philology and Morphology. She taught Honours English at the Convent of Mercy in Fitzroy in 1918 and 1919, and in 1919 taught and examined in English at the Convent of the Sacred Heart in East Melbourne, as well as teaching at the Sisters of the Sacred Heart School in East St Kilda. She taught Intermediate French at the Collegiate School in Hobart in third term 1919, and for one term in 1920, three terms in 1921 and one term in 1922. She subsequently taught High School Certificate European and Ancient History, Economics, French and Intermediate and Leaving Certificate English in 1926 and 1927. Her teaching record to 27 May 1927, when she sought permanent registration as a teacher in Tasmania, also included coaching French, Latin, Greek and English.

Keith survived the War as a Lieutenant in the 2nd Australian Tunnelling Company, returning to Australia in July 1919. Ralph enlisted a year after Keith, on 6 January 1916, and served as Sapper in the 2nd Australian Tunnelling Company with his older brother, returning to Australia on 20 December 1918. Athol, who enlisted on 28 February 1916, served as a Lieutenant in the 3rd Division Artillery, returning to Australia on 16 March 1919.

Lewis's younger brother, Owen Gower Lewis was educated at the Church of England Grammar School at Launceston and, from 1909 to 1913, at Wesley College. In 1914, he was studying studying Third Year Mining Engineering at Queen's College, Melbourne University, and was a member of the Melbourne University Rifles, where he held the rank of Sergeant and provisional Lieutenant. On 1 January 1916, he enlisted in the AIF as a sapper, was taken on strength in the 10th Field Company of Engineers on 29 May 1916, and embarked for the Front the following day. In April 1917, he transferred to the Australian Flying Corps, in which he served as an observer with number 3 Squadron. He was killed with his pilot George Best when their reconnaissance plane burst into flames after taking off near Amiens on 12 April 1918.

In *Our War,* a memoir of the period published in 1981, Phyllis Lewis's younger brother, Brian Bannatyne Lewis (1906-1991), recounted his family's responses to news of Owen's death, and his sister's subsequent recollections of scenes of childhood, along with her recurrent dreams of Owen, and her scepticism (and her mother's rejection) of a relative's offer to commune with Owen's spirit via séance. Phyllis, earlier engaged to be married to fellow Melbourne University graduate Bob (Robert Gordon) Menzies, broke off her engagement after her brother's death. Her elegiac poem *1918* was issued as a twelve-page pamphlet early in 1920.

Phyllis's name appears on electoral rolls for the suburb of Balaclava in Melbourne from 1916 until 1919 before she moved to Tasmania with her husband Raymond Freear Lade. Lade, a solicitor born at Launceston in 1889, had served as a Lieutenant in the 52nd Australian

Infantry Battalion, and for his bravery had been mentioned in despatches. Raymond and Phyllis were married by the Rev. David Graham McCrea, at the Armadale Presbyterian Church on 27 April 1920.

The couple's first child, Owen Gower Lade, born at Phyllis's parents' house, 'Remo', on 4 April 1921, lived only twenty-nine hours. There followed three children who lived to maturity: Owen Gower Lade (16 June 1922-2007), who later studied zoology and worked as a scientist before turning to art; then Aidan Freear Lade (born 10 May 1925), who later served as a Captain in the Royal Australian Navy); and Edith Katherine Bannatyne Lade (3 May 1938-10 October 2017), who married Anthony John Evenhuis and worked as an academic.

In May 1929, Phyllis gained Tasmanian registration as a teacher of high school English, Latin, French and Greek, on the strength of her academic record and a supportive reference from her former teacher Professor (and from 1925 Sir) Archibald Strong, Professor of Classics at Melbourne University, and she subsequently taught high school English and French.

In the 1930s, the family home was a house called 'Perdita', in Talune Street, Lindisfarne, a Hobart east-shore suburb on the Derwent River. By 1954, the family had moved to a house opposite the Mersey hospital at Torquay Road, Latrobe. Phyllis was an active member and honorary secretary of the local branch of the Country Women's Association and wrote spiritedly and with some wit on the organisation's location and role. A keen walker, she was also a supporter of the Guides movement. More than half a century later, older listeners recalled her talks on radio.

Phyllis's husband Raymond died on 30 October 1971, and Phyllis at Hobart on 5 October 1986. Their graves are in the Mersey Vale Lawn Cemetery, Devonport.

Lewis did not leave any other published poem apart from her elegy for her brother. In a brief notice of the appearance of the poem *1918*, the *Australasian* newspaper reported on Sunday 3 January 1920 that the poem, partly 'in blank verse and partly rhymes' was 'written with good feeling and expression'. Seen from the perspective of almost a century later, the poem *1918* shares the distinction, with Queensland-New South Wales poet Zora Cross' 1921 'Elegy on an Australian Schoolboy' (a lengthy poem about the death of her own younger brother), of being one of the most memorable poetic responses to the loss of a loved person in the Australian literature relating to the First World War.

Publication

Phyllis Lewis. *1918*. Melbourne: Specialty Press, 1920.

References

Australasian, Saturday 4 August 1894, p. 41 [Family Notices: birth of Phyllis Lewis at Curral Road, Elsternwick on 12 July 1894].

Brian Lewis, *Sunday at Kooyong Road*, Richmond: Hutchinson, 1976.

Brian Lewis, *Our War: Australia During World War I. A View of World War 1 from Inside an Australian Family,* Melbourne: Melbourne University Press, 1980, p. 305. [Penguin Australia also published *Our War,* as a paperback, in 1981.]

John Lack, 'The great madness of 1914-1918: families at war on Melbourne's eastern and western fronts', La Trobe Journal, No. 96, September 2015. https://www.slv.vic.gov.au/sites/default/files/La-Trobe-Journal-96-John-Lack.pdf, accessed 15 May 2018.

Michael Molkentin, *Fire in the Sky: The Australian Flying Corps in the First World War,* Sydney: Allen and Unwin, 2010, pp. 189-191; 250-252).

Argus, Saturday 22 May 1920, p. 13 [Family Notices: Marriages: Phyllis Lewis and Raymond Lade on 27 April].

Argus, Thursday 7 April 1921, p. 1 [Family notices: Death of Phyllis and Raymond's son, who lived 29 hours].

'In the Public Eye', *Herald* (Melbourne), Thursday 1 October 1914, p. 12 [Raymond Freear Lade admitted as barrister of the Supreme Court of Victoria].

'Miscellaneous Works', *Australasian,* Saturday 3 January 1920, p. 39 [Notice of publication of 1918].

'Owen Gower Lewis', Australian Society of World War 1 Aero Historians, http://www.ww1aero.org.au/database.html accessed 29 March 2018.

'Lade, Phyllis Cardin', Application for Registration as Teacher, Tasmania, 30 May 1927, Archives Office of Tasmania, ADRI CB23/6/1/380. https://linctas.ent.sirsidynix.net.au/client/en_AU/all/search/detailnonmodal/ent:$002f$002fARCHIVES_DIGITISED$002f0$002fCB23-6-1-380/email?qu=Phyllis&qu=Lade&d=ent%3A%2F%2FARCHIVES_DIGITISED%2F0%2FCB23-6-1-380%7E%7E0. Accessed 9 May 2018.

Phyllis Lade, Letter to editor, *Advocate* [Burnie, Tasmania], 10 November 1948, p. 4 ['Public Opinion': an amusing letter concerning 'a profound spiritual experience' of her own at the age of four when, to the mind of the Devon Hospital Board, she 'must have been an extraordinarily repulsive little insect' for taking something that did not belong to her].

'Devonport Guides Activities', *Advocate,* Friday 26 August 1949, p. 13 [Reference to Phyllis's work as leader of Latrobe Guides].

Phyllis Lade, hon. Secretary, Latrobe CWA, Letter to editor, *Advocate,* 22 March 1950, p. 4 ['Public Opinion': on CWA work in World War 2 and subsequent charity work, and repudiating allegations relating to opposition to a new town hall].

Advocate, 15 October 1986, p. 17 [Obituary for Phyllis Lade].

Anton Lade, Private communication [emails], 3 April 2018 and 4 April 2018.

Dr Chris Lade, Private communication [email], 8 May 2018.

Penny Lade, Private communication [email and telephone] 12 May 2018.

Mrs Dora Bramich, Private communication [telephone], 6 June 2018.

Phyllis Lewis
1918
To Owen Gower Lewis, A.F.C.

1

      The heath is all in bloom.
We saw it so in those half-faded years,
Half lit by memory's sunset splendours, when
We roamed together, hand in friendly hand.
We sought adventure, and our wishes wove
In one bright thread dreams of our future days.
Since we have wandered on those hills and felt
The keen wind our playmate, and looked down
On sunny breadths of river, now concealed
By hills and trees, now flashing into view,
No one, I think, has so much loved these woods.
Each year the heath budded and shone and died,
Awaiting our return; the berries hung
Their purple burden midst the shrubs and trees,
Or, straight upspringing from the ground, displayed
Fruit of such blue as might be seen on robes
Of Eastern Kings. To pleasure us, the Earth
Has spread her fairest treasures forth to-day.
I cannot see you by me, but can dream
That you are here, where you once loved to be,
Far from the squalid dreariness of towns,
Your light step pressing upwards, and your eyes
Fixed on the uplands. Ah, your feet are still,
And foreign soil presses the shining hair,
The cheeks I've kissed, the ardent, willing brain,
'But not,' a voice consoling cries, 'the soul;
For do you think, fond mortal, that the Power
That makes each heath-bell perfect of its kind
And leaves no lonely drop of rain to fall
Useless, but lifts it to the clouds again,
Think that it would waste those soaring hopes,
Those high designs for others' good, in dust?

He whom you mourn still haunts his old time loves
And whispers comfort, if they will but hear,
There is no death, no waste.'
                                  God make it so!
The smiling hills and rivers promise hope,
Each year these flowers know death, but spring again,
I pluck them for you now, my dear, my dear,
And lay their prisoned sunshine on the breast
Of Mother Earth, who holds you in her arms,
For she is yours, who died to keep her free,
And you are hers, held in her vast embrace;
These are her gifts and mine, these flowers you loved.

II

          It is all dark to-night.
The sleety wind is fretting on the glass,
A myriad forms of sorrow slowly pass,
          O God, is there no light
          And no release from grief?
Great grief makes small chafes large, till, hour by hour,
Life's song grows mute, and sweetest love turns sour;
          Mine eyes see no relief.
          What if the hope that men
Have cherished ever, be mistake, and death
Means that our spirit flies back, with our breath?
          To senseless air again?
          On either side the grave
Then, were no comfort; best it were to lie
At once on mother earth, 'neath some quiet sky
          And yield the life she gave.

          Have you lived all for naught?
Those years of effort, must they all be lost,
Those hopeful plans, nipt by an early frost,
          That love and life and thought?
          Oh lawless howling wind—
Oh darkness none can lift—Oh hopeless night—

Oh gibbering shadows making heavy flight—
        Oh soundless gloom of mind!
        Ye wise ones of the earth
Take not from us our simple early faith,
The balm of stricken souls, the holy wraith
        Who comes to us at birth.

        Long sorrow mutes the brain;
Your voice approaching laughs, "It was not true,
I never felt death's pangs, nor went from you."
        Quick ebbs the tide of pain
        Toward the uncharted deep,
The sun shines warm, and chill regret lies dead.
You take my hand again, and with me tread
        The flower-strewed fields of sleep.

III

Not to-day will the preacher ride
Up to the church on the mountain side,
Nor shall we children, drest
Befitting the Sabbath, all in their best,
Half pleased, half awed at sight of the grace,
That shines on the good man's holy face.
He will not come to-day, and so
We'll pass as of old, dear brother of mine,
Down the road where the grey wattles blow,
And sportive sunbeams dance and shine
'Midst the tree trunks. We hear the wild birds call
And watch the wavering shadows fall
Across the blue-veined purple hills.
The Sabbath quiets my heart and fills
The bush with peace. Who could despair
On such a day? No whit less fair
Is such a temple than the grand
Dim-lit cathedral, where men stand
To woo with gifts and praise a God
Who made these hills. Oft have I trod

These aisles, and in the shadows kneeled
And prayed for you, while rich notes pealed
From the organ's quivering heart. 'Ah, keep
Him safe, dear God!'
                    How can you sleep
So still? But will you never wake,
To see the bright-faced morning shake
Her tear-drops' spray from leaf and bough,
Or gather in her flock, the mist
That all night long the valleys kist
To the homestead height? Ah how
Could you lie mute, and never feel
These days that one by one reveal
Earth's treasures his from yester year?
E'en now, perhaps, you stir to hear
Her call and mine, and, sleeping, smile;
Or else you linger here, the while
I weakly mourn, and try to rend
This veil that sunders friend from friend.
Oh hills and skies! while we are sad,
How can you be so calmly glad?

IV

Could I but make my plaint, like his who mourned
The absent shepherd, or th'ethereal notes
Of him who sung his Adonais's death—
Then men would know you still, tho' many years
Passed your unmoving head, and grieve that you
had left this world that promised you so much.
No crude memorial carved in garish wise
Would tell your virtues lost, but they would live
And shed their radiance when stones were dust—
        Could I but sing as others!
                          When our souls
Which feel, but may not tell the things they feel,
Shall find their fleshy fetters flying free

And waking from their restless, weary dreams,
        Arise to satisfy long felt desires,
Then will you know the measure of our love.
Till then, we must not envy you your peace.
Oh ye, who would disturb our holy dread
To wring the secrets from those silent lips.
Take your dark powers to others; we can wait
To know the whole of what you tell in part.

Source: Phyllis Lewis, *1918,* Melbourne: Specialty Press, 1920, s.n. [19pp. pamphlet]

The Lewis Family in Melbourne, ca. 1907. Left to right: Ronnie, Phyllis, Ralph, Edith (seated, with Brian), Keith (at back), James (seated, with Neil), Athol (at back), Owen. Photo by courtesy of Penny Lade.

DOROTHY FRANCES McCRAE

Pencil portrait of Dorothy Frances McCrae by Elizabeth Wallwork (1882-1969), Christchurch, New Zealand, 1929. State Library Victoria. Permission to reprint courtesy of Wallwork family.

Dorothy Frances McCrae (1878–1937) was one of six children of the distinguished literary and artistic McCrae family of Melbourne. Her mother was Tasmanian-born Augusta Helen Brown (1850-1923), who married the poet and littérateur George Gordon McCrae (1833-1927). Her father's notable literary confrères included Henry Kendall, Richard Hengist ('Orion') Horne, Marcus Clarke and Adam Lindsay Gordon. George Gordon McCrae was eventually regarded as 'father of Victorian letters'. Dorothy's grandmother was the pioneer artist and diarist Georgiana Huntly McCrae (1804-1890, London-born natural daughter of George, marquis of Huntly, afterwards fifth Duke of Gordon). Georgiana married Andrew McCrae and migrated in 1841 to Australia where she recorded the vicissitudes of her life and her children through the ensuing twenty-four years. Georgiana's diaries were gathered and edited by her grandson, one of Dorothy's brothers, the poet, actor and artist Hugh McCrae (1876-1958).

Dorothy Frances McCrae was born at Hawthorn, and educated first at the 'Rolyat' school run by Jeannie, Lizzie and Carrie Taylor at Creswick Street, Hawthorn, and at Ruyton Girls' School at Kew. One of her teachers at the former school (the name is 'Taylor' spelt backwards) was Jeannie Taylor, later famous as Mrs Aeneas Gunn, author of *We of the Never-Never*. Jeanie Taylor had matriculated at Melbourne University in 1887, and Eliza Bromby, head of Ruyton, was the first woman to pass the matriculation with credit.

In 1907, Dorothy Frances McCrae married the Reverend Charles Elliott Perry, with whom she subsequently had four children: Charles Stuart Perry (1908-1982), Claire Gordon Perry (1910-1995), Peter Nicholas Maine Perry (1912-?), and Geoffrey Gordon McCrae Perry (1916-?).

Perry, the son of an Anglican minister, had attended schools in Melbourne and graduated with honours in history from St Johns College, Oxford in 1894, the year in which he was made deacon. He was ordained in Melbourne the following year, and served in several churches. At first an evangelical like his father, from 1897 he began to preach the Catholic faith according to the Church of England with enthusiasm and aroused contention in his several postings. His last Australian appointment was as vicar of St John's Anglican Church in Camberwell, before he was appointed vicar of St Michael's in Christchurch, New Zealand, in May 1916. St Michael's had turned Anglo-Catholic, and Perry encountered resistance from his sacristan and some of his parishioners who favoured elaborate ceremonial usage. By 1918, Perry, who emphasised the importance of confession and fasting before communion, was subject to charges laid against him by Archdeacon C.H. Gosset, which led to lengthy litigation in church tribunals and a rebuke by his bishop who nevertheless forbade only minor aspects of ritual. Perry felt vindicated but modified his practice very little; ceremonial aspects of St Michael's ceremony did not concern him so much as matters of faith.

Perry garnered a reputation beyond New Zealand for his preaching on many subjects, including the social gospel. He wrote for newspapers on many subjects and lectured in history for a time at Canterbury College. Though trenchant in his religious conviction, he attracted admiration for his gentle disposition, his erudition and love of 'literature and tobacco and picture theatres'. His general reputation stood high enough for him to be elected a Canon of Christchurch Cathedral in 1934. Dorothy, known as a poet as well as wife to a minister, also provoked a measure of controversy in her unconventional wider interests and opposition to playing the part of a clergyman's wife and engaging in parish work. Her poems appeared in the Sydney *Bulletin,* a paper still broadly regarded as the leading Australasian literary outlet but still not welcome in many conservative homes on account of its earlier radicalism. In 1927, the *Bulletin* published three of Dorothy's poems between April and August. That the Perrys still took the paper, let alone that Dorothy chose to publish in it, confirms their independence of thought.

Caedmon's Gift, McCrae's last book, reprinted poems from the *Bulletin* and elsewhere, but it is notable for the inclusion of poems that retell Maori legends ('Hinemoa and Tutaneki', and 'The Fairies of New Zealand', the latter a dream-narrative with a sequel) and poems descriptive of southern New Zealand ('A Word Sketch From Timaru, New Zealand') as well as accounts of miracles ('Caedmon's Gift', 'The Holy Coat of Treves') and other stories affirming the power of love.

The demographic nature of the Rev. Canon Perry's parish shifted, and the congregation shrank during the Depression, while Perry's health declined to the extent that he retired in October 1936, and he and Dorothy moved with their daughter Claire from Christchurch to Balmoral on Sydney's North Shore. They sought a suitable new home, but the Rev. Canon Charles Elliott Perry died on 8 January 1937 at Miller Street in North Sydney, and was buried the following day at the Northern Suburbs Church of England Cemetery.

Suffering from cancer and depression, Dorothy died by drowning in the bath at her Miller Street home on 9 April 1937, and the Sydney coroner returned a verdict of death by suicide.

In Christchurch, in later years, a street name was changed from Percival to Perry to memorialise the Rev. Charles Elliott Perry. The eldest of the Perry children, Charles Stuart Perry, studied Law in New Zealand, worked as a teacher during the Depression, and in 1933, joined the Wellington Public Library. As City Librarian in 1946, he was responsible for transforming the library from a pay service to a modern institution, and for encouraging the establishment of the National Library of New Zealand in 1964. He died in 1982. Dorothy's youngest son, Geoffrey Gordon McCrae Perry, served in the Australian Infantry in the Second World War.

§

Dorothy Frances McCrae wrote under her own name and as Mrs Cecil Perry and Mrs C.E. Perry, contributing poetry from 1901 to the late 1920s, to the Sydney *Bulletin, Steele Rudd's Magazine, The Bookfellow, The Lone Hand, Argus, Australasian* and other newspapers and magazines in Australia, besides New Zealand periodicals. Her earliest *Bulletin* poems and stories (1901-1903) were signed 'The Young 'Un' and 'Moth'. She achieved some renown as a writer of patriotic works during the War, especially for her two collections, *Soldier! My Soldier!* (published in mid-October 1914) and *The Clear Call* (July 1915, dedicated 'To the Mothers of our Soldiers'). When the first of these was published, with a dedication 'to Geoffrey Gordon McCrae, Captain, 1st Expeditionary Force', Australia's military involvement in the War had chiefly concerned the seizing of German New Guinea by a small force sent for the purpose. When the second book appeared, the full story and cost of the Anzac troops' engagement at Gallipoli was far from complete.

In a poem 'Killed at the Front! Oh, noble end', published in the Sydney *Bulletin* on 12 August 1915, McCrae heroises an imagined death. The actual death of her younger brother Geoffrey at the age of twenty-six in the following year, struck her much harder.

The Sydney *Bulletin* noted, on the appearance of the collection *Soldier, my Soldier!* that two of the poems had been previously published in the paper, and that the book contained 'little artifice' though McCrae had contrived 'to compress the feminine view-point of war into her simple metre', and 'the appeal of these verses is immediate. They are hurried jottings, rushed into publication; but their directness and simplicity give them a permanent value'.

McCrae's brother is commemorated beyond his sister's poetry in a stained glass window in Christ Church, Hawthorn, Victoria. The window portrays a sainted knight in antique garb, with shield and unsheathed sword, below the motto 'Fortitudine'.

Publications

Frances McCrae, *Lyrics in Leisure,* Melbourne: Lothian, 1909.

Frances McCrae, *Some Children's Songs* [with music by Marion Alsop], Melbourne: George Robertson, 1910.

Frances McCrae, *Soldier, my Soldier!* Melbourne: George Robertson, 1914.

Frances McCrae, *The Clear Call.* Melbourne: George Robertson, 1915.

Frances McCrae, *Caedmon's Gift and Other Verses.* Melbourne, Edward A. Vidler, 1926.

References

Norman Cowper, 'McCrae, Georgiana Huntly (1804–1890)', Australian Dictionary of Biography, National Centre of Biography, Australian National University, http://adb.anu.edu.au/biography/mccrae-georgiana-huntly-2392/text3157, published first in hardcopy 1967, accessed online 2 January 2016.

Sally O'Neill, 'Gunn, Jeannie (1870–1961), Australian Dictionary of Biography, National Centre of Biography, Australian National University, http://adb.anu.edu.au/biography/gunn-jeannie-6506/text11163, published first in hardcopy 1983, accessed online 4 June 2016.

Marie Peters. 'Perry, Charles Elliott' from the Dictionary of New Zealand Biography. Te Ara - the Encyclopedia of New Zealand, updated 7-Jan-2014 URL: http://www.TeAra.govt.nz/en/biographies/3p23/perry-charles-elliott Accessed 4 Jun 2016.

H.M. Bowron, 'Anglo Catholicism in the Diocese of Christchurch 1850-1920', Thesis submitted in partial fulfilment of the requirements for the Degree of Master of Arts in History at the University of Canterbury, 1975, especially chapters 7 and 8 [pp. 188-240].

Dorothy Frances Perry poems in the *Bulletin* in 1927: 'Pierette', 21 April, p. 6; 'The Garden', 2 June, p. 6; 'The Tryst', 25 August 1927, p. 6.

'McCrae, Geoffrey Gordon, Major (b. 1890-d. 1916', Australian War Memorial, https://www.awm.gov.au/collection/1DRL/0427/ Accessed 4 June 2016.

'To Live in Sydney', *Sydney Morning Herald,* Wednesday 6 January 1937, p. 9 [Article with photograph of Dorothy and her daughter Claire at Balmoral].

Sydney Morning Herald, Saturday 9 January 1937, p. 16 [Family Notices: Death of Rev. Canon Perry Charles Elliott Perry on 8 January 1937 at North Sydney].

'Woman's Death. Drowned in Bath', *Sydney Morning Herald,* Saturday 8 May 1937, p. 10 [death of Dorothy Frances Perry at 'age 56'].

'Perry Street', War Memorial Avenues, Papanui, Christchurch New Zealand, http://ketechristchurch.peoplesnetworknz.info/documents/0000/0000/0204/Onl03.MemAves.pdf. Accessed 1 May 2018.

Brian McKeon. 'Perry, Charles Stuart', Dictionary of New Zealand Biography, first published in 2000. Te Ara - the Encyclopedia of New Zealand, https://teara.govt.nz/en/biographies/5p23/perry-charles-stuart. Accessed 2 May 2018.

1917 Christ Church Anglican, Hawthorn Victoria. Stained Glass Australia. [Memorial: Major Geoffrey Gordon McCrae]. https://stainedglassaustralia.wordpress.com/category/brooks-robinson-co/. Accessed 2 May 2018.

Dorothy Frances McCrae
The Empire's Call

The Empire is calling, my son, my son.
    I heard it last night when I struggled to sleep.
Will you stand idle, with battles unwon?
    With comrades unburied? and kingdoms to keep?
Women have need of you, over the sea,
Soldier, my soldier, march forward for me.

The Empire is calling, child of my breast,
    Thrilling and urgent her resonant cry;
Enemies slaughter, and burn and molest.
    Buckle your sword, shoulder rifle, and fly—
Children have need of you, over the sea,
Soldier, my soldier, sail swiftly for me.

Source: Dorothy Frances McCrae, *Soldier, My Soldier,* Melbourne: G. Robertson, 1914, p. 9.

Dorothy Frances McCrae
The Shawl

Ah my shawl! My boy in Egypt sent it me,
Fine as though a fairy wove it cunningly,
Scented with an Eastern perfume, faint and sweet,
Bringing Egypt in a vision, sights and heat.

Would that I could go to Egypt, to my son,
Watch him drilling, guard him sleeping, duty done.
Would that I could join his army in the spring,
Be a man, and sling a rifle for the King.

For a woman's work's the hardest, duty bound
To the common task and daily dreary round,
Working, praying, keeping cheerful, making home,
While the surging soldiers muster o'er the foam.

Ah my shawl! A duty's hidden in each fold,
My boy wants no martial mother, stern and bold,
But a woman living bravely, day by day,
Serving God, and King, and country,—mother's way.

Source: Dorothy Frances McCrae, *Soldier, My Soldier,* Melbourne: G. Robertson, 1914, pp. 35-36. [David Holloway's *Dark Somme Flowing* anthology omits the first and last stanzas.]

Dorothy Frances McCrae
Second Thoughts

I wished you back at my breast
      When I saw this war descend,
Now I'd scour the east and west
      For another son to send;
Oh, that the parents, too, might go
To lead the way, and slay the foe.

I wished your toddling feet
      Played round the house again,
Now I want them strong and fleet, a
      And sure in the grand campaign.
Our prayers will follow you, my son;
God take you, then—His will be done.

I wanted your baby tongue
      To prattle with laughter gay,
Now give me an order flung
      Like a rifle-shot away—
Your parents' hearts are on the field—
Die if you must, but do not yield.

I wished you back at my breast
      When I saw this war descend,
Now I'd scour the east and west
      For another son to send;
Oh, that the parents, too, might go
To lead the way, and slay the foe!

Source: *Bulletin*, 22 October 1914, Red Page (p. 3). (Reprinted in *Bulletin* from her book *Soldier, my Soldier!,* Melbourne: George Robertson, pp. 27-28. [David Holloway's *Dark Somme Flowing* anthology omits the final stanza.]

Dorothy Frances McCrae
Geoffrey

I was dumb when we said Good-bye
    But you never saw my tears,
(I can weep when you're marching by
    And the air resounds with cheers,)
For a soldier's sister must not cry
When she spurs him on to Victory.

On the day that you volunteered
    We were smitten down by grief,
But skies have changed and winds have veered,
    And now—of our joys, it's chief,
For 'tis the greatest, grandest thing
To give a soldier to the King.

Source: Dorothy Frances McCrae, *Soldier, my Soldier!*, Melbourne: George Robertson, 1914, pp. 19-20.

Dorothy Frances McCrae
Gaba Tepe

With hopes, and fears, and rousing cheers
    They sped the flagship on her way,
With laughter, blessings, shouts, and prayers
    They played her out of Mudros Bay.

On through the quiet afternoon
    With leaping hearts and courage high,
Each man elate that he thus soon
    Should strike for God and Liberty.

They wait to hear man's order read,
    They pause to render God a prayer
With reverent mien and down-bent head,
    While hosts from Heaven hovered near.

All night they watched, that heavenly host,
    Above the troops stretched out to rest,
All night they watched, till like a ghost
    The sickle moon stole down the west.

Out swung the boats, towards the shore
    The gallant line in order crept,
A world of mystery lay before,
    As from life's peaceful paths they stept.

Slow moved the boats and very slow,
    Three battleships stole in behind,
There was no sound, no light aglow,
    Only the starlight, and the wind.

Oh mothers in your homes afar
    Pray! For your boy's great hour has come;
He leaps into the arms of War,
    And fights for Honour and for Home.

The blinding bullets fell like rain,
        They met the volleys with a cheer,
Leapt in the sea and charged amain,
        Sprang to the shore, and ran like deer.

Behind them boomed the cannon's roar,
        Before them hung the cliff's sheer side,
Men dropped, and staggered on once more
        Withy shot-torn breasts, and shouts of pride,

Rushed at the Turks with flashing steel,
        Triumphant laughed to see them fly,
While cannons thundered, peal on peal,
        And lightning-flashes rent the sky.

Weep, mothers, lest your hearts should break—
        Where soldiers fall, there heroes rise;
Their gallant charge the world will shake,
        . . . But in his blood your loved one lies.

They scaled the cliff, they faced the fire,
        They chased the foeman far and wide,
O'er sand and clay, thro' scrub and briar,
        While shells shrieked vengeance on each side.

Thro' fires of hell, the ridge was gained,
        Thro' fires of hell, the heights were kept,
Australia's honour was maintained
        As fighting, dying,—on! they swept.

But ah! those creeping piteous lines,
        Of stretchers borne towards the shore,
Where wounded men made feeble signs
        And cheered their comrades on once more.

Who dreamed, a hundred years ago,
        Our race so soon its spurs should win?
The deeds they did that day will show
        What homes our men were nurtured in.

Glad homes! Though some are sad to-day
    For those who will return no more,
Proud mothers, who thro' tears can say—
    Our sons helped Britain in the war!

Source: Dorothy Frances McCrae, *The Clear Call,* Melbourne: George Robertson, 1915, pp. 9-15.

Dorothy Frances McCrae
My Soldier

I love him for his ready wit and brain,
    His gallant mien, his spirit bold and free,
His strong right arm and honour without stain;
    But most I love him for his need of me.

The world sees how he plans and fights and dares,
    They hear him argue, struggle and agree;
Only to me he shows his doubt and tears;
    And so I love him—for his need of me.

They see him standing dauntless in the fight,
    I see him childlike, nestling at my knee;
My words alone can set his fears to flight—
    God! How I love him for his need of me!

Source: Dorothy Frances McCrae, *The Clear Call,* Melbourne: George Robertson, 1915, p.16.

Dorothy Frances McCrae
The Hero

Lieut. Alan D. Henderson, of the 7th Battalion, at the Dardanelles, continually impressed his men not to yield a foot. 'Remember, you're Britons, men,' he said again and again; 'we must not retreat, whatever happens.' He was shot through the chest later in the afternoon.

>Deep hidden in the scrub they lay,
>And we above them on the hill
>Lay tense and silent, grim and still,
>While haze hung brooding o'er the bay.
>
>All day their bullets hissed like rain,
>And crackling volleys rose and died,
>Shrieks echoed down the mountain side
>As swift we answered back again.
>
>'You're Britons, men,' our leader said;
>A steady fire was our reply
>Our comrades fell, we let them lie,
>They cheered us, as they lay and bled.
>
>... And when a moan rose 'neath our feet
>That froze our hearts, we made no stay
>But stood our ground and blazed away
>While gallant pulses ceased to beat.
>
>E'en when a bullet laid him low
>Like Britain's men we kept the line,
>While blood surged thro' our veins like wine,
>As (Britain's men!) we faced the foe.
>
>We held the field, we kept the line,
>Thro' fearful odds and fires of hell,
>Like Britain's men. But he? ah well,
>He lives in fields that are Divine!

Source: Dorothy Frances McCrae, *The Clear Call,* Melbourne: George Robertson, 1915, pp. 21-23.

Dorothy Frances McCrae
The Gift

All that I have, England, I give to you.
Gladly, through tears, I see my son depart.
You gave me all, so I, with grateful heart,
Give you my child, so loyal and so true,
Nor do I count my offering sacrifice,
Oh! tender guardian of our land and sea,
For in your flag that flames upon our skies
Lies our sole claim to life and liberty.

See! We to your defence with ardour run,
Strong arms, keen eyes, swift limbs, and sword and gun;
All to your service fondly, proudly, press,
A glad return for your dear gifts that bless.
All that I have, dear Motherland, I give
Who gave my son and me the right to live.

Source: Dorothy Frances McCrae, *The Clear Call,* Melbourne: George Robertson, 1915, p. 29.

GRACE ETHEL MARTYR

Grace Ethel Martyr. Photographer unknown.
Australian Woman's Mirror, 2 August 1927, p. 13.

Grace Ethel Martyr was born at Ballarat in 1888 and died at Bendigo in 1934. She was the sole child of James Kent and Grace Flora Martyr (née King), who had married the previous year. Her father, eldest son of Creswick pioneer James Martyr, was employed by the Bank of New South Wales, and served as a vestryman at St Augustine's Anglican church at Inglewood. Her mother was the third daughter of Dr James King of Ballarat and granddaughter of Captain King of the Bellisle, County Fermanagh Yeomanry and of the 49th Regiment.

Martyr first attended school at Inglewood and spent her early adult years in the central Victorian town of Maldon, for which she retained her affection though spending much of her working life in Bendigo. In 1902 she won prizes for Letter Writing and for a piano solo in a competition sponsored by the Australian Natives Association; in the following year, she came second in the Association's song competition. She matriculated at the Melbourne University examinations in June 1906, but commenced work in the Bank of New South Wales. In 1911, she became engaged to Lindsay Gladstone Webb, of Rathmines Road in the Melbourne suburb of Auburn, but the relationship appears to have failed. In July 1915, Webb enlisted in the AIF and served in the Second Field Artillery, returning to Australia on 5 April 1919.

Martyr was appointed to a position in the Castlemaine branch of the Bank of New South Wales in August 1918, where she would remain for four and a half years before leaving on account of ill health. While working at the bank, she published poems and entered competitions, winning commendation for works including the poem 'Afterwards' that provided the title-poem of her 1918 collection of patriotic poems, *Afterwards and Other Verses*, which she dedicated to her parents.

On the appearance of the book, the *Castlemaine Mail* noted 'Miss Grace Ethel Martyr is a Maldon lady, who of late has come into prominence as a writer of war poems. Her work is known and appreciated throughout the continent, a fact which is very creditable to the continent, and incidentally a high tribute to Miss Martyr's talent as a writer of verse. She has deserved the plaudits which have been showered upon her'. The book ran to two editions, and reviews appeared in several States: in the *Western Mail* (Perth), *Adelaide Observer* and *Advertiser*, the Brisbane *Daily Mail*, *Sydney Morning Herald* and *Sydney Stock and Station Journal*, the Launceston *Examiner*, the Victorian *Labor Call* and the *Socialist*. Conservative reviewers variously noted the book's 'noble', 'memorial' and religious sentiments, and Martyr's technical accomplishments as a lyric poet. Many writers quoted generous sections of poems, and entire poems continued to be reprinted in many papers. Exceptionally, the *Labor Call*, while noting Martyr's enthusiasm and energy, hoped that those qualities would be 'so exercised that, in the coming years, she will realise that fighting and dying for home and country ('when the cause is just and there is no other way'), though a great and noble deed, is not only—or necessarily the greatest—quest in which chivalry may be engaged'.

The *Socialist* went further, stating that the book was 'readable from a literary point of view, but, like most verse dedicated to Mars', was 'apparently written with the fallacious idea that war is right and manly and glorious, the author even going so far, in "Follow On", of placing on it the designation of "holy", and of otherwise associating it with the peaceful Nazarene'. The reviewer allowed 'merit in the title verse', poetry in 'Westward', and feeling in 'the dirge of "Rain"', but questioned Martyr's assumption that the Allied soldiers were determinedly fighting for 'the ideal of liberty against tyranny', and remarked that she 'doesn't admit such elements as love of adventure or economic conscription as impelling forces, and forgets or doesn't realise that the initiative of the man is lost when he becomes part of the military machine'.

Whether or not Martyr read or was even aware of such responses to her work, she returned to the theme of heroic Australian manhood in a poem she entered in 1920 Rupert Brooke Award, run by the Presbyterian Ladies College of Melbourne, for a poem on the theme of Gallipoli. Martyr's poem came second to one by the *Bulletin* editor David McKee Wright, in retrospect, a pity, since Wright's pompous poem sank forever after its initial publication in the *Bulletin*. Martyr's 'Gallipoli' and other wartime poems have less of bombast and heroics, and often employ subtler rhythm and rhymes that downplay glory at the cost of lives. In 1920, Martyr also published, in the *Woman* magazine, a poem commemorating the visit of the Prince of Wales.

After leaving the bank, Martyr embarked on writing to earn her living, and she became a prolific writer of poems, stories and serial novels for children, and travel sketches, short stories and serial fiction for adults, increasingly written under the name Ethel Martyr. Her fiction chiefly appeared in the *Australasian* and *Weekly Times* in Victoria; from 1919, stories also appeared in the *Queenslander*. Many of Martyr's stories concerned life in country towns (including New South Wales locations) and were characterised by precise details of natural settings, variations on romance themes, and shrewd, sometimes satirical depiction of social conventions, including children's behaviour. Several serials, including 'The Threshold' (1937), set in Victorian gold rush times, and her last short story, 'Twelve by the Clock', were published posthumously.

Martyr's post-War poetry output appeared in the *Bulletin* and the *Australian Woman's Mirror,* though regional papers were quick to reprint poems that appeared in major Melbourne papers as well as those from her book. In 1925, a meeting of the Australian Natives Association at Middle Park featured a recitation of the poem 'Afterward' as part of its annual Anzac Remembrance. In the same year, *The School Paper for Grades VII and VIII* republished her poem 'In Memory, April 25, 1915'.

Martyr worked as a journalist for the *Bendigo Advertiser,* where she edited the women's columns and the children's page up to a week before her death. At the same time, she was the Bendigo social correspondent for several Melbourne publications. A talented pianist, she gave a series of lectures in Bendigo on the great musicians, and collaborated with the Melbourne pianist and composer William James, writing stories and verses for the 3LO children's hour, with James setting the verse to music.

In 1927, Zora Cross wrote a profile of Martyr for inclusion in a series of articles on contemporary Australian women writers in the *Australian Woman's Mirror*. Cross and Martyr corresponded after Cross received a copy of Martyr's book during a chance encounter with a cousin of Martyr's who worked in a bank in Sydney. Cross thought the poems 'very good indeed', and that they were written at a time when Martyr 'was not taking writing very seriously'.

Martyr was, however, taking writing very seriously at the time of her correspondence with Cross. She told Cross that she was aiming to write a novel, even while Cross opined that Martyr's 'true vein' was writing stories and verse for children. Cross believed that Martyr was 'that rare writer, the one who never forgets that child-verse should also be poetry'. Cross nevertheless commended Martyr's turn to fiction for women and verse-production for 3LO, and concluded, 'It seemed only the other day that Miss Martyr was writing to me and asking me if I thought she should leave the Bank of New South Wales to become an Australian writer. How glad I have been since that I replied promptly, "Yes". Martyr wrote of the photograph she sent to Zora Cross, 'I suppose people will wonder who the Early Victorian with her "bun" is, but I am not as old-fashioned as all that'.

§

Martyr died at Quarry Hill, Bendigo, on Saturday 22 December 1934, and was buried at Maldon in her father's grave, where her mother was also later interred. Her father had died at Maldon on 19 July 1931, aged 78, and her mother died at a private hospital in Essendon on 9 September 1945. In August 1935, Dr Donald Baker, Anglican Bishop of Bendigo, dedicated a memorial cross to Grace Ethel Martyr in St. Paul's Church, Bendigo. The cross bears the inscription 'To the glory of God and in memory of Grace Ethel Martyr, a devoted servant of God and of this Church'.

Publications
Afterwards and Other Verses, Melbourne: Australasian Authors' Agency, 1918 (Reprinted 1918).

Reviews
'Afterwards, and Other Verses', *Castlemaine Mail*, Friday 3 May 1918, p. 4.
'Our Book Column—More War Verses', *Sydney Stock and Station Journal*, Friday 10 May 1918, p. 4.
'A Woman's Verse', *Socialist*, Friday 10 May 1918, p. 4.
(Untitled) *'Afterwards, and Other Verses'*, *Bulletin*, 16 May 1918, Red Page, p. 2.
(Untitled), *The Daily Mail* (Brisbane) Saturday 18 May 1918, p. 10.
'Poems of War-time', *Observer* (Adelaide), Saturday 18 May 1918, p. 2.
'Australian Verse', *Sydney Morning Herald*, Saturday 18 May 1918, p. 8.
'Afterwards, And Other Verses', *Examiner* (Launceston), Tuesday 21 May 1918, p. 3.
'Afterwards, and Other Verses', *Labor Call*, Thursday 23 May 1918, p. 11.
'Verses: *Afterwards, and Other Verses'*,*Western Mail* (Perth), Friday 21 June 1918, p. 31.
'New Poetry', *Ballarat Courier*, Saturday 3 August 1918, p. 7.
'Recent Publications', *Advertiser* (Adelaide), Saturday 20 July 1918, p. 3.

References
Ballarat Star, Thursday 3 March 1887, p. 2 [Family notices: marriage of James K. Martyr and Grace Flora King].
'Musical and Literary Competitions', *Bendigo Advertiser*, Friday 20 June 1902, p. 4 [Ethel Martyr, first in Letter Writing, and in under 16 Piano Solo (performing 'Le Papillon']; also listed in Age, 20 June 1902, p. 6.
'A.N.A. Competitions', *Bendigo Independent*, Thursday 11 June 1903, p. 3 [Ethel Martyr, second in Girls under 16 song competition].
Ballarat Star, Tuesday 19 June 1906, p. 3. ['Matriculation. Melbourne University Exams': Martyr's name included].
Table Talk, Melbourne, Thursday 4 May 1911, p. 7, and Australasian, Saturday 29 April 1911, p. 48 [Family Notices: Martyr's engagement].
Argus, Thursday 8 February 1912, p. 1 ['Silver Anniversary': details of Martyr's parents' ancestry].
'Maldon', *Castlemaine Mail*, Wednesday 7 August 1918, p. 1 [Report of Martyr's appointment to position at Castlemaine Bank of New South Wales]. .
Bernice May [Zora Cross], 'Grace Ethel Martyr', *Australian Woman's Mirror*, 2 August 1927, p. 13.
Daily Mail (Brisbane) Saturday 18 May 1918, p. 10 [Martyr's South Street Ballarat award for poem 'Afterwards'].
'Social Notes', *Table Talk*, Saturday 10 July 1920, p. 45 [Martyr's poem commemorating the Prince of Wale's visit noted].

Record (Emerald Hill), Saturday 25 April 1925, p. 6 [Report on Middle Park A.N.A. meeting and recitation of Martyr's poem, 'Afterwards'].

'Bendigo, *Age,* Friday 15 August 1930, p. 7 [Report of fifth public lecture at St Andrews Church Hall, Bendigo, on Wednesday 13 August by Martyr, on Schubert's life, and Mr. M.W. Allan, on Schubert's works].

Argus, Monday 20 July 1931, p. 1 [Family notices: death of James Kent Martyr].

Age, Monday 24 December 1934, p. 12 [Death of Grace Ethel Martyr].

Australasian, Saturday 29 December 1934, p. 6 [Death of Grace Ethel Martyr on 22 December 1934].

'Bendigo and District', *Argus,* Monday 26 August 1935, p. 4 [Memorial cross dedicated to Grace Ethel Martyr by Anglican Bishop of Bendigo].

Ethel Martyr, 'Darkey' (serial), *Queenslander,* 7 August-4 September 1926.

Ethel Martyr, 'Chums at Wunnamurra' (serial), *Queenslander,* April-May 1929.

Ethel Martyr, 'Twelve by the Clock', *Weekly Times,* Saturday 16 May 1936, p. 44.

Ethel Martyr, 'The Threshold: A Romance of the Bendigo Diggings in the Fifties' (serial), *Weekly Times,* May 1937.

Argus, Monday 10 September 1945, p. 2 [Family notices: death of Grace Flora Martyr].

'Sidney Rupert Green', The A.I.F. Project, https://www.aif.adfa.edu.au/showPerson?pid=118381. Accessed online 8 May 2016.

'Another Echuca Volunteer. Lieutenant Green', *Riverine Herald* (Echuca Vic., Moama NSW), Monday 17 May 1915, p. 3.

'Sergeant Green', *Riverina Herald* (Echuca Vic., Moama NSW), Wednesday 29 December 1915, p. 2.

'A Soldier's Death. How Sergeant Rupert Green Died. A Comrade's Tribute', *McIvor Times and Rodney Advertiser* (Heathcote), Thursday 1 March 1917, p. 3. *Echuca and Moama Advertiser and Farmers' Gazette,* Thursday 15 February 1917, p. 4.

'Wilfrid Richard Walters', The A.I.F. Project, https://www.aif.adfa.edu.au/showUnit?unitCode=INF21CD. Accessed online 8 May 2016.

Ronald McNicoll, 'McNicoll, Sir Walter Ramsay (1877–1947)', Australian Dictionary of Biography, National Centre of Biography, Australian National University, http://adb.anu.edu.au/biography/mcnicoll-sir-walter-ramsay-7436/text12945, published first in hardcopy 1986, accessed online 10 June 2018.

Grace Ethel Martyr grave site, Billion Graves. https://billiongraves.com/grave/Grace-Ethel-Martyr/13150782 Accessed 28 June 2018.

Keith Cole, *A History of St Paul's Cathedral Church,* Bendigo 1968-1993, Bendigo: Bendigo Anglican Diocesan Historical Society Incorporated, 1991, p. 73.

Grace Ethel Martyr
The Soldier

To 2152, Sergt. S. Rupert Green, 5th Battalion, A.I.F.,
of Maldon, who gave his life at Flers, France,
on 31st October, 1916.

He stood upon the morning road of Life,
And looked along its pleasant avenue.
The stately trees were arched above his head,
The sunlight flashed upon him thro' the leaves,
And like a silver ribbon ran the road
Far down the vista of the years to be.

But Duty called him from the frowning heights,
And, leaving all, he followed her, and climbed.
The breath of Fear was chill upon his face,
With danger ever round him like the mist
That clings and floats and lingers in the hills,
But with undaunted heart he followed on.

Until he looked into the eyes of Death;
And Death stood still, and met his eyes, and smiled,
Then moved aside to let him pass, and watched
To see him pressing up the Great White Way,
Where, 'mid the glory and triumphal songs,
The Christ, with welcoming hands, awaited him.

Source: *Afterwards, and Other Verses,* Melbourne: Australasian Authors' Agency, 1918, p. 9.

Sidney Rupert Green, a schoolteacher (born 1897, though he put his age up one year), was a school Cadet (Lieutenant) and member of the Citizen Forces before he enlisted as a private in the AIF on 10 April 1915. His parents were Charles Lewis Green (Postmaster, of Echuca) and Mary Ida Louise Green (née Wedel). Green embarked with reinforcements for Gallipoli in June 1915 and was promoted to Corporal and then Sergeant during the battle of Lone Pine. Falling ill, he was sent to England, where he was operated on for appendicitis in December 1915. Promoted to Company Quartermaster Sergeant in August 1916 in France, he reverted to the rank of Sergeant at his own request on 3 October, and was killed two weeks later. Other members of his family who served in the Dardanelles were Private Allan Green, Staff Nurse Doris Marion Green, and Lieutenant-Colonel McNicoll (Sir Walter Ramsay McNicoll, KBE, CBE, DSO, VD). Sidney Rupert Green is commemorated in Holy Trinity Anglican Church at Maldon by inclusion of his name on a list, beneath a stained glass window with the figure of St George, of 22 men of the parish 'who laid down their lives in the Great War'. A separate framed plaque on the opposite (west) wall was dedicated by his parents and bears the legend, 'In loving Memory of Rupert Green, C.Q.M.S. 3rd Batt, A.I.F., beloved only son of C. L. Green and M.I.L. Green, who died in the service of his country at Flers, France, on the 31st October 1916, aged 19 years, 5 months. Ready to do whatsoever my Lord the King shall appoint'.

Grace Ethel Martyr
Rain

I hear the sound of falling, falling, rain,
Like dead hands beating on the window-pane,
And still it sobs and sobs the same refrain —
And he is gone, nor will he come again.
Perhaps on such a drear night he has lain
Out in the darkness there, among the slain,
Uncovered, to the pitiless, falling rain.
I hear the moaning, crying wind complain.
The sound of pattering drops beats on my brain,
That I shall never see his face again,
But lonely wait and wait for him in vain;
And, weeping with the longing and the pain,
My tears are falling, falling with the rain.
He has preserved his honour without stain,
But all I hear is sobbing, driving, rain,
That beats and taps upon the window-pane,
I only know he will not come again.

Source: Grace Ethel Martyr, *Afterwards and Other Verses,* Melbourne: Australasian Authors' Agency, 1918, p. 24; *Register* (Adelaide), Saturday 25 May 1918, p. 4; *Observer* (Adelaide) Saturday 1 June 1918, p. 2.

Grace Ethel Martyr
Follow On

Follow on and follow up the path that lies ahead,
The path through all the ages where the bravest men have led,
From knights in shining coat of mail with helm and plume and lance
To men of ours in khaki on the far-off fields of France.

Straightway take your valiant place among the brave and strong,
With those who lived to help the weak and died to right the wrong,
For never knight went riding forth upon a nobler quest
Than this—to fight for home and King and country in the West.

Give your young and splendid strength for this most holy war,
Be worthy of your country and the men who went before,
Be straight and strong and undismayed, be chivalrous and true,
Be worthy of your women and the faith they have in you.

In the West your brothers wait, and they have waited long,
Then follow with a happy heart and ringing battle song,
And for the love you bear them, for the honour of the dead,
Oh! follow on and follow up the path that lies ahead.

Source: Grace Ethel Martyr, *Afterwards and Other Verses,* Melbourne: Australasian Authors' Agency, 1918, pp. 12-13.

Grace Ethel Martyr
To the Stretcher-Bearers
And especially to Wilfrid Richard Walters, 6th Field Ambulance, killed at Bullecourt, 3rd May, 1917.

They place no price upon their priceless lives,
    But all they have and are they freely give.
Each, brave and constant, self-forgetful, strives
    To help and heal. That other men may live
This perfect offering of themselves they make,
Their only thought, their only care to take
The burden and to ease the pain. They ask
For nothing for themselves except the task.

And He, who silently endured so much,
    With tender heart of love and ready will,.
Brings peace and consolation with his touch,
    And surely works and watches with them still;
Goes ever in and out with them unseen.
And in that Presence, still of soul, serene,
They work. And He, who set them thus apart
Will hold the stretcher-bearers in His heart,

Source: Grace Ethel Martyr, *Afterwards and Other Verses,* Melbourne: Australasian Authors' Agency, 1918, p. 24.

Private 992 Wilfrid Walters, of Korumburra, Victoria, enlisted on 3 February 1915 in the 21st Battalion, and embarked on 10 May 1915. He died of wounds at the age of nineteen while serving in the Royal Australian Medical Corps on the date indicated in Martyr's subtitle. The *Great Southern Advocate* newspaper (servicing Korumburra, Leongatha, Moyarra and Poowong) reported his death on Thursday 24 March 1917, adding that before enlisting, 'he was employed in the local branch of the savings bank, and took an interest in the fire brigade and other affairs. Private Walter's father is on active service in France. His mother now resides in Melbourne, and general sympathy is extended to her in the severe trial she is experiencing' (p.4).

Grace Ethel Martyr
Returned

He has returned with eyes that do not see,
    Nor ever will, and I am consecrate
To one great purpose—so to love that he
    May never miss one gladness, small or great,
can give—in this his hour of need;
    To stand beside, and strengthen him to learn
To live his life again; by word-and- deed
    To prove my need of him. So love will burn,
To light the dark. But how can any thing
    Reward or recompense him? How can words
The glory of the glowing sunset bring
    Before him; or the sudden flight of birds
Among the trees at dusk; how can they paint
    The distant mountains deeply blue and far,
Or the soft primrose at the dawning, faint
    And lovely in the East, where one great star
Shines palely; or the depth of velvet green
    In Spring; the red-gold of the Autumn
Richly sun-crowned; the silver-shining sheen
    Of rain-wet leaves, and all the happy ways
Of sunlight upon laughing water? These
    He loved ah, how he loved them. Not my touch,
Nor life of love, honours, nor victories
    Well won, can recompense him for so much.

Source: *Australasian,* Saturday 5 April 1919, p. 41.

MYRA MORRIS

Photograph of Myra Morris 1930/40.
Photographer unknown. State Library Victoria.

Myra Evelyn Morris was born on 15 May 1893 at Boort in northern Victoria, the second of five daughters of Bessie Lily Morris (née Sydenham) and her English-born husband Charles William Morris. Myra's sisters were Roma Louise Rosa (b. 1892), Vera Bessie (b. 1897) Alma Lily (b. 1900), and Irma St James (b. 1913). One brother, Nelson, was born in 1906.

Morris and her sisters saw a great deal of the Victorian western and central northern districts as a result of their father's business enterprises. Charles William Morris was a successful businessman who owned a succession of grocery and produce stores at Allansford, Warrnambool, Rochester, Maldon, St James and Camperdown. Like her mother and her siblings, Myra was at home in the natural surroundings of these towns that provide background for her later stories and poetry. Her paintings as well as her book *The Australian Landscape* (1944), focusing on Australian landscape artists, also reflect her delight in the natural world. (Morris was the aunt of Australian painter Rick Amor, whose work also seeks 'the intensely poetic character' that Morris had attributed to Melbourne half a century before his works such as 'City 6am'.)

Morris was encouraged in her literary interest by her mother and her English teacher at the Brigidine Convent at Rochester, near her birthplace Boort, where she was chiefly educated. She also briefly attended Miss E.M. Fuller's Church of England Girls Grammar School at Warrnambool. By 1916, her verse had appeared in the Melbourne *Australasian* and the Sydney *Bulletin*, and in 1918, she published her first, patriotic collection, *England and Other Verses*.

Morris moved in 1922 with her youngest sister Irma (called 'Goblin' by the family) from St James, in northern Victoria, to Melbourne, following publication of her serialised novel *Us Five*. Five years later, she moved again, with her parents and elder sister Roma to 'Charlecote', a beachside house at Frankston, which would remain her permanent home. From that time, water imagery, first-hand accounts of seaside pursuits and sights, ocean travel and dreams of maritime action in past and contemporary times became characteristic of Morris's poetry.

Morris's sister Alma, who also wrote poetry and published in the *Australasian*, later joined a religious order and took the name Sister Patricia. Nelson and Irma Morris became members of 'The Passers-By', a theatre company that later became the Frankston Theatre Group (and, from 1942, the Frankston Players). In 1937, Nelson married the sisters' friend and fellow actor Elsie Lloyd, and the following year, Irma Morris married the schoolteacher and artist Robert James Amor. In a 2012 interview, the artist Rick Amor recounted that his aunt Myra 'knew a lot of artists and writers, and her house was full of paintings and books'.

In the 1920s, Myra was a prolific contributor of verse to journals and papers including the *Lone Hand, Triad, Australasian, Bulletin* and *Australian Woman's Mirror*. From the 1920s, her short stories appeared with more frequency in the *Bulletin, Australasian, Australian Journal, Home,* and *Sydney Morning Herald,* to which she also contributed reviews and non-fiction. From 1918, she had published Anzac Day commemorative poems in the *Argus, Australasian* and other papers, and in 1922, her poetry was anthologised in *The Little Track and Other Verses,* a collection containing poems by Morris, her friend Capel Boake (Doris Kerr), Cecil Doyle, Gertrude Hart and Bernard Cronin.

On 7 May 1930, following a large farewell party organised by the Association of Australian Authors, Morris travelled to England on the *Jervis Bay*, with the intention of making a cycling tour of southern counties and gathering material from districts that provided background for the fiction of the English writer Sheila Kaye-Smith. En route, she had an affair with the ship's captain. On her return to Australia, she told the *Horsham Times* that she had discovered the English were not interested in Australian literature or the classics. She subsequently published articles extolling the beauties of South Devon, the Isle of Man, the New Forest, Somerset and other English districts, together with accounts of other destinations, in the 'Tourist' section of the *Australasian*. Morris also became increasingly active in artistic and literary circles, publishing essays and editing, but chiefly writing short stories. She was one of the founders of the Melbourne branch of P.E.N. International.

Morris was considered a talented woodcarver, and she had studied art with the painter and art historian William Colquhoun. At home with her parents in Frankston, she insisted on paying rent and contributing to housework. She was a keen gardener and enjoyed sport, bushwalking and swimming, like her sister Irma.

A composite portrait of Morris, culled from newspaper accounts by those who knew her, highlights her affection for her family, her artistic enthusiasms and work on behalf of other authors, and her vivacity in company. Belying her claims of indolence, her litheness was matched by keen observation and questioning relating to the natural world and topics bordering on religious experience. Transience and spirituality appear in many images. Some reviewers of her poetry and later fiction spoke of her failure to move beyond conventional observations, but her work shows a serious questioning of the necessity to respond to every impulse, and a compassionate portrayal of others' lives.

Morris's novel, *The Wind on the Water* was published in 1938, and in 1939, she completed another, *Dark Tumult*. In 1942, her father died aged 84 at Frankston. Two years later, her interest in landscape art resulted in publication of the book *Australian Landscape*. The following year, her best friend Doris Kerr ('Capel Boake') died, and Morris suffered a nervous breakdown soon after. Following receipt of a Commonwealth Literary Fellowship, she later published a selection of her short stories in *The Township* in 1947, and in 1949, she contributed the introduction to the *Selected Poems of Capel Boake*.

In all, Morris wrote over 100 stories and published more than 300 poems. Her work was broadcast on Australian and British radio and on Australian television, and translations were published in Germany,

Austria and Switzerland. To her frustrations with her work were added the crippling effect of Paget's disease of the bones. She died at Frankston on 18 August 1966 and was cremated with Anglican rites.

§

On the appearance of Morris's *England and Other Verses,* the *Australasian's* anonymous book reviewer endorsed the high quality of her verse, 'already familiar' to readers of that paper:

> She has experimented in quite a number of metres, some of them by no means the easiest to handle successfully, but in none has she failed to reach a comparatively high level of attainment. Her poems, however, are much more than mere poetic exercises.
>
> They are adorned with delicate touches of fancy, and some of them display deep thought as well as warm feeling, especially when, as in 'The Seeking' and 'Expiation,' the theme is some vital problem of man's relation to God and the universe. There is great beauty in some of the scenic descriptions, such as those, for example, woven into the fabric of the dainty love lyric named 'Golden River'.

Other reviewers were quick to claim the sophistication of Morris's language. *The Graphic of Melbourne,* for instance observed 'A fine craftsmanship is revealed in all the verses, and in the introductory piece, "England", the idea is lofty, well sustained, and the 'language noble'. The reviewer concluded, With this volume, which we trust is the forerunner of others, Myra Morris takes her place amongst the foremost women poets of Australia'. The Adelaide *Mail's* famously pedantic critic adopted a characteristic sour note, claiming that

> One cannot help noting the frequent use of compound words so usual in Tennyson and Keats, and there is something of a search for epithets suggested at times. 'Christ', the longest and most rambling poem in the book, is in blank verse, which is more forceful than impressive. The verse is artificial, not varied enough in caesura, and cleaving too much to the stopped line. 'The Seeking' is a neat little thing, seemingly influenced in idea (and in diction to a point) by Francis Thompson's 'Hound of Heaven'.

... There is an absence of originality, but much that will please is contained in the verses.

Closer to home, the *Warrnambool Standard* noted 'a strong, religious vein, coupled, as is usual in young writers, with a sense of doubt and dissatisfaction', as well as the echoes of Thompson's poem, but claimed that the best pieces in the volume were 'Daffodils' and 'Ode to the Magpie', which had 'a true lyrical note; the poems as a whole had 'definiteness, melody and imagination; further, they do not employ slang and gutter language to produce their effects—a sure note of decadence in literature now as always'.

Publications

England and Other Verses, Melbourne: Australasian Authors' Agency, 1918.
Us Five [children's fiction], Melbourne: Melbourne Publishing Company, 1922.
White Magic, Melbourne: Edward A. Vidler, 1929.
Enchantment [novel], serialised in *Australian Woman's Mirror,* 1 October–24 December 1929.
The Little English Girl [novel], serialised in *Australasian,* 7 April–1 September 1934.
The Wind on the Water [novel], Adelaide: Rigby, 1938; Adelaide: Rigby, 1960.
Dark Tumult [novel], London: Thornton Butterworth, 1939.
Australian Landscape, Sydney: J. Sands, 1944.
The Township [stories], Sydney: Angus & Robertson, 1947.

References

D. J. Jordan, 'Morris, Myra Evelyn (1893-1966)', Australian Dictionary of Biography, National Centre of Biography, Australian National University, http://adb.anu.edu.au/morris-myra-evelyn-7660/text13399. Published first in hardcopy 1986, accessed online 28 January 2016.
Warrnambool Standard, Saturday 3 January 1914, p. 9 [Note on Miss E.M. Fuller, Principal of the Church of England Girls Grammar School, Warrnambool].
'Miscellaneous Works', *Australasian,* Saturday 21 September 1918, p. 50 [Review of Morris's *England and Other Verses*].
Graphic of Melbourne, Thursday 3 October 1918, p. 14. [*Review of England and Other Verses*].
'A New Writer', *Mail,* Saturday 5 October 1918, p. 3 [*Review of England and Other Verses*].
Warrnambool Standard, Monday 14 October 1918, p. 3 [*England and Other Verses* reviewed, with note on Morris's attendance at Miss Fuller's school in Canterbury Road].

Benalla Standard, Friday 21 October 1921, p. 4 [Marriage of Vera Bessie Morris to Edwin Jane of Waggarandall. Myra and Irma were bridesmaids].

Warrnambool Standard, Thursday 5 December 1918, p. 3 [Miss E.M. Fuller relinquishes connection with the Church of England Grammar School].

Rick Amor, 'The City 6am (1989-90)', Deutscher and Hackett catalogue: Important Australian + International Fine Art Melbourne 9 May 2007, http://www.deutscherandhackett.com/auction/1-fine-art-auction/lot/city-6am-1989-90. Accessed 5 March 2018.

The Little Track and Other Verses, Melbourne: Robertson & Mullins, 1922.

Alma Morris, 'O, Little Girl', *Australasian,* Saturday 20 January 1923, p. 54.

'Women in the World', *Australian Woman's Mirror,* 1 February 1927, vol. 3, no. 10, p. 20.

Age, Tuesday 29 April 1930, p. 7 ['Miss Myra Morris Farewelled by Society of Australian Authors'].

Frankston and Somerville Standard, Saturday 12 April 1930, p. 4 [Morris's travel plans].

'English People Not Interested', *Horsham Times,* Tuesday 9 December 1930, p. 2.

Jennifer Phipps, 'Colquhoun, Alexander (1862–1941)', Australian Dictionary of Biography, National Centre of Biography, Australian National University, http://adb.anu.edu.au/biography/colquhoun-alexander-5742/text9721, published first in hardcopy 1981, accessed online 24 May 2016.

Myra Morris, 'Seeing Rustic England on Wheels', *Australasian,* 12 December 1931, p. 51.

Myra Morris, 'The Isle of Man', *Australasian,* Saturday 20 August 1932, p. 44.

Myra Morris, 'The Great Moors: Exmoor and Dartmoor. No. 2. Dartmoor', *Australasian,* Saturday 29 April 1933, p. 43.

Myra Morris, 'Ceylon: Pearl of the Orient', *Australasian,* Saturday 5 August 1933, p. 47.

Myra Morris, 'The New Forest', *Australasian,* Saturday 21 December 1935, p. 47.

Myra Morris, 'Charm of Somerset: Beauty and Legends', *Australasian,* Saturday 25 April 1936, p. 47.

'Three Melbourne Poets. Elsie Cole, Frederick Macartney, Myra Morris', *Age,* Saturday 23 January 1937, p. 4.

Frankston and Somerville Standard, Friday 10 September 1937 ['About People': Marriage of Nelson Morris and Elsie Lloyd].

Australasian, Saturday 18 February 1939, p. 43 [Account of Morris to accompany pencil portrait by Esther Paterson].

Argus, 15 June 1942, p. 2 [Family Notices: death of Charles William Morris at 375 Melbourne Road Frankston].

Frankston Standard, Wednesday 5 October 1949, p. 19 ['Frankston Theatre Group'].

Myra Morris, 'The Shadowy Woman' and 'The Little Old Woman', *White Magic,* Melbourne: Edward A. Vidler, 1929, pp. 119-120 and 123].

Josephine Rowe, 'Rick Amor is a Painter' [interview with Rick Amor], Dumbo Feather, Third Quarter 2012. http://www.dumbofeather.com/conversation/rick-amor-is-a-painter-2/ Accessed 25 May 2016.

Myra Morris
The Old Mother

He'll come no more an' softly kiss
    This shaking head,
    This old grey head.
I can remember nought but this—
    That he is dead.
    He's killed—he's dead.
The sun shines on the broken wall,
An' dances where the poppies fall:
Him that was big an' brown an' tall,
    Is gone—is dead!

I saw the glint of yellow hair
    When lie went by,
    Tramp, tramping by.
The grey old street stones were astare,
    I heard them sigh,
    Sing-sobbing sigh.
I listen where the willows shake,
An' hear the bending grasses quake,
An' still, my moaning for his sake,
    Nor breathe one sigh.

Dry-eyed I sit beside the door
    Where cobwebs swing,
    An' watch them swing,
I beat my old feet on the floor,
    An' rock an' sing.
    An' only sing,
For him, the sands as winding-sheet,
Only the wild sea at his feet,
An' weary waves that still their beat
    To hear me sing.

> An' on the roof when night is come,
> 　　　An' sheoaks drop—
> 　　　Tip-tapping drop—
> Their acorns down, I hear his drum,
> 　　　That will not stop,
> 　　　'Twill never stop!
> I see him tramping thro' the rain;
> An' if these eyes be wet with pain,
> I only sing my song again,
> 　　　An' never stop.

Source: *Australasian,* Saturday 3 February 1917, p. 37; *Queensland Times* (Ipswich), Saturday 24 February 1917, p. 4.

Myra Morris
To the Glorious Dead

Hark, hark, ye glorious dead who sleep
'Neath distant skies;
Who everlasting vigil keep,
By windy waste and frowning steep,
By flow'ry field and sandy shore,
And gentle rise—
The day of peace is come, know ye,
Whose blood was spilt
Unquestioning, that this might be!
That on your living flesh and bones
This Day is built!

Source: *Record* (Emerald Hill), Saturday 28 December 1918, p. 2; *Ovens and Murray Advertiser* (Beechworth), Wednesday 4 December 1918, p. 4; *Benalla Standard,* Tuesday 3 December 1918, p. 3.

Myra Morris
England

England is mine, and I am England's own!
All that is best within me lives for her alone.
That which is base and vile I spurn from me
Lest she with her unsleeping eyes should see,
And me condemn. She bore me in her womb
Where wild winds blew; and through the storm-lashed gloom
    Came ocean's boom.
And I was wove a living thread here strung
    In the vast loom.
She was my mother mighty-voiced. I hung
Upon her breasts, and greedy-mouthed did drink
Her noble sustenance. And on the brink
Of secret things I stood, when sweet and high
Her slumber songs lulled me to sleep, and I
Heard through their mounting cadence, wild and free,
The low andante beating of a sea.

England is mine, and I am England's own!
I am a singing harp, and hers the hand alone
That plays the strings. Without, I am a thing
Dead, dumb, inanimate. So shall I sing!
Here at the doorway to her room I keep
A ceaseless watch, untouched by straying sleep—
    Dream-shadowed, deep.
A living flame of fire from out its sheath
    My sword shall leap,
If I should hear her proud soul moan beneath
A weight of woe. My voice shall beat the stars
And thundering shake the might of heaven's bars
Till earth's dark caverns echo with the cry:
'Here, mother, mighty-souled, O England, I
am here to serve! Born of the wind and sea
I give thee back the life thou gav'st to me.'

Source: Myra Morris, *England and Other Verses,* Melbourne: Australasian Authors' Agency, 1918, pp. 1-2.

Myra Morris
Remembrance
Anzac Day

In ancient days upon the Trojan plain
    They warred—Homeric men of whom the breeze
    Aegean-born croons yet. Not less than these
Are they who stormed mid ruthless death and pain
The ridged front, and struggling to attain
    The towering heights heights, piled by the strange old seas,
    Fresh glories for the Golden Chersonese—
The heaped-up hecatombs of countless slain?

Such do not die! Not for a little day
    Shall they be with us. Ages shall not shake
the grandeur of Gallipoli. Who bled
    For us, like shining spectre-shapes shall stay
Among us; and our memories shall make
    The mighty mausoleum for our dead.

Source: *Argus*, Friday 5 April 1919, p. 6.

Myra Morris.
Going Home

'So you are going home,' they said,
    'Where your forefathers' bones are laid;
And you will see the Thames roll by
    From sunlight into purple shade
And walk beneath an English sky
    On sounding roads the Romans made.

And as you swing down London streets
    The past will brush you with its wings.
And you will feel against your face
    The breath of old romantic things,
And see in their dim, hallowed place
    The carven tombs of English kings.

And you will tramp historic shores
    That fringe a sea with glamour veiled.
Where Viking prows once pierced the mist.
    And pirates' tattered banners trailed
Where Spanish walls and English kissed,
    And lordly Drake and Nelson sailed!'

Oh, steeped in story England's stones ...
    And yet I'm thinking, it will be
(All delicately dreaming up)
    A crinkled poppy by the sea.
That deep within its silken cup
    Will hold all England's heart for me!

Australasian, Saturday 19 April 1930, p. 44.

NINA MURDOCH

Sir John Longstaff 1861-1941. Portrait of Nina Murdoch, 1920.
oil on canvas, 63.2cm x 36.3cm.
http://nla.gov.au/nla.pic-an2268336 Accessed 3 January 2016

Nina Murdoch (1890-1976, birth name Madoline Nina Murdoch) was born on 19 October 1890 at North Carlton, Victoria, daughter of Rebecca Murdoch (née Murphy), and John Andrew Murdoch, a Clerk of Courts in Melbourne and Wangaratta. Murdoch's family moved to Woodburn near Lismore in New South Wales when she was young, and she first attended a school where her mother taught, before the family moved to Neutral Bay.

In an interview by the Adelaide *News* in 1930, Murdoch stated that her first literary effort, written at the age of eight, was an acrostic on the name conferred on her in honour of her Spanish great-grandmother: 'Madoline'. Murdoch also told the newspaper that she had written 'mushy verse' at school', but her first real success 'was the winning of a prize for a fairy tale' in the magazine of the school she attended in Sydney. The prize was Robert Louis Stevenson's *Virginibus Puerisque*, which gave her 'the first realisation of thinking for myself, and the sense of words'. The book was, she said, 'my Bible for years'.

Murdoch completed her education between 1904 and 1907 at Sydney Girls High School, whose headmistress, Lucy Garvin, encouraged many students' pursuits of professional careers: Lilith Norman (later author of a history of the school), Lilian Burwell—author, as Lilian Turner, of *An Australian Lassie*)—and Lilian's younger sister Ethel Turner (author of *Seven Little Australians*). Murdoch's contemporaries also included the Mack sisters, Louise (who became a war correspondent in World War One) and Amy (a prolific nature writer), and Zora Cross. Cross and Murdoch would later stage fundraising events in Sydney during World War One. In the latter period, Murdoch would be elected to the committee of the Old High School Girls' Union in 1917.

Murdoch first taught with her mother at Sydney Boys Preparatory School before a meeting with the *Sun* journalist Adam ('Dum') McCay, persuaded her to join the paper in 1914. Trained by the paper's innovative editor Montague ('Monty') Grover, Murdoch became a popular and even celebrated journalist. Her attitude to the War in some measure coincided with that of the sceptical Monty Grover, who opposed Billy Hughes's Conscription campaign. By the time she left the paper at the end of 1917, the newspaper's owner Hugh Denison had installed McCay as editor of the daily *Sun*, leaving Grover to conduct the Sunday edition. On Murdoch's departure, Grover described Murdoch as the ablest woman reporter he had ever known, one equally at home reporting in the economics of a meat trust or describing a man who bit the tails off dogs for a living. Murdoch had also written political articles under her own byline. The *Australian Journalist* summed up her contribution to the press as 'brilliant'.

Murdoch's engagement with the *Sun* newspaper had two significant results. She met her future husband, a fellow *Sun* journalist, Duncan Brown (George Duncan McKay Brown, b. 1886), who introduced her to George Saintsbury's *English Prosody*. She attributed her poetical development to Brown, with whom she vied in writing sonnets for the monthly competitions run by the *Bulletin's* Red Page. Murdoch remarked, in a 1930 interview, 'I won four.'

Murdoch's poetry of the War period reflects her versatility; she had already written a winning sonnet on the subject of Canberra in the

Bulletin in 1913, and she subsequently produced memorable poems on the Australian seasons and wildflowers, on social conditions (including what a reviewer called 'the real goods', a 'propagandistic, socialistic, if you like', poem called 'Song of the Slum Woman', concerning a baby and a rubbish-tin 'huddled side by side' in Sydney's Central district), and patriotic verse including the admired and much-reprinted 'Socks', conveying the thoughts of a knitter on the fate of her sons.

§

Murdoch's employers and reviewers were at first distracted by her appearance and underrated her abilities. Montague Grover confessed that he had initially thought Murdoch would be a failure as a competent journalist because she was 'a nice looker' though he admitted in 1917 that he had never been so wrong in his judgment. Reviewing her first book of poems, the *Maitland Daily Mercury* described Murdoch as 'a shy, pretty, petite girl, who scribbles on a daily for her crust' and said of her book that it was 'full of dainty gems, lyrics really, and the sort that women can read, for most people know that the average woman doesn't know an epic from doggerel'—but the reviewer allowed that 'the Miss Murdoch hits are so good that they're going to educate us, along the lines we should follow'. The *Freeman's Journal*, announcing Murdoch's engagement in March 1917 to Duncan Brown, referred to her as 'this sweet-faced young journalist' who 'gave promise of a brilliant career'. Even the *Yass Courier's* report of her wedding in 1918 spoke of her in patronising manner as 'that clever little presswoman' who 'has built her nest in just the romantic spot one would expect a poetess to choose'.

§

In spite of the infantilising tone of the foregoing descriptions, Murdoch was a member of a social circle that included some independent-minded Sydney press and literary identities, and her presence at a reception for Sir Rider Haggard at Government House in April 1916 pointed to her easy incorporation in an effectual Who's Who of prominent New South Wales writers, journalists, academics, politicians, clerics and business leaders. Haggard was on tour in a supposedly unofficial role—which the *Sun* declared to be in fact as 'authorised delegate from the Royal Colonial

Institute'—to sound out the possibilities of post-war settlement schemes for returned English servicemen in Australia. He received similar official welcomes to those he had met with in Canada and South Africa, where he played on identical racial fears of the white population. Murdoch's response to Haggard's investigation is matter for conjecture, but the *Sun* was clear on the matter, embracing the idea of settling English as well as Australian returned soldiers, and stated, 'We want British stock in the Commonwealth. We are a white nation, with no race divisions to perplex us, and no colored majority. The *Sun* does not grow weary of saying that Australia is the most purely British country on the planet—not even excepting the United Kingdom itself'.

Earlier in the same year, however, Murdoch's extracurricular activities had focused on support for Australian nurses and returning Australian soldiers. On 11 March 1916, the North Sydney District Comedy Club performed Charles Hawtrey's long-running farce *The Private Secretary*, in aid of the Nurse Cavell Memorial Home for Nurses. At this show, the popular actress Frances Ross recited a poem by Murdoch in honour of Cavell. Murdoch, along with many of her journalistic and artistic peers, took part in a Sydney presswomen's entertainment at the Repertory Theatre in March 1917, to raise funds for a cottage at the Frenchs Forest settlement for wounded and disabled soldiers. With Zora Cross, Murdoch designed and wrote a 'Muses Pageant' for the occasion, with music by Sydney composer May Summerbelle (1868-1949). Cross took the part of the chorus, and Murdoch that of Euterpe, goddess of lyric poetry. Jean Curlewis represented Terpsichore, and Nora Kelly (New Zealand-born Nora McAuliffe, *Bulletin* journalist and poet), Ella McFadyen (children's fiction writer, and journalist), Blanche D'Alpuget (social editor of the *Daily Telegraph*), and other Sydney women journalists performed roles of the other Muses. The cast members were coached by Bertram Flohm, 'Professor of Elocution and Voice Culture' of St Andrews College, Sydney University. Several prominent artists including the *Bulletin's* cartoonist 'Hop' (Livingston York Yourtee Hopkins, 1846-1927) contributed publicity and other illustrations to the show that also featured the renowned Scottish-Australian baritone Andrew Black (1859-1920).

Murdoch's poetry received praise from an unusual quarter in June 1917, when Henri Verbrugghen, foundation director of the Sydney Conservatorium, explained to a concert audience a movement of Ravel's 'Pantoum', performed by members of his own Quartet, by reading a verse from a Murdoch poem and comparing its metre with Ravel's unusual timing.

Later the same year, Murdoch's verses were featured in a Red Cross Society Christmas calendar, elegantly designed by the *Bulletin's* illustrator D.H. Souter (1862-1935). In November 1917, Murdoch wrote a *Sun* feature article on the favourable view of Conscription expressed by the returned Army chaplain, Rev. Professor John Laurence Rentoul (1846-1926). Her article was signed in accordance with the electoral act provisions associated with the Conscription Referendum. One month later, the *Sun* reported that Murdoch had resigned her position 'in view of her approaching marriage'.

§

Duncan Brown and Nina Murdoch married on 19 December 1917 in St Philip's Anglican Church at Church Hill (in Sydney's York Street), with Brown's friend, political cartoonist Hal Eyre, enrolled as best man. The *Daily Telegraph* described Murdoch as the 'youngest daughter of Mrs R. Murdoch of Yeo Street, Neutral Bay' (The previous year, her mother's address was listed in *Sands Sydney Directory* as 77 Ben Boyd Road, Neutral Bay.)

Murdoch's husband (born 1886) was the only son of Margaret Ann (née Duncan) and James Andrew Brown, first engineer of the Wimmera Water Works. Duncan Brown had worked as a teacher and had lost an arm before he became a journalist on the *Sun*. The *Freeman's Journal* called him 'a fine athlete' who had 'several championships in sport to his credit'. Following their marriage, Murdoch and her husband took up residence at 'The Lyn' (or 'The Lynn') on a cliff with an uninterrupted view of the Pacific Ocean, at Tamarama near Bondi. Their neighbours included Montague Grover, who lived at Bondi, and closer to their own house, what the *Australasian* called 'quite a colony of well-known Sydney artists', among whom were the painters Elioth Gruner and Julian Ashton. The Browns' house and gardens became the site of social gatherings reported in the Sydney, Melbourne, and rural press in following years.

On 18 February 1918, Melbourne *Table Talk* reported her marriage and noted that on her departure from the *Sun*, Murdoch had been presented with a silver purse 'well lined with notes'. The paper also declared, somewhat confusingly, that Murdoch's husband, 'after a spell on the *Sun*, runs a preparatory school at Coogee'. In September and October of the same year, Murdoch was guest of Ruby Doyle at the Doyles' property 'Kirriki', near Dungog, and shortly afterwards, Ruby Doyle visited Sydney. Doyle, at the commencement of a career as short story, serial-writer and novelist, was one of Murdoch's extensive circle of women writers in Sydney. Doyle was an assiduous worker for the war effort, and her adventurous nature was much akin to Murdoch's. Doyle wrote about Australian touristic and holiday locations, and her accounts of her travels in Asia, America, England, Ireland, Scotland and Europe in the mid-1920s appeared in several Australian newspapers. The author of short stories, literary essays, reviews, and plays (*The Man from Murrumbidgee*, and *The Family Tree*) were chiefly set in Australia. Doyle also wrote two romantic novels, *The Winning of Miriam Heron* (1919) and *The Mystery of the Hills* (1923), on which her reputation rests.

In 1919, Murdoch and her husband moved from Sydney to Melbourne, to work on the *Herald* and, from 1922, Hugh Denison's *Sun News-Pictorial*. Duncan Brown was appointed cable editor, and Murdoch became the first woman reporter to cover the Senate debates. In 1927, she travelled alone in Europe, gathering material for her first travel book, *Seventh Heaven*, which conveyed her delight at localities and people she encountered in Italy, Switzerland, France, Belgium, Holland and England. Her combination of historical anecdote, details of landscape and regional manners, and alertness to the changing political situations in each country established her reputation as an astute observer and witty raconteur. *Seventh Heaven* rapidly ran into four editions.

Returned to Australia, Murdoch joined the *Melbourne Herald*, and when retrenched with other women staff at the beginning of the Depression, joined Radio 3LO (later taken over by the Australian Broadcasting Commission), where, from 1932, she ran the 'Children's Corner' and conceived the idea of the Argonauts Club, a program that would feature work written by children. When she left the ABC in 1934 to join her husband, who was working as associate editor of the Adelaide *News*, the Argonauts program folded, to be revived in 1941 until discontinued in 1972.

Murdoch's book *Seventh Heaven* (1930) was followed by *Miss Emily in Black Lace*, a novel concerning a young woman's conducted trip in Europe and subsequent romantic engagement. Two sequels were eventually published. Murdoch was preoccupied with reportage, and her further European travels in the 1930s resulted in *She Travelled Alone in Spain* (1935), an account that largely focused on regional customs while casually alluding to her own Spanish great-grandmother, and a third travel book, *Tyrolean June: A Summer Holiday in Austrian Tyrol* (1936). The latter contained characteristically enthusiastic accounts of the Austrian landscape and many of the people, together with less admiring details of the rise of Nazi sympathies in Innsbruck (where she stayed for a month) and other localities. She reported on the anger of Austrian inhabitants of the North Tyrol, over the surrender of the South Tyrol to Italian rule in 1913, and Mussolini's treatment of the non-Italian minority. Her articles, printed at length in the Adelaide *News*, outlined in detail the extent of the German menace to Austrian independence. On her return to Australia, she became active in movements to alert Australians to the dangers of Nazism and Fascism, and she recommenced broadcasting in radio as well as undertaking war work on the outbreak of World War Two.

While Murdoch travelled in the 1930s, her husband was engaged in journalism in South Australia, and among his accounts of social and political developments was a series of articles on the Northern Territory, where, in 1935, he flew with the director of the Transcontinental Airways Ltd, Mr T. Kelly, and Sister Eileen Styles of the Northern Territory Medical Service, on the pioneering air mail flight of the aeroplane 'Faith in Australia'.

In 1942, Murdoch and her husband moved to Victoria, where from 1943, she cared for her blind mother (who lived till 105) and her husband, a sufferer from asthma, who died in 1957.

In 2008, the Australian Capital Territory's Division of Franklin (named for Miles Franklin) named many streets after Australian writers; several commemorate Murdoch's women contemporaries: Jeannie Gunn, Emily Coungeau, Nettie Palmer, Ruth Bedford, Margaret Trist, and Kylie Tennant. A major road encircling these and others is named Nina Murdoch Crescent.

§

Between 1913 and 1922, Murdoch published 80 poems in the *Bulletin*, several under her pen name 'Manin'. She also employed the pen name 'Madolin'. Her first collection of poems, *Songs of the Open Air* (1915), was followed by *More Songs in the Open Air* in 1922. As well as her three travel books originally published in the UK, and her three 'pot boiler' novels published by Halstead in the UK and Angus & Robertson in Australia between 1930 and 1937, Murdoch published, in 1948, a biography of her friend Sir John Longstaff, whose portrait of Murdoch, painted in 1920, was hung in the Reading Room of the National Library of Australia at Canberra.

§

As the 'song' titles of her two collections indicate, Murdoch's poetry published around the time of World War One embraced many subjects and themes, and was predominantly lyrical predisposition. The 'open air' she celebrated was redolent of the Australian hinterland and the coastal bush and shoreline. The poems in the present anthology reflect that lyric bent, though their matter is darker: the deaths of admired service men and the sorrows of their partners provide a sombre counterpoint to ostensibly insouciant manner.

Poems
Songs of the Open Air, Melbourne: William Brooks, 1915.
More Songs in the Open Air, Melbourne: Robertson and Mullens, 1922.

Novellas
Miss Emily in Black Lace: A Christmas Tale in which the Heroine is Plain and Perilously Near Forty and the Good Fairy has Bushy Eyebrows and Green Eyes, Sydney: Angus and Robertson, 1930.
Portrait of Miss Emily: A Tale in Which the Heroine from Birmingham is invited to a French Wedding, Upsets Another and is Responsible for a Third, Sydney: Angus and Robertson, 1931.
Exit Miss Emily: In Which Emerges the Hero, Who, with the Aid of the Green-Eyed Fairy, Makes Willing Captive the Heroine from Birmingham, Sydney, Angus and Robertson, 1937.

Travel titles
Seventh Heaven. Sydney: Halstead, 1930.
She Travelled Alone in Spain. London: George G. Harrap, 1935.
Tyrolean June, A Summer Holiday in Austrian Tyrol. London: Harrap, 1936.
Vagrant in Summer, Holiday Memories of Nine European Towns: London, Harrap, 1937.

Biography

Portrait in Youth of Sir John Longstaff (1861-1941). Sydney and London: Angus & Robertson, 1948.

References

Suzanne Edgar, 'Murdoch, Madoline (Nina) (1890–1976)', Australian Dictionary of Biography, National Centre of Biography, Australian National University, http://adb.anu.edu.au/biography/murdoch-madoline-nina-7694/text13469, published first in hardcopy 1986, accessed online 3 January 201; Wikipedia Commons, https://en.wikipedia.org/wiki/Nina_Murdoch accessed 3 January 2016.

Lucy London, 'Madoline (Nina) Murdoch 1890-1976 Australian WW1 poet', Female Poets of the First World War. http://femalewarpoets. Blogspot.com/2014/10/madoline nina Murdoch.1890-1976.html, accessed 26 September 2018.

'Writes Charming Books of Travel', *News* (Adelaide), Wednesday 20 May 1930, p. 10 [details of Murdoch's earliest literary efforts].

'Morning', *Wangaratta Chronicle*, Wednesday 22 December 1915, p. 16 [Review of *Songs of the Open Air*; includes reference to John Murdoch, Clerk of Courts at Wangaratta, and notes on local references in Murdoch's poems].

'Some Recent Books', *Sun* [Sydney], Sunday 10 October 1915, p. 13 [A review of *Songs of the Open Air* with remarks on Murdoch's appearance and her 'socialistic' poem, 'Song of the Slum Woman'].

'Sydney Week by Week', *Maitland Daily Mercury*, Thursday 14 October 1915, p. 3 [Review of *Songs of the Open Air*, Murdoch's 'hits' and appearance].

'Sir Rider Haggard's Visit', *Sun*, Tuesday 18 April 1916, p. 6.

Norfolk in World War One, https://norfolkinworldwar1.org/2017/10/10/henry-rider-haggard-and-the-imperial-war/ Accessed 15 December 2018 [Sir Henry Rider Haggard's tour of British Dominions, to discover attitudes to postwar settlement of English servicemen].

'The Nurse Cavell Matinee', *Sydney Morning Herald*, Saturday 11 March 1916, p. 20; 'For Women', *Queensland Times* (Ipswich), Saturday 25 March 1916, p. 6 [Report on Nurse Cavell fundraising event at North Sydney].

'Personal', *Daily Telegraph*, Saturday 29 April 1916, p. 8 [Report on guests of the State Reception by Governor Sir Gerald Strickland and Lady Edeline Strickland for Sir Rider Haggard].

'For Women', *Daily Telegraph*, Monday 19 February 1917 [Account of preparations for the Zora Cross and Nina Murdoch 'Muses sketch' for the Repertory Theatre concert], p. 7.

'In the Winter Garden', *Freeman's Journal*, Thursday 22 February 1917, p. 28 [Report on the concert's success]; also reported in *Sydney Morning Herald*, Saturday 17 March 1917, p. 7, and *Sunday Times*, Sunday 18 March 1917, p. 27.

'In the Winter Garden', *Freeman's Journal*, Thursday 25 September 1924, p. 20 [Note on Blanche D'Alpuget's impending move from the *Daily Telegraph* to the *Australian Women's Mirror* D'Alpuget was the great-aunt of the novelist and biographer of the same name, born in 1944.]

Joy Damousi, *Colonial Voices: A Cultural History of English in Australia, 1840-1940*, Melbourne: Cambridge University Press, 2010, p. 152 [concerning Bertram Flohm, teacher of elocution].

'Women's News', *Sunday Times*, Sunday 4 March 1917, p. 11; *Sydney Morning Herald*, Saturday 17 March 1917, p. 7; 'Presswomen's Concert', *Sunday Times*, Sunday 18 March 1917, p. 27: reports on rehearsals and performances at Murdoch and Cross's fundraising concert.

Sunday Times (Sydney), Sunday 18 March 1917, p. 27 ['Engagements': announcing Murdoch's engagement to Brown, his background and current employment as 'a master at the Coogee Preparatory School'].

Freeman's Journal, Thursday 22 March 1917, p. 28 [Announcing Murdoch's engagement to J.D.M. Brown].

Sydney Morning Herald, 'Social', Saturday 31 March 1917, p. 8 [Report on annual meeting of the Old High School Girls' Union and Murdoch's election to the committee].

Nina Murdoch, 'Professor Rentoul Outspoken. Men in Trenches Were Misled', *Sun*, Sunday 11 November 1917, p. 2.

J.R., 'Musical Notes', *Sunday Times*, Sunday 1 July 1917, p. 17 [Verbrugghen compares Ravel and Murdoch].

Sunday Times, 30 September 1917, p. 16 [Reports Murdoch's contribution to Red Cross Society calendar].

'From Near and Far', *Sun*, Wednesday 12 December 1917, p. 7 [The *Sun* announces Murdoch's resignation].

'City Weddings', *Daily Telegraph* (Sydney), Thursday 20 December 1917, p. 9 [Includes Murdoch's mother's address].

'Personal', *Table Talk* Thursday 18 February 1918, p. 7 [Montague Glover's farewell speech, on Murdoch's departure from the Sydney *Sun*, and his remarks and those of the *Australian Journalist* on her career].

'Pars About People', *Australian Worker*, Thursday 7 March 1918, p. 10 [Grover's comments on Murdoch's 'looks'; the *Australian Worker* called Murdoch 'one of Sydney's most brilliant lady inkslingers'].

'Society Doings in Sydney', *Australasian*, 16 March 1918, p. 34 [Description of the Browns' sea-side residence and neighbours].

'A Sylvan Retreat', *Yass Courier*, Monday 18 March 1918, p. 2 ['Local and General': an account of the Browns' residence].

'Home and Society', *Sunday Times*, Sunday 19 May 1918, p. 15 [Murdoch entertains Australian and New Zealand visitors prior to their departure for America].

'Personal', *Table Talk*, Melbourne, Thursday 18 February 1918, p. 7 [Source of Grover's remark on Murdoch, and report of Murdoch's marriage to Duncan Brown, who 'runs' a preparatory school at Coogee'].

'Talk of the Town', *Sunday Times*, Sunday 7 December 1919, p. 13 [Ruby Doyle's return to Kirriki from her visit to Sydney].

'*Miss Ruby Doyle Home Again*', *Dungog Chronicle: Durham and Gloucester Advertiser*, Tuesday 12 January 1926, p. 5 [Account of Doyle's world tour in 1925-26]. Doyle had earlier visited Colombo in 1924; she sailed again for Europe in 1935 and settled in England, where she died in 1943.

Montague Grover, *Hold Page One, Memoirs of Monty Grover, Editor,* edited and introduced by Michael Cannon, Main Ridge, Victoria: Loch Haven, 1993, p. 27 [Brown and Murdoch appointed by Monty Grover to Hugh Denison's *Sun News-Pictorial* newspaper].

'Plays and Talks', *Advertiser* (Adelaide), 24 February 1940, p. 15 [Murdoch's ABC radio talk, 'Stormy Weather']; *Advertiser,* Saturday 18 May 1940, p. 9 [Murdoch talk on 'Lost Arts']; 'Over the Air', *Kadina and Wallaroo Times*, Wednesday 14 May 1941, p. 1 [Murdoch's talk on station 5CL, 'The Painters Are in the House']; 'Today's Radio', *Advertiser,* Thursday 18 September 1941 [Murdoch's talk on station 5CL, 'The Amazon'].

'Portrait in Youth', *News* (Adelaide), Saturday 4 December 1948, p. 2 [Review].

Rhonda Chrisanthou, *Sir John Longstaff: Portrait of a Lady,* 18 February to 22 April 2012, Education Resource Kit, Shepparton Art Museum. http://www.sheppartonartmuseum.com.au/assets/files/downloads/Portrait_of_a_lady.pdf.pdf. Accessed online 9 May 2016.

Nina Murdoch
Socks
(Inspired by the appeal of Mrs. Joseph Cook to Australian women to knit socks for the 20,000 expeditionary sldiers.)

Two plain, purl two,
It's little else a woman can do
But bear sons and watch them grow
Till marching out of her life they go.

Knit five, purl one,
I doubt if ever a mother's son
In war's cause hacked and cleft,
Knows half the hurt of the woman that's left.

Slip one, purl eight,
There's nothing left but hope and wait,
And the seven tasks of Hercules
Would count as little compared with these.

Turn, slip, then the heel,
Out of sorrow comes haply weal,
But fair times are far away,
And there's many weep for their men to-day.

Cast off, the thing's done!
Many a husband and many a son
Find death in a hapless war,
Nor ever know what they fought it for.

Two plain, purl two,
It's little else a woman can do
But bear sons and watch them grow
Till marching out of her life they go.

Source: *Sun*, Thursday 13 August 1914, p. 1. Subsequently reprinted in the following:

Sydney Stock and Station Journal, Friday 4 September 1914, p. 2.
Ararat Chronicle and Willaura and Lake Bolac Districts Recorder, 30 September 1914, p. 6.
Heyfield Herald (VIC.), Thursday 1 October 1914, p. 4.
Colac Reformer, Saturday 10 October 1914, p. 6.
Mortlake Despatch, Saturday 10 October 1914, p. 2.
Murchison Advertiser and Murchison, Toolamba, Mooroopna and Dargalong Express, Friday 21 May 1915 p. 2.
The Australian Worker, Thursday 3 June 1915, p. 11.
Southern Star (Bega, NSW), Saturday 22 August 1914, p. 1.
Queensland Figaro, Thursday 27 August 1914, p. 7.
Gippsland Times, Thursday 1 October 1914, p .6.
Ballan Times (Vic.), Thursday 1 October 1914, p. 4.
Lilydale Express (Vic.), Friday 2 October 1914, p. 2.
Heyfield Herald (Vic), Thursday 1 October 1914, p. 4.
The Romsey Examiner (Victoria), Friday 2 October 1914, p. 4.
Violet Town Sentinel (Vic.), Tuesday 6 October 1914, p. 4.
Rupanyup Spectator and Lubeck, Banyena, Rich Avon and Lallat Advertiser (Vic), Thursday 8 October 1914, p. 4.
Boort Standard and Quanmbatook Herald, Thursday 8 October 1914, p. 4.
Heytesbury Reformer and Cobden and Camperdown Advertiser (Vic.), Friday 9 October 1914, p. 4.
Seymour Express and Goulburn Valley, Avenel, Graytown, Nagambie, Tallarook and Yea Advertiser, Friday 9 October 1914, p. 6.
Stratford Sentinel and Briagolong Express, Friday 16 October 1914, p 4.
Malvern News, Saturday 3 October 1914, p. 4.
Omeo Standard and Mining Gazette, Friday 9 October 1914, p. 4.
Lone Hand, vol. 19, no. 91 (n.s. vol. 2, no. 12), 2 November 1914, p. 417.
Nina Murdoch, *Songs of the Open Air*. Sydney: William Brooks & Co., 1915, pp. 71-72.

Nina Murdoch
Unfit

If you had loitered at home, Johnny,
And made no move to go
With the others over the foam, Johnny,
You would have shamed me so!

I could fancy no worse disgrace, Johnny,
Than the others for battle begirt,
And you too frightened to face, Johnny,
The toil and the heat and the hurt.

When you went to volunteer, Johnny,
My heart stood still that day.
For love of you and for fear, Johnny,
And for pride that fought dismay.

Till you came back homeward at night, Johnny,
With your brows darkly knit,
And your eyes robbed of their light, Johnny,
By the bitter word, Unfit.

The Gods they know that I tried, Johnny,
To put me in your place,
And my mouth and my eyes that lied, Johnny,
Feigned sorrowing for a space,

While the shameless heart of me sang, Johnny,
Sang as a bird in the spring,
Knowing no grievous pang, Johnny,
Tho' you hold it an evil thing.

You had shown the spirit was there, Johnny,
What blame that knowing you so,
My heart like a bird of the air, Johnny,
Rejoiced that you could not go?

Source: *Sun,* Sunday 30 March 1915, p. 19; *Northern Star,* Saturday 5 June 1915, p. 3; *Sydney Stock and Station Journal,* Friday 14 January 1916, p. 2.

Nina Murdoch
Army Nurses

There are, in addition, seven nurses on board, and a number
of other details, bringing the total complement to 412.
(Following a list of names of soldiers returning by a hospital ship.)

We volunteered for service, and when we'd struggled through
A labyrinth of red tape, on bank accounts we drew
To buy gum-boots for Egypt, as officials told us to!

We took it as a compliment to be allowed to pass,
And felt extremely flattered when they sent us second class,
Where the mercury was rising ever upward in the glass.

Our feet have travelled blithely Ghezireh's stony floors,
No hand of ours has been withheld from mean and lowly chores,
For we are but the servitors behind the pomp of wars.

And we have nursed the wounded into manhood out of pain,
And patched the shattered that they might turn homeward once again,
And even Death we softened, so we have not worked in vain.

And now the news is published of the ship that journeys back,
With Sergeant This and Private That upon the homeward track,
But of us and other details the report is rather slack.

Officialdom is like a proud and very haughty dame
Who would not that her well-bred lips should ever deign to frame
The title of her cook, and so — we come without a name!

Source: *Maryborough Chronicle, Wide Bay and Burnett Advertiser,* Friday 19 November 1915, p. 2; *Daily Post* (Hobart), Saturday 20 November 1915, p. 4.

Nina Murdoch
Colored Bows

*(Women of the Royal Naval House wear coloured bows
to signify to which boats their men belong.)*

The cruisers and destroyer have borne our men away;
Perhaps ten thousand miles divide our men from us today.
They may be in the North Sea, they may be near at hand,
We only know for certain that we wish them safe on land.

O' it's red for the *Australia*
      The little *Penguin*'s blue,
It's white for the *Encounter*
      And the *Sydney*'s purple hue;

But it's black, plain black if your husband or son
Went out of Sydney Harbour in the AE1.

We're not afraid of hardships, and we're not the sort to shirk,
If the pay we get is not enough, we simply look for work;
And some have gone to service to raise an extra pound
To put towards a cottage or perhaps a piece of ground.

So it's not the fear of struggling with hunger at the door,
And it isn't that we're lonely—we've been through that before!
But it breaks a woman's spirit when there's trouble for her mate,
And for her the helpless knowledge she can only work and wait.

O' it's red for the *Australia*
      The little *Penguin*'s blue,
It's white for the *Encounter*
      And the *Sydney*'s purple hue;

But it's black, plain black if your husband or son
Went out of Sydney Harbour in the AE1.

Source: *Sun*, Sunday 14 February 1915, p. 18; Nina Murdoch, *Songs of the Open Air*, Sydney: William Brooks, 1915, p. 74.

Note. The battle cruiser HMAS *Australia* joined the Australian Naval Station in Sydney Harbour on 4 October 1913, and on 9 November 1914, engaged and sank the German raider *Emden* in the Cocos Islands. On 17 February 1915, HMAS Australia joined the Grand Fleet and remained in the Atlantic for the rest of the War. On 31 October 1916, the battle cruisers HMAS *Sydney* and HMAS *Melbourne* were also assigned to the Grand Fleet. HMAS *Penguin* was parent ship of the Royal Australian Navy's two E-Class submarines, *AE1* and *AE2*, commissioned in the RAN on 29 February 1914. AEI had a history of mishaps from the time of setting off from its British construction yard to Australia. On 14 September 1914, while on patrol off New Britain, the submarine was lost with all crew and without trace. In 2017, the submarine was located 300 metres under water near the Duke of York Islands in Papua New Guinea.

On 30 April 1915, Turkish naval vessels in the Sea of Marmara, close to the Turkish coast, sank the submarine *AE2*, which had been despatched to the Sea of Marmara with orders to 'run amok generally' among Turkish shipping. News of the sinking of the *AE2* [near the coast of Gallipoli] was announced in Australia on 18 May 1915. (T.R. Frame & G.J. Swinden, *First In, Last Out: The Navy at Gallipoli*, Kenthurst: Kangaroo Press, 1990, pp. 33-49; ABC News 21 December 2017: http://www.abc.net.au/news/2017-12-21/hmas-ae1-submarine-found-after-century-long-search/9278782; . The Royal Navy's light cruiser HMS *Encounter*, which formed part of Australia's new navy in 1913, patrolled the Pacific throughout the War.

Nina Murdoch
A Toast

    Charge your glasses and drink to the dead,
Our dead, whatever their birthplace be,
Who have fought and suffered that such as we
Might live our little lives over sea.
Pledge a toast to the memory
    Of the brave blood shed!

    Lift your glasses and let the toast pass!
Yet haply if at the board there be
One who taken his liberty
And paid no tithe of the nation's fee
In coin or labor or sons, 'tis he
    Must lower his glass!

                    Sydney

Source: Nina Murdoch, 'A Toast' ['Charge your glasses and drink to the dead'], in Franklin Paterson, ed, *Melba's Gift Book of Australian Art and Literature*, Melbourne: George Robertson, 1915, p. 28.
Also in the following:
Queenslander, Saturday 16 October 1915, p. 3 ['Literature'].
Brisbane Courier, Wednesday 20 October 1915, p. 9 ['In Bookland'].
Nina Murdoch, *Songs of the Open Air,* Sydney: William Brooks & Co., 1915, p. 73.

Nina Murdoch
The News

I used to say: 'When Victory is won
I shall go out with laughter and with song;
Touch hands and shout and mingle with the throng,
From blazoned dawn to glorious set of sun.

Till, shining-eyed, one ran to me and said:
'Victory is ours!' — I laughed a moment's space,
Then, groping strangely, sought a hidden place,
And wept, and thought all day upon the dead!

Source: *Sun*, Sunday 17 November 1918, p. 15; *North Western Advocate and the Emu Bay Times* (Tasmania), Thursday 21 November 1918, p. 1.

Nina Murdoch
The Two That Stayed

At the Anzac Buffet an old man was waiting to welcome home a nephew.
'Two sons of mine are still in France' he said. 'At Bretonneux.'

'Two sons of mine stay on in France!'
The old man cried with kindling glance.
'And where they are, the mellowed field
Will always bounteous harvests yield.

They fought like god and turned the tide.
They'll stay on now', he proudly cried,
'At Bretonneux!' He bowed his head.
And then we knew his sons were dead

Source: *The Farmer and Settler* (Sydney), Tuesday 8 July 1919, p. 8; Nina Murdoch, *More Songs of the Open Air*, Melbourne: Robertson & Mullens, 1922, p. 68.

JOICE M. NANKIVELL

Photo of Joice NanKivell Loch by Clarke Hilwood Studios London, c. 1920-22. State Library Victoria

Joice Mary NanKivell (24 January 1887–8 October 1982) published under several variants of her birth and married names: Joyce NanKivell, Joice Mary Loch, J.M. Loch, Mrs Sydney Loch, Joice M. Loch, Joice M. NanKivell, and Joice NanKivell Loch. She gave different birth dates in several literary and other documents, varying as much as six years from that given above.

NanKivell was the daughter of Edith Ada NanKivell (née Lawson, born in Jersey 1866, died at Windsor, Victoria 1951) and George Griffith NanKivell (born at St Kilda 1859, died at Richmond, 1941). Edith and George had two children, Joice and Charles George (called Geoffrey by the family). Joice's father managed a sugar plantation at Farnham, near Ingham in North Queensland on behalf of his father, Thomas NanKivell, who was considered Australia's richest man.

Joice grew up and worked on the family plantation, where her sympathies lay with the disenfranchised as a result of the treatment she saw accorded to Kanaka labourers. Her family's fortunes collapsed when the importation of black labour was abolished, and her parents walked off the property. The family moved to rural Victoria, where Joice's father took a job managing a property in Gippsland, where she also worked until her mid-twenties.

Joice was educated by governesses and, during an interlude in Melbourne, at a school in Brighton, where she began to write verse and children's stories. By her teen years, she was a regular letter writer to children's sections of the Melbourne *Leader* newspaper and others, and a winner of prizes for essays. One of many stories she contributed to the Melbourne *Leader* newspaper's Children's Page concerned a trip from Mars aboard the space ship 'Flying Fox', to a world where she and a companion named Dorothy encounter former British sovereigns as far back as King Arthur. The editor, Mary Grant Bruce, and other readers were sometimes prompted to remark how they enjoyed Joice's letters and stories.

Her poems of early adulthood revealed a patriotic slant on contemporary events, and one such work, 'Peace', published in the Melbourne *Leader* newspaper at the conclusion of the Boer War in 1902, with the byline 'Joice NanKivell, aged 15' proclaimed

> The long, hard war is over, and we have peace once more,
> And may we long have unity twixt German, French and Boer;
> A peace with all, as brethren should, but never had before,
> So long may peace embrace the world, from sea to sea, from shore to shore.
>
> When first the Boers decided our countrymen to kill
> We were ashamed of them, you know, and took their challenge ill;
> We thought we soon will settle them, they soon will get their fill,
> And then we'll take their country, and make them pay the bill
>
> But when we went to fight them, they showed what they could do;
> We tried our best to beat them, and wide our thunder threw;
> And after years' hard fighting, we made them pretty blue,
> So let's have Peace and Unity mixed up in Irish stew.

Family finances prevented her from pursuing medical studies, but she nevertheless moved to Melbourne, taught herself touch-typing, submitted and published poems in several papers and magazines, and applied for and obtained a job as secretary to Dr Alexander Leeper, Warden of Trinity College and Head of Classics at Melbourne University. Her record as author of reviews in the Melbourne *Evening Herald* newspaper, and children's fiction and poetry (one of her earliest publications was in the Melbourne journal *Contrast*) impressed Leeper, who hired her without interviewing others. She consequently read widely in ancient history and classical literature that Leeper made available from his extensive library. In 1916, she published *The Cobweb Ladder,* her first book for children.

Joice's patriotic fervour was still expressed in poems like 'The Eleventh Hour', published in the *National Leader* newspaper in Queensland in December 1916. The poem, addressed to waverers, concluded with the lines 'Every ounce of your strength is needed— still you are standing deaf and dumb. / How can you pause?The cry is urgent: 'God of Nations, when will they come?' A note at the poem's conclusion stated 'Miss NanKivell's only brother, who left Australia with the 4th Battalion, was killed at Pozières'.

When the Melbourne *Evening Herald* editor Guy Innes asked her to review a memoir of war experience, *The Straits Impregnable*, by 'Sydney de Loghe' (London-born Frederick Sydney Loch, a former jackeroo, who had been wounded at Gallipoli and returned to Australia), Joice wrote a glowing account of his book. Published by the Australasian Authors' Agency in Melbourne in 1916, *The Straits Impregnable* had been initially banned by the censor on the grounds that it would impede enlistment. The London firm of John Murray published the book in revised form the following year. Loch's first-hand report on Gallipoli gave Joice an insight into the events in which her brother, Sergeant Charles George ('Geoffrey'), had played a daringly significant part before he went to France, where, aged twenty-eight, he was killed in action at Pozières. (He was awarded the Military Medal.)

Following the appearance of her review, Joice was introduced to Loch, and they discovered many shared cultural interests. Loch was also deeply sympathetic with NanKivell's grief at her brother's death. Their friendship resulted in their marriage at the Methodist manse in Royal Parade, Carlton, in Melbourne on 22 February 1919. Joice was worried that her family might not approve of the union on account of her age. Two years older than Loch, she had stated her age as twenty-six rather than thirty-one at the time of her marriage.

The couple wanted to travel abroad and work as journalists and writers, and when Guy Innes guaranteed that Joice could work as a freelance correspondent, she and her husband left Australia in 1920 for London. When Innes moved to London to take up a position with Lord Northcliffe's newspapers, Joice's journalism increasingly appeared in English papers.

With a contract from John Murray to write on events in Ireland, the Lochs carried on to Dublin, despite Joice's relatives' warnings about the danger involved, to cover the Sinn Fein war. Sydney worked on another book, and Joice wrote for the *Edinburgh Review* and *Blackwood's Magazine*, as well as for the Melbourne papers. Their jointly authored book, *Ireland in Travail,* appeared in 1922, and in Australia, under the rubric 'Points for the Propagandist', the *Worker* newspaper quoted from the book an aphorism indicative of the distance Joice had travelled since her early effusive verse: 'Patriotism, how it limits a man in judgment, in sincerity, in his horizon'.

Following their Irish experience, Joice and Sydney volunteered to assist with a Quaker relief organisation for refugees in Poland, where, after a trip to Moscow, they worked among displaced and homeless refugees. The Quaker Relief Movement was particularly concerned with people suffering from damage inflicted on that country by Lenin's troops. The Lochs' jointly authored book, *The River of a Hundred Ways: Life in the Devastated Areas of Eastern Poland* (1924) and their newspaper reportage witnessed the desperate conditions of refugees. For their part in practically assisting humanitarian work, Joice and Sydney were awarded medals by the President of Poland.

In 1923, they went to Greece as aid workers following the burning of Smyrna. For two years, they worked in a Quaker-run refugee camp on the outskirts of Thessaloniki before renting a Byzantine tower by the sea in the seaside village of Ouranoupoli, near Mt Athos. Joice provided medical aid and a program to educate girls and to help the poverty-stricken villagers, who included Greek Orthodox Turks who had settled after the expulsion. Joice and her husband purchased looms and made others so the women could work to revitalise the rug industry. She and her husband sourced local wools and dyes and designed the new Pirgos rugs using motifs from ancient Byzantine manuscripts in the monasteries at Athos. They sourced the dyes and wool and later sold the rugs in Greece, England and Australia. Joice also acted as a medical orderly and held regular clinics for the villagers.

In 1940, Joice and Sydney joined the Friends Relief Service in Bucharest to assist refugees fleeing from Poland. They provided food and other relief and helped organise the refugees' escape; Joice took a group of 1000 refugees by ship from Constantinople to Palestine, and worked for the remainder of World War 2 with Polish and Greek refugees in Palestine. In 1945, the Lochs returned to Greece to help with reconstruction work. When Sydney died in 1954, Joice continued her rug-making projects, free medical clinics, and used royalties from her writing to provide a water supply to her village.

For their work in Greece, the couple were awarded medals by the King of the Hellenes, and Joice was later the recipient of other awards by governments of Greece, Romania, Serbia, Poland, and Britain, for humanitarian work saving Polish and Jewish refugees. In 1972, the Australian government belatedly awarded her the Order of the British Empire in recognition of her work for international relations. She died at Ouranoupolis and was buried with Greek Orthodox rites. Kallistos Ware, the Greek Orthodox Bishop of Oxford (now Metropolitan Kallistos) named her 'one of the most significant women of the 20th century'. The tower in which the couple lived and worked is now a museum.

Joice's later non-fiction works, *A Life for the Balkans* (1939) and *Prosporion, Uranopoulos Rugs and Dyes* (1964), reflect her interest and connection with that country, as do her later poems.

§

Joice's husband Sydney Loch (1888 or 1889–Greece, 1954 or 1955 according to different sources) had come to Australia in 1905, and worked as a jackeroo before enlistment. As well as his account of Gallipoli, he published several novels in 1916 and 1917, under the name Sydney de Longhe, and another, *Three Predatory Women*, under his own name in 1925 (London: George Allen & Unwin). A further Australian publication was *'One Crowded Hour': A Call to Arms* (Melbourne: Australasian Authors' Agency, 1918), a compilation of newspaper articles about his War experience. His last publication was *Athos: The Holy Mountain* (London: Lutterworth, 1957), a travel book that Joice completed as a tribute to him, but requested the omission of her name.

§

Joice published several children's books under the name Joice M. NanKivell, commencing with *The Cobweb Ladder* (1916). Her book of sketches of her childhood bush and city life, *The Solitary Pedestrian* (1918), includes reminiscences of her family, including her brother Charles George (who appears in the book under the name 'Robin'). Later books published under her married name include those already mentioned and *The Fourteen Thumbs of St Peter* (about Russia). Her autobiography, *A Fringe of Blue*, was published in 1968 and her *Collected Poems* two years before her death. The royalties of Joice's and Sydney's books went to further their causes.

§

The 1915 poem, 'To You Who Should Follow', a product of Joice's early patriotism before she acquainted herself with the truth of Gallipoli, was syndicated widely, following its first appearance in print in Victoria. The poem's patriotic sentiments are conventionally expressed in an appeal to men to enlist. She returned to the theme in other poems that were widely republished up until the result of the second Conscription Referendum in December 1917 put an end to the issue of conscription.

Joice's post-World War One poems are at once more sophisticated in form and historical consciousness. She came to regard war as less a matter of glory than of abiding pity, and poems such as 'Lake Narocz' express a sweeping concern for all suffering humanity—a concern enacted in her practical deeds. Beside the enduring tone of fellow feeling for the victims of war and famine, her later poems attest to her sense of wonder at the dramatic seasonal phenomena she experienced in Eastern Europe and the Mediterranean.

Publications
Children's fiction
The Cobweb Ladder, Melbourne: Lothian, and London: Limpkin, 1916.
The Fourteen Thumbs of St Peter, London: John Murray, 1926.
The Hopping Ha'penny [as J.M. Loch], London: Methuen, 1935.
Tales of Christophilos, Boston: Houghton Mifflin, 1954.
Again Christophilos, Boston: Houghton Mifflin, 1959.

Nonfiction
Ireland in Travail [with Sydney Loch], London: John Murray, 1922.
The River of a Hundred Ways: Life in the Devastated Areas of Eastern Poland, London: Allen and Unwin, 1924.
The Fourteen Thumbs of St Peter, London: John Murray, 1926.
A Life for the Balkans: The Story of John Henry House of the American Farm School, Thessaloniki, Greece [as told by his wife to J.M. NanKivell], New York: Fleming H. Revel Co., 1939.
Prosporion, Uranopoulos Rugs and Dyes, Istanbul: American Board Publication Dept, 1964.

Autobiography and memoir
The Solitary Pedestrian, Melbourne: Australasian Authors Agency, 1918.
A Fringe of Blue, London: John Murray, and New York: Morrow, 1968.

Poetry
Collected Poems, Burford UK: Cygnet Press, 1980.

References
Ros Pesman, 'Loch, Joice Mary Nankivell (1887–1982)', Australian Dictionary of Biography, National Centre of Biography, Australian National University, http://adb.anu.edu.au/biography/loch-joice-mary-nankivell-14347/text25418, published first in hardcopy 2012, accessed online 4 January 2016. (Article first published in hardcopy in *Australian Dictionary of Biography,* Volume 18, (Melbourne: Melbourne University Press), 2012.
Susanna De Vries, *Blue Ribbons and Bitter Bread; The life of Joice NanKivell Loch,* Sydney: Hale and Iremonger, 2000; Brisbane: Pandanus Press, 2004.
Susanna De Vries, *Great Australian Women,* Pymble: HarperCollins, 2001.
Joice M. NanKivell, 'Peace', *National Leader,* Saturday 19 July 1902, p. 42.
Joice M. NanKivell, 'The Eleventh Hour', *National Leader* (Brisbane), Friday 22 December 1916, p. 5.
Joice NanKivell, Letter to the Children's Page, *Leader,* Saturday 18 October 1902, p. 42 [Prize Letters; Joice's letter from Quick Silver, September 14th].
Jake De Vries & Susanna De Vries, eds, *To Hell and Back: The Banned Story of Gallipoli,* Sydney: HarperCollins, 2007.
'George Griffiths [sic] NanKivell', From Edinburgh to Hobart Town. The Young and Murray Families. http://www.cocker.id.au/murray/george_griffiths_nankivell.php Accessed 16 April 2018.
'Charles George NanKivell', The AIF Project, https://www.aif.adfa.edu.au/showPerson?pid=220353 Accessed 16 April 2018.

'Points for Propagandists', *Worker* (Brisbane), Thursday 9 November 1922, p. 1.
John Arnold and John Hay, Eds, *The Bibliography of Australian Literature,* vol. 3, St Lucia: University of Queensland Press, pp. 212-213.
Bellinda Kontominas, 'The Great Heroine Australia Forgot', *Sydney Morning Herald,* 8 July 2006.
Wikipedia. https://en.wikipedia.org/wiki/Joice_NanKivell_Loch accessed 3 January 2016.

Joice M. NanKivell
To You Who Should Follow

Over the rim of the ocean, beyond the stretch of the sky,
Stand brothers, husbands, and lovers, who count it their glory to die.
Broken, unbeaten, heroic, torn limbs and quivering breath,
Day after day, night after night, shoulder to shoulder with death.

Shoulder to shoulder with death! Would we keep them safe at our side,
Saved by the blood of their brothers who followed their duty and died?
Safe, though dead voices are calling, and wounded men beckon in pain,
Do you, who should follow, care nought? Have they hewn you a pathway in vain?

They fight as our forefathers fought, and they died as our forefathers died;
Raw and reckless they rushed to the fight, and they came out well proven and tried.
The zip and the bite of the bullet, the thunder, the shriek of the shell—
Yet they surely find glimpses of Heaven even in uttermost Hell.

Will ye close your eyes to the call, the whisper that thrills through and through,
Will you close your eyes to the beck'ning, the hearts that are broken by you?
For every tear that is falling, and for all the blood that is spilt,
Blame only yourselves, oh, ye slackers, for the guilt is mostly your guilt.

Then buckle your armour and follow, over the ways they have won;
Tread if you can, in their footsteps—their voices are urging you on.
Think: you could join battalions, and they are so pitiful few.
Their King and their country have claimed them, and now they are calling on you.

Source:
Brunswick and Coburg Leader (Victoria), Friday 24 September 1915, p. 1.
Ballarat Star, Saturday 30 September 1915, p. 2.
Townsville Daily Bulletin, Wednesday 3 November 1915, p. 4.
Northern Miner, (Charters Towers Queensland), Wednesday 3 November 1915.
Queensland Times (Ipswich), Saturday 6 May 1916, p. 11.
Register, (Adelaide), 17 March 1917, p. 10.

Joice M. NanKivell
We Are Not Schooled in Vengeance

We are not schooled in vengeance, we count all men are free.
Strange roads we sought and opened, threw wide, both land and sea,
And we are slow to anger, but the blood ye spilled is wet.
Though slowly we remember, more slowly we forget.

We are not schooled in vengeance, but—learn and know our way,
We shall not doff our armor till drop for drop ye pay;
And render unto Caesar the price of stricken years,
Disgorging all ye plundered, full toll for blood and tears.

The brand of Cain is on you, marked deep on soul and brow,
An outcast from the nations, with broken faith and vow;
Ye sat at all our councils, ye smoked the pipe of peace,
Ye broke bread with the nations, and swore that strife, should cease.

We are slow to anger, but we shall not sheathe the sword,
Until you render tribute for the blood that you outpoured;
Can ye break our might, slow gathered?—hold back the turning tide?—
We are not schooled in vengeance, but—our sons have fought and died.

Source: *Herald* (Melbourne), Friday 21 July 1916, p. 1; *Daily Herald* (Adelaide), Saturday 17 March 1917, p. 3.

Joice M. NanKivell
Where Are You Going To?

'Where are you going to, pretty man?'
'To the football field as fast at I can.
And then I shall go to the cinema show.
War on a pictured screen, you know,
Brightened by farces two or three,
With a girl at my side, is enough for me.
So off to the football field I go, where the shouting
      drowns the crying.'

'Where are you going to, soldier men?
To the fields of France and back again?'
'We have heard the call of the brotherhood,
And whatever comes we shall count it good,'
A handful only we take the track,
And the chances are we shall not come back,
But we shall fight as our brothers fought, and fall
      where our mates are lying.'

Where are you going to, do you know?
Some are going where strong men go,
But the others have trampled beneath their feet
The British Flag as they stroll the street.
They heard, but they chose Life's easy ways,
And their souls are branded for all their days—
They have dinned the Motherland, and the broken men,
      and the dying.

Source: *Brisbane Courier,* Monday 18 June 1917, p. 8.

Joice M. NanKivell
Lake Narocz

Where in the winter of 1916, 60,000 Russian soldiers crashed through the ice and were drowned in a vain attempt to reach the German lines on the other side.

The breeze ruffles your surface
And you laugh up to the sun,
The wind stirs your brown depths deeper,
And still you laugh to the sun,
And your laughter wakes not the sleeper
Where the great pike bask in the sun
That drifts down from your surface.

Waves jostle the reed in the shallows,
And spend themselves on the shore,
Fretting in needless anger,
Stirring the stones on the shore,
But they rouse you not from your languor
In the fast embrace of the shore.
Waves jostle the reeds in the shallows.

In the winter the ripples are stilled,
Smooth and white in the pall on the water,
A pall laid to cover the dead,
The dead who lie under the water,
Did you stir in your sleep at their tread?
To comfort them under the water
Until all their crying was stilled?

At the crashing of ice did you stir?
Why should your slumber be broken?
In spring the ice grinding, complaining
Gives you sign that the winter has broken,
That the sun his old power is regaining.
Should the spell be so suddenly broken?
That the crashing of ice made you stir?
And what is the crying of men?
Smooth is your bed for the sleepers.

Did you think it the wolf or the wind
That howled o'er the couch of the sleeper,
When guiltless and those who had sinned
Fell asleep in the arms of the sleeper
And hushed was the crying of men?
And you stirred not in your dreaming,

Still clasped in the arms of the winter,
By never a ripple disturbed,
Calm as the breath of the winter,
Unconquerable and unperturbed,
Still as the stillness of winter,
You heard not nor woke from your dreaming.

Source: Joice NanKivell Loch, *Collected Poems*, Burford, Cygnet 1980, pp.11-12.

NETTIE PALMER

Nettie Palmer. Photographer unknown. State Library Victoria.

Janet Gertrude Palmer was born on 18 August 1885 at Sandhurst (Bendigo), the only daughter of Irish-born John Higgins, a draper and later accountant, and his wife Catherine (née MacDonald). The family moved to Armadale in Melbourne, where Esmonde MacDonald, Nettie's only brother was born in 1897. (In 1917, Esmonde enlisted in the AIF and served as a gunner in the Field Artillery Battery during World War One.)

Nettie was educated at home by her mother and at a Miss Rudd's Seminary at Malvern before she attended Presbyterian Ladies College. Her school friends included Hilda Bull (later radical intellectual and wife to playwright Louis Esson) and Christian Jollie Smith (later solicitor, anti-Conscriptionist, foundation committee-member of the Communist Party of Australia, and tireless defender of working-class interests).

Nettie's first writing was a response to her parents' strict Baptist beliefs, and she began to publish verse and prose while still at school. She matriculated with honours in Latin, French and English, with strong results also in history. Enrolling at the University of Melbourne in 1905, she graduated BA in 1909 and MA in 1912, gaining a scholarship and honours results. From 1905, against her parents' efforts to restrain her interests, she engaged in political events that were bolstered by her association with poet and cultural nationalist Bernard O'Dowd, whom she regarded as a sage and with whom she shared a passionate sense of affiliation with the Australian bush. O'Dowd's lecture and pamphlet *Poetry Militant* as well as his poems collected in *Dawnward?* (1903), *The Silent Land* (1906) and the long poem *The Bush* (1912) inspired many radical women and men besides Nettie Higgins: Katherine Susannah Prichard left one of his lectures 'almost too exalted exhilarated to speak'.

Nettie wrote and published at first under several names including 'Bendigo', Owen Roe O'Neill, and Shalott. Later names would include Janet Gertrude Palmer, N.P., N.Q., and Nettie Palmer.

In 1909, she met the writer Vance Palmer, who had embraced radical Australian nationalism in Queensland, where he wrote an essay on 'An Australian National Art' for *Steele Rudd's Magazine*. He subsequently worked as a journalist in London, returning via Russia and Japan. In Melbourne in 1909, he met many members of literary circles and engaged in activities with the Victorian Socialist Party prior to returning to Queensland to work as a tutor and bookkeeper before again travelling in England and France between 1912 and 1915, apart from a return via America and Mexico in 1912 and 1913. He supported himself through astonishingly prolific literary work, while encountering writers including Katherine Mansfield, Ezra Pound, Frank Harris and expatriate artist Will Dyson.

Nettie was meanwhile assisted by her father and uncle to travel to Europe in furtherance of her academic career. Her uncle, Henry Bournes Higgins, Judge of the Arbitration Court, defender of the Labor movement, advocate for women's tertiary education and member of the Melbourne University Council, was a notable supporter of the arts, and in 1904 had donated £1000 for a poetry scholarship. (Nettie later published an admiring biography of her distinguished uncle.)

Nettie studied for the diploma of the International Phonetics Association in Germany, France and England from 1910 until 1912, during which time she and Vance, who had been engaged since 1911, married in London on 23 May 1914 and went on a honeymoon to France. When war was declared, they returned to England, where their first child, Aileen, was born, and then, one month after the sinking of the *Lusitania,* left for Australia, where they continued their literary and political activities, including campaigning against censorship and the Conscription plebiscite. Their second daughter, Helen, was born at Katherine Susannah Prichard's cottage (formerly inhabited by Louis and Hilda Esson), at Emerald, southeast of Melbourne, in the Dandenong Ranges.

§

Nettie published two collections of poems in England, in 1914 and 1915. In Melbourne, she and Vance would eventually become one of Australia's outstanding cultural partnerships.

Nettie's journalism and talks provided income while Vance wrote fiction and, with her, edited short fiction and such classics as Joseph Furphy's *Such is Life.* Nettie's diaries, critical studies and biographies were crucial in the promotion of an Australian cultural tradition. Nettie produced regular book reviews for Melbourne newspapers, especially the *Argus* and *Australasian,* and gradually appears to have abandoned verse (apart from a translation of a poem by Verlaine in the early 1920s). Her earlier poems reappeared in anthologies while her literary journalism was both essential for the family income and persuasive in foregrounding the more outstanding Australian writers of her own and earlier generations.

Nettie Palmer's pre-World War One verse received mixed reviews. A sensitive 1915 reviewer of *The South Wind,* which appeared in the Melbourne *Herald,* observed that 'in more than one verse, the mere suggestion of shadow and shine prefigures an entity for ever escaping, much as the melody of Dvorak's "Humoreske" indicates the existence, present yet always unrevealed, of a being not of this earth, but of the dales of Arcady of old time. Some of Richard Hovey's wonderful woodland verses furnish a parallel, but lack the absolute and certain human touch that thrills in "Transformation," "The Hour", and "The Prisoner". Not less in things said, but in the mastery of the word unspoken, lies Mrs Palmer's sincerity and charm'.

Elsewhere, the *Sydney Morning Herald's* reviewer treated Palmer's poetry patronisingly in 1916, lauding Vance's first collection, *The Forerunners,* while faintly praising Nettie's *Shadowy Paths.* Vance was commended for 'his power of producing a vivid impression in a few lines' and his ability to 'make us share' his 'mental vision'. The reviewer asserted that Nettie's volume, 'contains less of intrinsic importance', but 'there is much in it that is distinguished by genuine charm and gracefulness', and that 'Miss Palmer's muse is not one of force, nor does she aim at the highest peak of Parnassus. But within her limitations her verse is excellent. She brings to it a sympathy, a delicacy of feeling, and a sense of melody, and above all a tender simplicity which carry her far when more ambitious flights might have failed'.

Palmer nonetheless continued to produce lyrical verse throughout the War.

Her poem 'Birds' (1916) and others appeared sporadically but her sense of the urgency of the task she embarked on with her husband, to encourage recognition of Australian literature, remained a priority.

§

Nettie's cousin Mervyn Bournes Higgins, sole son of Justice Henry Bournes Higgins and his wife Mary, enlisted in the army while his family was in England at the outbreak of the War, and he survived Gallipoli only to die, a Captain in the 8th Australian Light Horse, at Magdhaba, Egypt, on 23 December 1916, aged 28. His desolated parents created a scholarship in his name at Melbourne University.

Vance Palmer might have avoided joining the army during the War on the grounds that he was a married man and parent of two daughters, but he felt compelled to enlist, and in March 1918, did so. He was sent with reinforcements for the fourteenth Battalion to France, arriving three days after the Armistice. He found army life agreed with him, seeing it as a guild or 'band of brothers'. After spending some time in France, England and Ireland, he returned to Australia, still a private soldier, and was discharged in Melbourne on 4 November 1919. The army experience informs Vance's second collection of poems, *The Camp*, published in 1920, which contains his most celebrated and much-anthologised poem, 'The Farmer Remembers the Somme'.

Among other immediate postwar writing and journalism, and a number of plays for the Melbourne Pioneer Players, Vance contributed articles to the soldiers' magazine *Aussie*, under the pen name 'Rann Daly', and, on foreign affairs, to the Catholic newspaper the *Advocate*.

The Palmers lived in Caloundra in Queensland from 1925, but returned to Europe on occasion after the War. Vance went to promote his work in 1930, and the couple went together in 1935 and 1936, when they were closely involved in supporting the Republican cause in the Spanish

Civil War. Back in Australia after a brief sojourn in Spain, the couple were active in the cultural fight against Fascism. Nettie became Victorian editor of a Sydney anti-Fascist journal for women, and a member of a branch of the International Refugee Emergency Committee, while teaching migrants English, and undertaking other literary activities.

Vance, a liberal socialist like his wife, made his last overseas trip in 1955 as a delegate to the World Peace Council. He died at his home at Kew on 15 July 1959, a few days before *Meanjin* magazine published a special issue in honour of both Nettie and Vance. In poor health, but nevertheless caring for ill and elderly relatives through the 1940s and 50s, Nettie Palmer died at Hawthorn on 19 October 1964.

Publications

Henry Bournes Higgins: A Memoir, London: Harrap, 1931.
Modern Australian Literature, Melbourne: Lothian, 1924.
Talking It Over [essays], Sydney: Angus & Robertson, 1932.
Fourteen Years: Extracts from a Private Journal 1924-1939, Melbourne: Meanjin Press, 1948.
Australians in Spain: Our Pioneers Against Fascism (with Len Fox), Sydney: Current Book Distributors, 1948.
Henry Handel Richardson: A Study, Sydney: Angus & Robertson, 1950.
The Dandenongs, Melbourne: Ron Edwards, 1952.
Bernard O'Dowd (with Victor Kennedy), Melbourne: Melbourne University Press, 1954.
Letters of Vance Palmer and Nettie Palmer 1915-1963, ed Vivian Smith, Canberra: National Library of Australia, 1977.
Nettie Palmer: Her Private Journal 'Fourteen Years', Poems, Reviews and literary Essays, ed Vivian Smith, St Lucia: University of Queensland Press, 1988.

References

D. J. Jordan, 'Palmer, Janet Gertrude (Nettie) (1885–1964)', Australian Dictionary of Biography, National Centre of Biography, Australian National University, http://adb.anu.edu.au/biography/palmer-janet-gertrude-nettie-7948/text13835, published first in hardcopy 1988, accessed online 19 February 2018.

Chris Wallace-Crabbe, 'O'Dowd, Bernard Patrick (1866–1953)', Australian Dictionary of Biography, National Centre of Biography, Australian

National University, http://adb.anu.edu.au/biography/odowd-bernard-patrick-7881/text13701, published first in hardcopy 1988, accessed online 19 February 2018.

John Rickard, 'Higgins, Henry Bournes (1851–1929)', Australian Dictionary of Biography, National Centre of Biography, Australian National University, http://adb.anu.edu.au/biography/higgins-henry-bournes-6662/text11483, published first in hardcopy 1983, accessed online 20 February 2018.

Geoffrey Serle, 'Palmer, Edward Vivian (Vance) (1885–1959)', Australian Dictionary of Biography, National Centre of Biography, Australian National University, http://adb.anu.edu.au/biography/palmer-edward-vivian-vance-7946/text13831, published first in hardcopy 1988, accessed online 30 May 2018.

Ann Vickery, 'Nettie Palmer: Another Path Taken', *Stressing the Modern: Cultural Politics in Australian Women's Poetry,* 2007, pp. 263-308.

'Australian Verse', *Sydney Morning Herald,* Saturday 29 January 1916, p. 8 [Anonymous review of *The Forerunners* and *Shadowy Paths*].

'Birds', Weekly Times Annual, Saturday 4 November 1916, p. 15.

'A Woman's Verses', *Herald,* Tuesday 2 March 1915, p. 8 [review of *The South Wind*].

Nettie Palmer
The Mother

In the sorrow and the terror of the nations,
In a world shaken through by lamentations,
Shall I dare know happiness,
That I stitch a baby's dress?

So: for I shall be a mother with the mothers,
I shall know the mother's anguish like the others,
Present joy must surely start
For the life beneath my heart.

Gods and men, ye know a woman's glad unreason,
How she cannot bend and weep but in her season,
Let my hours with rapture glow
As the seams and stitches grow.

And I cannot hear the word of fire and slaughter;
Do men die? Then live, my child, my son, my daughter!
Into the realms of pain I bring
You for joy's own offering.

Source: Nettie Palmer, *Shadowy Paths.* London: Euston Press, 1915, p. 30.

Nettie Palmer
The Barrack Yard

A sack of straw suspended from a tree,
    Soldiers with bayonets in the barrack-yard,
    In turn they lunge and thrust and stand on guard,
Their faces rigid, fraught with destiny.

A summer wind is moving dreamily,
    The sack a hundred times is gashed and marred,
    In the tree-shadows by the railings barred
The city children stare and laugh to see.

What of life's glory, what of memory's glow!
What of he boon of song, the great word written,
    The highest peak our dreamers ever saw!
We learn to slay our kind. Ah, might we know,
Dying, that every foe our hands had smitten
    Was but a mute and soulless man of straw.

Source: Netttie Palmer, *Shadowy Paths*. London: Euston Press, 1915, p. 49.

Nettie Palmer
Birds

I know a place where birds are wild and swift,
   And strange and splendid,
   Hills where their sweetest songs are never ended,
And those that have no song may fare adrift
Attired like clouds at sunrise, rift on rift.

Across the high, bright orchard where there hung
   Late apples glowing,
   Came lories, red and blue, like small waves flowing,
Came later yet rosellas, and among
The smooth, bare branches like a garland swung.

And ah! the birds that sang, the soft, grey birds,
   The twilight feathered,
   Moving with tiny leaps like silken tethered
Singers to some great prince whose glance rewards
Each long-drawn call and all the wavering chords!

They sang, the grey-garbed mountain thrushes sang,
   And we two listened,
   Rapt on some rain-washed evening while there glistened
A sudden leaf a-tremble: you would hang
Clematis round me or the wild pea's fang.

At morning, when white clouds like leaves drop down
   Filling the hollows,
   And make vast, milk-white lakes and silence follows,
There on a stump some laughing jackass clown
Stiller than wood thought all the world his own.

But all the world was ours! The birds were ours,
   Because we knew them,
   The trees were ours, because our love passed through them,
And every dome of cloud and all the flowers
And mountain mists that built our silent bowers.

Enough, we had been jubilant too long,
    The gods have judged us,
        Such vital joy their tranquil eyes begrudged us.
You fight in France: here when the thrushes throng
How can I bear alone to hear their song.

Source: *Weekly Times Annual*, Saturday 4 November 1916, p. 15.

Nettie Palmer
The Hero

Billy hath done one braver thing
    Than all the worthies did.
To tell a lie he doth forbid;
    He maketh laws to sting.

That Roman judge example gave
    In dealing equal law;
His son the lot of death did draw,
    The father would not save.

But Billy's strength who will gainsay
    When lies, a crime we call,
He first beneath the law will fall;
    He gives himself away!

Source: *Labor Call*, Thursday 27 December 1917, p. 4.

CLARA LEONAR PATEY

Clara Leonar Patey was the youngest of four children (Thomas, Harry, Mary Ellen—'Nellie', and Clara) of Thomas Rapson Johns and Annie Johns. Her parents, Thomas Rapson Johns (born in Cornwall in 1848) and her mother Annie Bolitho (born in 1847) were married in the Helston district in Cornwall before they migrated to Adelaide on the *Glamis* in 1883. Thomas worked successively as a gold miner, copper miner and commercial traveller, and spent time in South Australia and elsewhere before settling at Bendigo. Association with mining seems a common thread in Clara's family. Her brother Thomas (1865-1951) worked in Bendigo and in Western Australia mining districts; her sister Nellie (1877-1952) spent 56 years at Moonta, South Australia (Australia's 'Little Cornwall', so named for its population of predominantly Cornish and Welsh immigrants working in the copper mines) before moving to Broken Hill.

Clara's husband, John Packwood Patey, derived his middle name from the family of John Packwood, a partner in the coaching and carrying firm of Snow and Packwood, which traded between Melbourne and the gold diggings at Bendigo and Central Victoria. Packwood is believed by later members of the Patey family to have assisted in John Patey's rearing. This seems likely, given that the Packwood and Patey families were related by marriage. John Packwood had married Louisa Gill (whose mother's name was Heard) in 1866; John Patey's father William Henry had married Isabella Eliza Heard in 1868, and they had two children: a daughter in 1869, followed by John. Isabella died in 1873, and William Henry Patey two years later. Relations between the Packwood and Patey families remained close for many years. Clara, together with John Packwood's daughter-in-law, engaged in assistance and comfort work for servicemen, independent of any official organisation during World War 1.

Clara's husband had first worked as a mining crew's tool man, and later taught elocution and drama. The Pateys lived at 'Glen Rhyl' in Murdock Street, California Gully, in North Bendigo. They had one son, Leonard, who served for four years with the British and American navies and died of epidemic pneumonia at the age of twenty-two, at the Marine Hospital in Boston on 1 October 1918. His death was perhaps the Pateys' crowning tragedy. Before the turn of the century, they had adopted an infant in poor health, named Stella Blackburn, but the child had died of gastroenteritis at their home in February 1899.

Clara was ill at the time of Leonard's death, and the Pateys inserted a notice in the local papers thanking the Eaglehawk Patriotic League, the California Comforts Club, friends and fellow workers 'for visits, letters, cards, messages, and for all kind expressions of sympathy tendered to them in their recent sad bereavement'. They found it impossible to respond individually by post to the volume of messages of sympathy. This is hardly surprising. During the War, the Pateys, civic-minded and philanthropic by nature, and popular for their contributions to public recitation and choral performances, had established the Comforts Fund to send parcels of food, clothes and other materials to serving men abroad. Besides Mrs Packwood, Clara's niece Rosie Johns was also a contributor of parcels for soldiers at the front.

In March 1917, the *Bendigonian* newspaper reported that Clara and her friends had sent 'several petrol cases full of good things to the front', and the paper printed a sample of the letters they had received via Lady Mary Hennessy's Patriotic League. (The Lord Mayor of Melbourne, Sir David Valentine Hennessy and his wife were 'formidable' philanthropists and fund-raisers.)

The effect of the Pateys' work is suggestive of the appreciation other servicemen felt as a result of the contributions of so many of the women poets I have surveyed; part of the *Bendigonian* record runs as follows:

> Dear Mrs. Patey, Just received your most welcome billy full of good things, also your nice letter, and must say thanks indeed for all. Well, we kept up our Christmas Day on 19th December, travelling all day, and got our billies at night; pushed off two hours afterwards, and have not stopped since. On the 23rd December we were up with the Turks. We captured two important towns and about 2000 prisoners, and we have not stopped yet. I suppose the papers will tell you all about our battles, so I will not waste your time describing them. Well, this is my third Christmas at the war, and it looks like a few more yet, but it's just like home to us now, so it does not matter how long it lasts. Corporal E. Simper'; 'Egypt, 28th December, 1916—Dear Mrs. Patey, I thank you for the lovely Christmas Billy which I received from you. I do think it is so kind of you dear ones in Australia to send

us boys such nice things for Christmas. No doubt you have friends of your own in this great war, but I suppose all would get a billy. I have never been over to Victoria. My parents live in Western Australia. If ever I have the luck to get back to Sunny Australia it will always do for me. Arnold C. N. Quartermaine'; 'Tel-el-Kebir, Egypt—Dear Mrs. Patey. Many, many thanks for your most thoughtful gift re writing wallet, which I received today. We (the troops) cannot say enough in praise of our people in Australia. We are always receiving gifts from them. Speaking of myself, I know I have received my share of good things. F.G. Solly'; 'France—Dear Jack, Thanks for the cigs and tobacco. They came just in time to save our tea supply, as we were starting on that. Syd Price, from Brunswick, Victoria'; 'France—Dear Jack, Your cigarettes and tobacco came just in time. The boys had been picking up butts for three days. Many thanks. Yours, 'Pat Sammy' from Auburn, Victoria.'

After Leonard's death, the Pateys moved from Bendigo to 'Fernlea', in the Melbourne suburb of Seaford on the eastern side of Port Philip Bay. They ran 'Fernlea' as a guesthouse, and cared for Clara's mother Annie, who died there on 1 February 1926.

Clara died on 28 September in the same year, at Dr Maxwell's private hospital 'Maxwelton', and the *Frankston and Somerville Chronicle*, to which she had frequently contributed verse, wrote that she 'possessed considerable literary ability and she published a book of poems of which over 1000 copies were sold for the Bendigo soldiers' memorial home'. John's farewell notice listed her name as Clara Jane, and carried the farewell remark, 'A noble soul called home'.

John Patey continued to teach elocution and dramatic arts, and on 1 June 1940, at St Barnabas Church of England, at Seaford, he married Nellie Riley Gunn, a widow, mother of four children (Edith Gunn, Ralph Gunn, Kenneth Patey and Shirley Patey). Nellie Gunn was an accomplished musician, who studied with the celebrated concert pianist and composer Una Bourne. John and Nellie continued to operate 'Fernlea' as a guesthouse, until her death on 16 August 1954. John Patey died in 1958.

Reprinting Clara Leonar Patey's poem 'Remembrance Day' in November 1926, the *Frankston and Somerville Standard* noted 'This poem was written originally by the late Mrs. Clara L. Patey for the Bendigo

Soldiers' Memorial, and published in her book of verse, entitled *Rosemary*. The late Mrs. Patey, during her residence in Seaford, was a regular contributor to the columns of the *Standard'*.

Publications

"Rosemary" for Remembrance: Soldiers' Memorial Souvenir. Bendigo: Cambridge Press, 1921 [37 poems, 42 poems, nine on war-related themes, including a C.J. Dennis-like narrative 'Billjim and Me (by 'Juliahann', pp. 28-29].

References

Elizabeth Conner, Re: Packwood of Coleshill, England 1755-1900. 27 July 2001.

http://www.genealogy.com/forum/surnames/topics/packwood/87/ Accessed 4 June 2016.

'Moonta, SA' Aussie Towns, http://www.aussietowns.com.au/town/moonta-sa, Accessed 5 June 2016.

National Trust South Australia, Moonta Branch. http://www.moontatourism.org.au/area-history. Accessed 5 June 2016.

Australasian, Saturday 16 June 1866, p. 29 [Marriage of John Packwood to Louisa Gill, youngest daughter of Robert Ballard Heard of London].

Leader (Victoria), 3 April 1869, p. 26 [Birth of a daughter to the wife of W.H. Patey at Sandhurst on 27 March; also advertised in Family Notices, *Illustrated Australian News for Home Readers,* 24 April 1869, p. 99].

'California Hill Methodist Church Choir Concert'. *Bendigo Advertiser,* Saturday 13 May 1899, p. 3 [John Patey's part in a 'capital programme'].

'Soldier's Friends. Comforts Appreciated', *Bendigo Independent,* Tuesday 27 February 1917, p. 8.

Mrs J.P. Patey's Organisation', *Bendigonian,* Thursday March 1 March 1917, p. 26 [responses from servicemen to gifts in Comforts Fund].

'Comforts for Soldier's. Girl's Fine Record', *Bendigo Advertiser,* Wednesday 27 February 1918, p. 7 [Rosie Johns's contribution to the war effort; includes a letter from Corporal Samuel Dales, writing from France].

David Dunstan, 'Hennessy, Sir David Valentine (1858–1923)', Australian Dictionary of Biography, National Centre of Biography, Australian National University, http://adb.anu.edu.au/biography/hennessy-sir-david-valentine-6640/text11439, published first in hardcopy 1983, accessed online 16 April 2018.

Argus, Tuesday 2 February 1926, p. 2 [Death of Annie Johns, aged 79].

Argus, Wednesday 29 September 1926, p. 1 [Death of Clara Jane Patey].

Clara L. Patey, 'Mistland Fairies', *Frankston and Somerville Standard*, Friday 9 July 1926, p. 3.

Age, 29 June 1940, p. 11 [remarriage of John Patey].

'For Freedom's Cause', *Bendigo Advertiser,* Tuesday November 26 1918, p. 4; Bendigonian, 28 November 1918, p. 3. [Death of Leonard Patey].

Bendigo Advertiser, Saturday 21 December 1918, p. 8. [Public notice, duplicated in *Bendigonian* newspaper, on Leonard Patey's death].

'Obituary: Mrs Clara Patey', *Frankston and Somerville Standard,* Friday 1 October 1926, p. 2.

Note to Patey's poem 'Remembrance Day', *Frankston and Somerville Standard,* Friday 22 April 1921, p. 1 (reprinted 12 November 1926, p. 2, with attribution 'The late Clara Leonar Patey').

Age, 29 July 1940, p. 11 [Patey-Gunn marriage at Seaford].

Emerald Hill Record, Saturday 28 August 1954, p. 1 [Death of Nellie Patey at Seaford].

Argus, Tuesday 17 August 1954, p. 13 [Death of Nellie Patey, at 90 Nepean Highway, Seaford].

Liz Conner. 'John Packwood Patey of Cornwall', Genealogy.com. 28 July 2001. http://www.genealogy.com/forum/surnames/topics/patey/79/ Accessed 6 June 2016.

Peter Burgis, 'Bourne, Una Mabel (1882–1974)', Australian Dictionary of Biography, National Centre of Biography, Australian National University, http://adb.anu.edu.au/biography/bourne-una-mabel-5307/text8961, published first in hardcopy 1979, accessed online 6 June 2016.

Clara Patey
Welcome All

There's a clarion cry resounding through the land,
    From the city and the town it's ringing clear,
And the country seems to waken,
       Just as if the earth were shaken,
       And the backblocks catch the echo, with a cheer.

'Tis the cry of welcome ringing through the land,
    And it sounds from north to south, from east to west.
For the brave boys are returning,
       Over whom all hearts are yearning;
       They have fought the fight, and nobly stood the test.

So this joyful note is heard, right through the land,
    And its sound is all triumphant as it goes,
For victory it's tolling,
       Won by heroes brave, excelling,
       Any other feats of valour, history shows.

There's another call, that's sounding through the land,
    As it sounded, day by day, for four years past,
And 'tis tho call to 'Carry on'
       Until the need for work has gone,
       And to stand by every soldier till the last.

There's a sound of many sighing, through the land,
    Though with smiles they'll greet our soldiers when they meet,
But to mar these days of gladness,
       There's a lonely kind of sadness,
       But there's One said, 'Lay thy burden at my feet'.

                  27/12/18 — Clara Patey

Source: *Bendigo Advertiser,* Saturday 28 February 1918, p. 10;
Riverine Herald (Echuca, Vic; Moama NSW) Friday 10 January 1919, p. 4.

Clara Leonar Patey
Boys in the Navy Blue

Over the rolling waves they sailed, our boys in the navy blue,
Down in the depths 'midst submarines they fought grim battles through,
And never a line for months they'd get from loved ones far away,
While years might pass e'er a message came from those in the battle's fray;
But nothing e'er daunted those hearts so true,
Naught could discourage our boys in blue.

They faced grim death in every shape, those boys in the navy blue,
'Twas lurking near them day and night, but still with courage true
That has made for our Australian boys a never-dying name,
They stuck to their posts, carving their names high on the scroll of fame;
But little thought they of the fame in view—
'Tis duty that counts with boys in blue.

Who is there could forget the thrill they dealt when the boys in blue,
Tackling the treacherous Emden, sank her and prisonered her crew;
And who of us could ever forget the Zeebrugge's grand blockade,
When they ran their concrete-laden ships 'neath a fearful cannonade,
Right up the canal, and they blocked it, too—
That was the work of our lads in blue.

They played the game when the need was great, those bonny boys in blue,
Stranded in ice-bound seas were they, but they hacked a passage through;
Anon in the Jutland battle they put up a record fight,
Sinking the enemy's battleships and putting the Huns to flight;
Whilst a debonair mirth-loving crew,
Happy as sand-boys are they of the blue.

Never a book could hold the deeds so brave of the lads in blue.
They 'who go down to the sea in ships' to fight our battles through,
And never a sailor man was there that put him out to sea
But his life was risked a hundredfold through the Hunnish treachery;
And there's many a seaman staunch and true
Lies, shrouded in death, in navy blue.

Source: Clara L. Patey, 'Boys in the Navy Blue', *Mornington Standard* (Frankston), 4 June 1920, p. 1, and *'Rosemary' for Remembrance: Soldiers' Memorial Souvenir.* Bendigo: Cambridge Press, 1921, pp. 17-18.

Note.
Zeebrugge (Belgium). Thirteen Australian sailors from HMAS *Australia* volunteered to join the Royal Navy's attempt to destroy the German defences at Zeebrugge with landing parties from surface ships, and a submarine filled with explosives, on 23rd April 1918. The raid failed to destroy defences, and the principal British assault ships were sunk before completing their tasks. The raid was famous for the audacity of its conception and the bravery of the participants. Several Australians received medals: Lieutenant-Commander Edgar, the Distinguished Service Cross, three Australian seamen on HMS *Vindictive*, the Distinguished Service Medal, and one of the stokers on the blockship HMS *Thetis*, the Belgian Croix de Guerre. 'Australians at Zeebrugge'. Naval Historical Society of Australia. http://www.navyhistory.org.au/australians-at-zeebrugge/ Accessed 8 November 2011.

Clara L. Patey
Remembrance Day

'Lest we forget' heroic sacrifices,
'Lest we forget' the fearful price they paid,
'Lest we forget' the debt that looms colossal,
'Lest we forget' those promises we made
Or memory, enfeebled, stray,
Give us, we pray, Remembrance Day

Ours now the right of liberty and freedom,
Bought with the life blood of Australia's best,
Then as we hope for mercy at the Judgment
Must each with honour issue from the rest.
Our word shall be our bond indeed,
Or we for mercy dare not plead.

'If ye break faith with us who, died, we shall not sleep'.
Rest! rest! dear hearts; we must keep faith with thee,
Or, conscience, dying, our, every path would haunt—
Still grim and gaunt, marring eternity,
Sleep! sleep! in all good faith we'll keep,
Thy memory with reverence—sleep.

And monuments of love and pride upraising,
A people's tribute to our gallant dead
Shall prove true homes of rest for war-worn comrades,—
What temple could a holier radiance shed?
Each hallowed stone might breathe a prayer,
Being wrought for selflessness so rare.

Australians, all the debt is still unpaid,
But golden opportunities out spread—,
Oh make these sanctuaries of rest all worthy
A Nation honours thus her noble dead,
And grateful hearts might truly pray,
God's blessing on Remembrance Day.

Source: *Frankston and Somerville Standard*, Friday 22 April 1921, p. 1 [also 12 November 1926, p. 2, with attribution 'The late Clara Leonar Patey'].

MARIE E.J. PITT

Marie E.J. Pitt. Photographer: Monteath, Melbourne.
State Library of New South Wales.

Marie Elizabeth Josephine Pitt was born on 6 August 1869 at Bulumwaal, a gold-mining town north of Bairnsdale in East Gippsland, Victoria. She was the eldest of seven children of Irish goldminer Edward McKeown and his Ayrshire-born wife Mary Stuart McIver (née Dawson), a widow and schoolteacher. The family lived at first in a bark-roofed slab house until they moved a little further south to the farming district of Doherty's Corner, soon to be named Wy Yung, on the Mitchell River.

Two schools were in existence in the 1870s, and though Pitt later claimed that she had learnt most from her natural surroundings (a claim largely supported by the detail and lyricism of her verse and prose descriptions of the Victorian rural scene), she had four years of sporadic formal education at Doherty's Corner. Her domestic childhood duties included tending crops, feeding pigs and milking cows until she was eleven years old. The poems of Burns and other balladists were familiar to her from infancy, and in spite of intermittent schooling, by age eleven she had gained a primary certificate. Aiming to become a teacher like her mother, she continued studying when she could.

In 1887, she failed her teaching competency examination, and, ill with neuralgia and incipient anaemia, she left her home for Bairnsdale and worked as a photographic retoucher. At Bairnsdale, on 18 March 1893, she married William Henry Pitt, a farmer from Longford in Tasmania, and moved with him to live for twelve years in mining camps. Three of their ensuing four children survived infancy.

Pitt published her first poems in local newspapers when she was fourteen. By 1900, she achieved national publication in the *Bulletin* with a satiric poem on the South African War, and in 1902, she won the English *GoodWords* competition for a song of Empire.

A supporter of the union movement, Pitt became vice-president of the Workers' Political Association at Mathinna, a north-eastern Tasmanian mining town named after the Aboriginal girl earlier patronised by Sir John and Lady Jane Franklin. When Pitt's husband contracted pthisis (pulmonary tuberculosis), the family moved back to Victoria, first to Bairnsdale in 1905 and then Melbourne, where Henry Pitt died in 1912.

Marie supported her family by clerical work, writing for newspapers, and reading for publishers. Between 1910 and 1948, she also received support from a Commonwealth Literary Grant. She associated with the Victorian Socialist Party thereby coming in contact with Louis Esson and his wife Hilda Bull (a medical graduate from Melbourne University in 1913), Vance Palmer and Nettie Higgins (later Palmer), propagandists and union activists Tom Mann and Robert Samuel Ross, and the radical poet, librarian at the State Library and later parliamentary draftsman, Bernard O'Dowd (1866-1953).

English-born Tom Mann was a founder and secretary of the Victorian Socialist Party, and first editor of the *Socialist* weekly paper; Ross was a union organiser, former editor of the radical *BarrierTruth* paper at Broken Hill, and Mann's successor as editor of the *Socialist*. Pitt was a regular contributor to the Socialist, and when Ross resigned, Pitt and the Rev. Frederick Sinclaire became joint editors, though both resigned when factional fighting split the movement in 1912. Sinclaire, a former Unitarian minister, had founded the Free Religious Fellowship, which espoused a Shavian, non-Marxian socialist orientation that attracted the

Essons, Palmers, O'Dowd, Frank Wilmot (who wrote poetry under the pen-name 'Furnley Maurice'), Lesbia Harford and other writers disenchanted with traditional political parties and the nascent Labor Party.

Bernard O'Dowd left his wife and family in 1907, and thereafter lived with Pitt though O'Dowd's wife, a Catholic, refused to divorce him. From 1924, Pitt and O'Dowd lived in an imposing Italianate house that Pitt named 'Marienfels', at 155 Clarke Street, Northcote. Pitt and O'Dowd held different views concerning the First World War, Pitt abjuring the propaganda surrounding the Anzacs and Gallipoli. She maintained a strong anti-war conviction, and in her poem 'The Mercy', published in her 1925 collection, wrote

> Oh, was it dream, or was it trance,
> or was it I was there
> And saw Hell's host of devils dance
> on bloody Sari Bair?

Pitt's literary and journalistic contributions to the *Socialist* addressed industrial conditions, class antagonism, State and Federal politics, religion, contraception, and the state of the press. Her writings were inflected with early experience of rural hardship and the living conditions of miners and their families, and was correspondingly realistic in mode and trenchant in tone. Her poetical writing was contrastingly couched in lyrical and balladic forms, reflecting her earliest (and many of her contemporaries') taste for Romantic and Victorian verse and language conventions. Her poetry rarely advanced beyond her earlier stylistic habits, but she published three major books after the First World War: *Bairnsdale* (1922), and two retrospective collections. As a consequence of her adherence to older forms, Pitt's poetry did not command critical attention through her later life. The East Gippsland historian Paul Gardner, in a brief biography of Pitt, calls her an 'Australian poet, socialist, feminist, ecologist and anarchist', and remarks that, though mocked for its archaic sentimentality by Chester Eagle (in his Bairnsdale memoir *Hail and Farewell*), her poetry

> 'falls into two fairly distinct types—the romantic and somewhat nostalgic lyrical ballad and the angry and sometimes bitter political poems. Whilst the former poems have dated badly [...] the latter are often as valid as when they were penned'.

Despite the efforts of Pitt's major biographer, poet Colleen Burke, by the end of the twentieth century, Pitt's name had receded from critical studies of Australian literature to the extent that her name did not even appear in the Oxford Literary History of Australia. Like Gardner, I think it regrettable that Pitt's independence of mind and prescience concerning the nature of work and governance in Australia continue to be ignored.

Pitt died on 20 May 1948 at Kew in hospital, where she had spent two years after suffering a stroke. Throughout her illness, she was daily visited by O'Dowd, who died aged 87 in 1953. At O'Dowd's death, his family destroyed his literary material including Pitt's correspondence.

Shortly before Pitt's death, a plaque was unveiled by the Gordon Lovers' Society at the Mechanics' Institute at Bairnsdale—now the East Gippsland Shire Library—to commemorate her birth, and shortly afterwards, another memorial was hung in the Unitarian Church (now named Melbourne Unitarian Peace Memorial Church) at 110 Grey Street, East Melbourne.

Publications:

Marie E.J. Pitt, *The Horses of the Hills and Other Verses*, Melbourne: Thomas Lothian, 1911.

Marie E. Pitt, *Bairnsdale, and Other Poems*, Bairnsdale: Back to Bairnsdale Committee, 1922.

Marie E.J. Pitt, *The Poems of Marie E.J. Pitt*, Melbourne: Edward A. Vidler, 1925.

Marie E.J. Pitt, *Selected Poems by Marie E.J. Pitt*, Melbourne and Sydney: Lothian Publishing Co. Pty. Ltd, 1944.

References:

Hugh Anderson, 'Pitt, Marie Elizabeth Josephine (1869–1948)', Australian Dictionary of Biography, National Centre of Biography, Australian National University, http://adb.anu.edu.au/biography/pitt-marie-elizabeth-josephine-8057/text14059, published first in hardcopy 1988, accessed online 16 March 2018.

Colleen Burke, *Doherty's Corner: The Life and Work of Poet Marie E.J. Pitt*, North Ryde: Angus & Robertson, 1985.

Chris Wallace-Crabbe, 'O'Dowd, Bernard Patrick (1866–1953)', Australian Dictionary of Biography, National Centre of Biography, Australian National University, http://adb.anu.edu.au/biography/odowd-bernard-patrick-7881/text13701, published first in hardcopy 1988, accessed online 16 March 2018.

P.D. Gardner, *Five Years of Mountain Echoes,* Ensay: Ngarak Press, 2001.
P.D. Gardner, 'Marie E.J. Pitt, 1869-1948', https://libcom.org/history/marie-ej-pitt-1869-1948 Accessed 17 March 2018.
Chester Eagle, *Hail and Farewell: An Evocation of Gippsland,* Melbourne: Heinemann, 1971, pp. 73-74. http://www.trojanpress.com.au/assets/A4_HailAndFarewell.pdf accessed online 16 April 2018.
Marie Elizabeth Josephine Pitt', Monument Australia. http://monumentaustralia.org.au/themes/people/arts/display/96554-marie-elizabeth-josephine-pitt/photo/1 Accessed 17 March 2018.
Catharine Cuthbert, 'Lesbia Harford and Marie Pitt: Forgotten Poets', *Hecate: An Interdisciplinary Journal of Women's Liberation,* vol. 18, no. 1, 1982, pp. 33-48.
Paul Michell, 'Marie E.J. Pitt (1969-1948) – "Clarke Street Lefty", Lyrical & Romantic Poet, Socialist, Feminist, Pacifist, Christian', 2005, revised 2014, Northcote History, https://northcotehistory.weebly.com/uploads/8/3/1/7/8317304/marie_pitt.pdf, accessed 19 July 2018.

Marie E.J. Pitt
The Mercy

Oh, was it dream, or was it trance,
    Or was it I was there.
And saw the sickly sunlight dance
    On steel-starred Sari Bair?

'Al-Allah!' through the battle smoke
    Shrilled loud the Moslem cry.
And where the Crescent phalanx broke
    Death's ruddy stream ran high.

And 'God for England!' fierce I prayed,
    And 'Allah for his own'
Prayed each behind the grisly blade
    That stripped an English bone.

Oh, fear for him and pride of him!
    Oh, love that slew despair!
Ye bore me swift as swallows skim
    That day on Sari Bair!

Yea, heel and spur that clips the heel,
    We clove that hiving swarm:
Where reddest ran his leaping steel,
    I nerved his flagging arm!

Nor tigress of the jungled dark
    With young beside her knee
Knew love so fierce or hate so stark
    As burned the soul of me.

They struck; they fell; to Heaven assigned
    Their fighting souls flew free ....
I heard the sound of a rushing wind.
    And the cry of the Banshee.

A hand of ice was at my throat,
    A black mist on my brain;
He lurched, and even as they smote
    I heard the call again!

I shrieked his name unto the skies,
    Nor answer came to me,
But a flitting flame before my eyes
    And the cry of the Banshee.

Oh was it dream or was it trance,
    Or was it I was there
And saw Hell's host or devils dance
    On bloody Sari Bair?

And he? Alive? Nay, read again!
    Before my frenzied eyes
I see him where the huddled slain
    Sleep under brooding skies!

Not dead? Not dead?—O God of love.
    Who hast delivered me,
Stretch still Thy conquering arm above
    Shell-torn Gallipoli!

The night watch pales to dawn of joy.
    To rose has turned the rue.
An alien mother mourns the boy
    My victor's bayonet slew!

Source: *Bulletin*, 26 August 1915, p. 47; *Socialist*, Friday 12 November 1915, p.3.

Marie E.J. Pitt
With the Guns at Charleroi
(An Incident of the War, as told by a
Special Correspondent.)

It was told on board a troop train
    (In an hour of little joy)—
We were bringing in the wounded
    From the fight at Charleroi.

* * *

'Faith 'twas a day of death and drouth
    With little to atone,
The blind black cannon's blistered mouth
    Spat Hell's own mad cyclone,
And the rifles bit like beaks of birds
    That flayed us to the bone.

A British battery held the hill
    Against the German fire,
All day Death on the shrapnel's shrill
    Ran like a singing wire,
Till to the spent survivors came
    The order to retire.

'Fall back!' Their leader's muffled shout
    Rang faint above the fray;
To lead the ragged remnant out
    There was no drum that day,
For underneath 2's offside wheel
    The little drummer lay.

'Twas here life's wasted ebb dripped slow
    Where broke the war-wave dun,
'Twas here the leaden hail of woe
    Wrought vengeance of the Hun,
And a gallant two of all her crew
    Were left to serve the gun.

Aye, here life's sluggish ebb lay dark
    In gapped ravines of Loss,
Here many-guised, with fingers stark,
    Death tore the trampled moss,
And a shrapnel shard had found its mark
    In a man from Charing Cross.

'Fall back!' The gunner turned his head—
    In a little hollow dip
Behind the gun, all rent and red,
    Lay life's whole fellowship,
His mate from far-off Charing Cross
    He bit his blackened lip.

'But look at 'im, sir; 'im they killed!'
    His blood shot eyes were dim,
As straining from his smutted face
    They sought their leader's grim.
''E was my pal! Don't ask me, sir!—
    God's truth, I carn't leave 'im!'

'Come on! The order is "Retire!"—
    The guns are doomed to loss,
Fall in!' The gunner's eyes shot fire,
    No time was this to gloss;
'You go to 'ell, sir!' firmly said
    The man from Charing Cross.

They doubled 'neath the flinty hill,
    Where blazed the lights of Hell,
That fragment of a battery corps—
    Then from a sheltered dell
Looked back—the man from Charing Cross
    Was cramming home a shell.

And low behind the battered screen,
    Calm as on Grand Review,
There crouched that silent other man
    To swing the breech-block to ...
... Then back they charged and saved the guns,
    As Honor bade them do!

* * * *

So they told it on a troop train,
    'Twas a wintry gleam of joy
To us bringing in the wounded
    From the field of Charleroi.

Source: *Weekly Times Annual,* Thursday 4 November 1915, p. 41.

Marie E.J. Pitt
The Ringers

[If conscription is carried, the Christmas bells will ring the single men out of Australia.]

    Muffle the bells ... the bells ...
  The Christ is dead ....
    His star that lit the hills
  Has fled... has fled ..
And in life's holy place walks Antichrist instead!

    Toll, toll, the heavy bells ...
  Hollow and slow;
    O'er war's red citadels,
  And woman's woe,
And all things brave and bright and beautiful laid low!

    Mothers of men ... of men,
  Valued and priced,
    Like dumb beasts in the pen,
  For slaughter triced...
Up! limb from groaning limb; rend this foul Antichrist!

    Clang out the bells ... the bells
  Of victory!
    O'er passing giant man-made hells,
  Ring in the heaven to be.
The golden age, whereof the gods gave US the key!

Source: *Labor Call,* Thursday 26 October 1916, p. 6.

Marie E.J. Pitt
Transports

Slaves, purple, peacocks, apes and ivory!
    How long till Retribution's tide-race roars
Above Man's greed, and Ocean's caverned floors
        Like hollowed hands hold Love's poor tragedy?
How long? How long? O bitter years to be! ....
    Since on grey Carthage Scipio's flashing oars
Launched javelined hate—upon the world's wan shores,
        Sat never grief like this beside the sea.

Without the heads if lean hulls take the roll
    Of the Pacific, and the smoke-trails swart
Like hooded pythons crawl across the Bay.
        Ah, God! Each trail, each hull-down ship of grey—
A red drop welling from Australia's heart,
        A slow flame falling from her splendid soul.

Source: *The Poems of Marie E.J. Pitt,* Melbourne: Edward A. Vidler, 1925, p. 131.

PHILADELPHIA NINA ROBERTSON

Photo: 'Miss Philadelphia Robertson O.B.E.',
Who's Who in the World of Women: Victoria Australia 1930, Melbourne:
Reference Press Association, 1930, vol. 1. State Library Victoria.

Philadelphia Nina Robertson was born at Wangaratta, Victoria, on 27 February 1886. She was one of six children of the Scottish-born pioneer minister Rev. John Dickson Robertson (1832–1915) and his English-born wife Amelia Spencer. Her father was successively charged with the parishes of Wangaratta, Horsham, Geelong, Yarrawonga, and Canterbury. In 1896, he was Moderator of the General Assembly. One of Philadelphia's brothers was Hume James Robertson (1860-1921), who studied theology at Ormond College at the University of Melbourne, and became a minister, serving in parishes including Mia Mia, Castlemaine (in the 1890s and early 1900s) and Brighton Beach. He enlisted in the AIF in 1915 as a Chaplain-Captain and in 1916 left for overseas service; wounded in 1917, he returned to the front and was promoted Major in

May 1918. Returning to Australia in August the following year, he died after a long debilitating illness.

Philadelphia Robertson was educated at the Presbyterian Ladies College in Melbourne, and like many outstanding alumnae, would achieve renown in her profession. The school's distinguished former pupils include Dame Nellie Melba (Helen Mitchell), Ethel Florence Lindesay Richardson (the author Henry Handel Richardson), and the suffragettes Marion Phillips (1881-1932, later graduate of the London School of Economics, co-worker with Beatrice Webb on a Commission investigating the Poor Laws, and Labour candidate and first woman to win a seat in the English Parliament), and Vida Goldstein (1869-1949), an uncompromising opponent of the White Australia policy, staunch pacifist during WWI and first woman to stand for election to the Federal Parliament several times from 1903 until 1917.

Robertson learned typing and shorthand, and took up secretarial work. She also completed first-aid classes, run by the St John Ambulance Association, at Castlemaine. She travelled in Palestine and Europe with her sister and brother-in-law, and at the outbreak of war, volunteered her services to the British Red Cross Society and the Order of St John, which employed her as a clerk until November 1914, when she returned to Australia.

Back in Victoria, the British (Australian branch) Red Cross employed her as secretary to the general council and its president Lady Helen Ferguson, wife of the Governor-General Sir Ronald Munro Ferguson (Viscount Novar of Raith). Robertson worked at the Red Cross headquarters in Government House, and with the aid of a small staff (two paid typists and several volunteers) managed the overseas business of the organisation, communicated with State divisions, edited bulletins and kept minutes of meetings. She oversaw the sending of parcels to prisoners of war in Germany, the provision of comforts to inmates of military sanatoria and homes, collection of funds for relief of wounded soldiers, and the convening of the Red Cross Book Depot for the collection, transport and dispatch of cloth-bound books from book bins at Geelong, Ballarat, Bendigo, St Kilda and metropolitan railway stations, for which she gained the services of the State railways for free transport. For her war work, she was awarded OBE in 1918.

In 1921, Robertson became general secretary of the revised Victorian division of the Red Cross and continued as secretary to the central council in 1922, when the national and State headquarters moved into a refurbished building in La Trobe Street. She visited London in 1925, interviewing officers of the British Red Cross Society, and again in 1930 as Australian delegate to the British Empire Red Cross Conference. She was the Australian delegate in 1938 to the 16th International Red Cross Conference, staying with her long-time correspondent, Lady Novar.

Among notable work in the 1920s, she organised collection of clothing and food for distribution by the International Red Cross to destitute people in Europe from 1919, continued assistance for veterans and their families, and relief for victims of natural disasters in Australia (such as floods in Launceston in April 1929). Twenty committees of the Red Cross were still active running hospitals or assisting district hospitals and specialist repatriation hospitals, including the Mont Park military hospital and another at Bundoora for mental patients.

In the 1930s, Robertson also worked to raise funds for a memorial sculpture to John Simpson Kirkpatrick. An article, 'The Human Touch', in the *Argus* newspaper, on 24 October 1933 recorded her appeal in the following terms:

> Almost all officers and soldiers who fought in the Great War have tales of heroism to relate—vivid incidents noted at the time but never appearing in official records—stories of men losing their lives in the effort to bring in a wounded comrade, stories of men sticking to their posts in the face of certain death. Each and every one of these gallant men might justly have a monument erected to his memory. It was to honour these and the multitude of others who made the supreme sacrifice that the Shrine was created, and to their memory it stands imperishably sacred and alone— transcending all human records in its universal appeal.
>
> A monument to Simpson the donkey man will be of a different nature. It will provide the human touch—exemplifying in simple fashion the everyday kindness of the common soldier, the Good Samaritan touch of the Red Cross. It will recall the healing hand of the doctor and the nurse and the splendid endurance of the wounded. The patient donkey with the Red Cross brassard below his long ears adds an inimitable touch to the whole picture. Children seeing the Shrine will be awed into reverence by its greatness. Simpson with his donkey and its pathetic burden will appeal to the child's natural love of animals and sympathy with all

suffering. To all of us amid the stress and turmoil of everyday life, the memorial with its gentle story, should lead our thoughts into the quiet ways of compassion and kindness.

A sculpture of 'The Man with the Donkey' created by Wallace Anderson, was eventually set up in the grounds of the Shrine of Remembrance in Melbourne.

In December 1938, Robertson resigned her Red Cross offices, and the central council and the Victorian division both granted her life membership. Her retirement was brief, and she returned as honorary director of the Victorian branches, coordinating and expanding their work through the Second World War. She retired again in 1946, and at the time of her death four years later, was living at 'Oaks Villa', 67 Park Street, South Yarra.

Robertson belonged to the Victoria League, the Alexandra Club and the Albert Park Golf Club. In 1950 a home for seriously disabled ex-servicemen, in Clarendon Street, East Melbourne, was named after her. Also in 1950, Robertson published *Red Cross Yesterdays*, an autobiography that outlined the history of the Australian Red Cross. Her account included humorous anecdotes such as that of a serviceman who received a pair of Red Cross socks, and wrote

> Madame, Thanks for the socks—they fit—
> One for a helmet, one for a mitt.
> Thank the Lord you are doing your bit,
> But why the hell don't you learn to knit?

Robertson died early in the following year.

§

Robertson's poetry appears to have been in chief a product of the War years. She published little after the patriotic verse of *An Anzac Budget*, a small booklet (6 x 4 inches) of 32 pages, containing twenty-two poems previously printed in the *Age, Argus, Book Lover* and *Bulletin*. The title poem is an invitation to a soldier to accept this 'billy'. The second poem 'On the Voyage / A Billy Corroborree' is a playful effort wherein different billies speak their part—the Pompous Billy, Billy the Nut, the Poetical

Billy, and so on. Her poem 'Exiled' (pages 24-25) recounts ten years in England, exiled from Australia. The following lines give the general tenor

> A horsewhip cracks in the yard nearby—
> I wake—and look at the poplars tall,
> And the misty grey of an English sky!
> ...
>
> I long for the scent that used to blow
> in wattle time from the long lagoon.
> (p. 25)

A postwar miscellany, *Shreds and Patches* (1924), contains prose sketches as well as a few poems republished from *An Anzac Budget*.

Publications

An Anzac Budget and Other Verses, Melbourne: Australasian Authors' Agency, 1916.
Shreds and Patches, Melbourne: Veritas Publishing Company, 1924.
Red Cross Yesterdays. Melbourne: s.n., 1950.

References:

H.J. Gibney and Ann G. Smith, *A Biographical Register* 1788-1939, vol. 2, Canberra: Australian National Dictionary of Biography, Australian National University, 1987. vol 2, p. 219.
'Death of a Pioneer Minister', *Benalla Standard*, Friday 19 Feb 1915, p. 3.
'Red Cross Society: Work of the Dimboola Branch', *Dimboola Banner and Wimmera and Mallee Advertiser,* Friday 28 January 1916, p. 2.
'Red Cross Book Depot', *Swan Hill Guardian and Lake Boga Advocate* (Victoria), Thursday 6 December 1917, p. 5 [and also the *Gippsland Mercury, Rainbow Argus* (Euroa), and 36 other regional newspapers, Friday 7 December 1917, p. 5.
'Wounded in Action. Chaplain Hume Robertson', *Castlemaine Mail*, Monday 22 October 1917, p. 1. 'Invalid Soldiers', *Age,* Monday 18 November 1918, p. 6, and *Argus,* 19 November 1918, p. 6.
'The Children of Europe', *Argus,* Monday 24 November 1919, p. 6.
'Red Cross Society', *Traralgon Record,* Tuesday 2 December 1919, Supplement, p. 1.

'Red Cross Branches', *Age*, Saturday 2 September 1922, p. 16.
'Military Mental Patients', *Argus,* Saturday 14 March 1925, p. 31.
'To Miss P. Robertson', *Australasian,* Saturday 28 March 1925, p. 50.
'The Human Touch', *Argus,* 24 October 1933, p. 6.
'Story of Red Cross Told with Humour', *Argus*, Wednesday 26 April 1950, p. 9.
Argus, 13 January 1951, p. 15 [Death notice].
Age, 27 July 1951, p. 13 [Law Notice: probate].
'The Man with the Donkey 1935'. Shrine of Remembrance. http://www.shrine.org.au/Exhibitions/The-Shrine-Collection/Man-and-donkey accessed 7 January 2016.
K. FitzPatrick, *PLC Melbourne: The First Century 1875-1975.* Burwood: Presbyterian Ladies College, 1975.
'Hume James Robertson', Heritage Guide to the Geelong College. http://gnet.geelongcollege.vic.edu.au:8080/wiki/ROBERTSON-Rev-Hume-James-1860-1921.ashx?HL=and accessed 9 January 2016.
Melanie Oppenheimer, 'Robertson, Philadelphia Nina (1866–1951)', Australian Dictionary of Biography, National Centre of Biography, Australian National University, http://adb.anu.edu.au/biography/robertson-philadelphia-nina-11544/text20599, published first in hardcopy in *Australian Dictionary of Biography,* Volume 16, Melbourne: Melbourne University Press, 2002, accessed online 8 January 2016.

Philadelphia Nina Robertson
'More Men, and Yet More, are Wanted'

'More men, more men, they want more men—it's up to you to go!'
These were the words his horse's hoofs beat out on the road below,
Whether he trotted along the trail, or cantered across the plain,
Or galloped the length of the sandy track, it was still the same refrain.

'There are plenty of chaps to go,' he said, 'who haven't won their way
by dogged graft from year to year—all work, no time to play.'
But the voice beat on as he rode along, while the evening sun sank low,
'More men, more men, they want more men, it's up to you to go!'

'I'm to be boss of the shed this year when shearing time comes round,
I've earned the billet, and it's mine,'—but still he could hear the sound—
Hear it above the singing breeze, and the creek with its spring-tide flow—
'More men, more men, they want more men—it's up to you to go!'

Then he thought of the boys at the Dardanelles—of all they'd dared and done,
Of the silent graves on that blood bought cliff, and the battles not yet won,
And he thought of the trenches there in France, and of Belgium trodden low,
And he looked it square in the face at last—it was up to him to go.

The wattles are fringing the creek with gold, the bell-bird pipes to his mate,
Somebody strange rides out to-day down the track from the homestead gate,
Someone else in camp has a lot to learn, but this he'll always know,
Whatever comes in the days to be—it was up to him to go!

Philadelphia N[ina] Robertson, *An Anzac Budget,* Melbourne: Australasian Authors'
Agency, n.d, [1916], pp.15-16.

Philadelphia N. Robertson
Killed at Gallipoli

Dead—and that is all!
His portrait smiles from the wall,
And the spikes of the bulbs he set
Have not pierced the brown earth yet.

Dead! Some say 'at rest,'
Ah no! That were not the best—
Death could not quench the zeal
That flamed for his Empire's weal.

Dead! But oh, my heart,
Still shall do his part,
Still he shall hold his post—
One of a Shining Host.

Dead—but he shall go
Wherever our bugles blow,
And his gallant soul, set free,
Shall help on each victory.

Philadelphia N[ina] Robertson, *An Anzac Budget,* Melbourne: Australasian Authors' Agency, n.d, [1916], p. 18.

JOAN TORRANCE

Photo of Joan Torrance by Talma, Melbourne.
State Library Victoria.

Joan Torrance (who also published as Joan Kerr and Mrs Kerr) was the third daughter of Captain John Torrance (1831–1872) and Janet Coulter (1836–1915), of Stanraer on the shores of Loch Ryan in Western Scotland. Captain John Torrance and Janet Coulter were married in 1861, and Joan was born at Stanraer on 12 September 1867.

Joan's mother was a dressmaker, and her father a master mariner, described as 'a careful intelligent seaman', and one 'who was much respected by all who knew him'. The son of master mariner Robert Torrance (1801–c.1860), Joan's father was successively captain of the schooners *Sarah Jane, Isabella Reid,* and the *Isabella*. He had purchased the latter in 1866, and in June 1871 (1872 by some accounts) committed suicide by leaping overboard from the ship. Another member of the same family (William Torrance) had died in similar circumstances when he leaped overboard from the steamer *Albion* in February 1871.

Two years later, Janet Torrance married James McMurdo, who had succeeded as captain of the *Isabella*. McMurdo died at sea following a collision with another ship near Loch Ryan in 1874. Janet's only son, Hamilton McMurdo, was born in the same year.

Four of Janet Torrance's siblings had earlier migrated to Australia: William Coulter (1832–1888), Archibald Coulter (1838–1885), James McDowall Coulter (1840–1872), and Margaret Coulter (1834–1904). William, who arrived first, mined for gold near Maryborough and for a time went into partnership with his brother Archibald near Talbot. James worked in the Customs Department in Melbourne, and Margaret married a brush manufacturer in the city.

In August 1876, with her daughters and her son, Janet also migrated to Melbourne, on the ship *True Briton,* from Gravesend, travelling under the name McMurdo. Later, Janet and her son changed their surname to McMurdie while the girls retained their father's surname: Jessie Stevenson Torrance (1862-1883), Margaret Coulter Torrance (1864-1902), Joan Torrance (1867–1943), and Marie Torrance (1870–1925). The girls' half-brother Hamilton McMurdie (1874–1954) would later work as an accountant and company director.

Joan Torrance, the future poet, therefore grew up in a colony already peopled with several of her mother's relatives and their families. Her mother Janet settled first at Albert Park where Joan and her sisters attended the Albert Park School. By 1888, Janet's brother William also resided with her at Albert Park.

On 12 September 1889, at the Clarendon Street Presbyterian Church in South Melbourne, Joan married Harold Bertram Kerr, an engineer and gold mining manager. Kerr was the second son of Scottish-born Peter Kerr (1820–1912), a Fellow of the Royal British Institute of Architects, who had migrated to Australia in 1852 and worked in the Public Works Department, designing the Post Office, Law Courts, Government House, Customs House and other landmark Melbourne buildings.

Torrance and her husband lived at 3 Raleigh Street, Windsor, and had one son, Charles ('Charlie') Tennyson Allen Kerr (1892–1963), and a daughter, Jessie Helen Agnes Kerr (1890–1970).

Throughout the 1890s and into the new century, Torrance built a substantial reputation as a writer of graceful lyrics and commemorative and eulogistic verse, and as a writer of scenic prose celebrating the countryside around Melbourne. Her commemorative poems included tributes to Henry Kendall, Adam Lindsay Gordon, the Scottish-New Zealand poet William Gay (who died at Bendigo in 1897), and others. She was a supporter of proposals by the Australian Literature Society and other organisations to honour the memory of Australian poets, and was proud of her native Scotland's bards. Numerous poems celebrated British heroes of the South African War, such as Lord Roberts, Kitchener, and Baden-Powell. For the arrival of Lord Hopetoun as Governor-General, she wrote a welcoming ode in Scots dialect, which Hopetoun declared she should print in her next collection of verse. She attested to her Australian and British patriotism in several poems associated with the African War, the Queen's birthday, Australian Federation and other signal events. She wrote an anthem for the Australian Natives Association, replete with references to the passing of the Aborigines and their supplanting by the 'overflow of old world strife / In Europe's crowded mart'. In addition, Torrance published, in newspapers and single-card souvenirs, so great a number of commemorative poems on public and sacred occasions as to be considered something of a Melbourne laureate. She was a talented reciter and performer at church and civic functions. At a Presbyterian Concert in the Mechanics Hall at Broadford, in north-central Victoria in 1904, the local paper reported that Marie Torrrance, a Shakespearean reciter and 'sister of the well-known Miss Joan Torrance, author of "Sons of the Southern Sea"' gave a charming recitation', and Joan recited 'Tit for Tat', a humorous Irish love story that occasioned a comic encore that brought roars of laughter. Like her mother and aunt, Torrance's daughter Jessie later became a popular performer, reciting her own poems, and acting in John Gilmour Swan's 1912 drama, *Herod Agrippa: A Tale of Palestine and the Roman Empire*.

Torrance's published works include songs, composed by W.R. Furlong and Joseph Gillott, for which she supplied the lyrics. She provided music for the annual Austral Salon conducted under the patronage of Lady Madden (wife of Chief Justice Sir John Madden).

The religious strain in her work became increasingly evident. She issued an annual 'Yuletide Card', and her Christmas and Easter poems appeared in papers in and beyond Victoria. The Rev. G.R. Jones read from her poem 'Easter Tide' at the Broadwood Presbyterian Church on Sunday 15 April 1900; her later sacred verse includes 'An Invocation' (1917, included in this anthology) addressed to Mary as 'Queenly Mother' and 'the Seamen's Star'. During World War One and into the nineteen twenties, Torrance published many poems in the Catholic weekly *Advocate* newspaper, celebrating the pious lives of particular nuns and priests, as well as Thomas Joseph Carr (1839–1917), second Archbishop of Melbourne (appointed 1886), the predecessor of Daniel Mannix. Her poem called 'The Triumph of Erin', published in the *Advocate* in 1922, welcomed Irish independence. Her version of 'Who shall roll away the stone', based on St Mark's Gospel, was sung at Easter in St Andrews Presbyterian Church at Bendigo in March 1919. Torrance appears to have struck a remarkably ecumenical note in such verse.

Some of her memorials to favourite poets and statesmen are gathered in her volume, *'Twixt Heather and Wattle: Poems 1911*. A greater number, such as her welcome poem to the Victorian singer Ada Crossley (1871–1929) on the singer's brief return visit from England, Europe, America and New Zealand in 1903, are mood-pieces that adapt their measure to the occasion. A few poems concerning local tragedies ('In Memoriam of the Members of the Mornington Football Team', for example, concerning the death by drowning of fourteen footballers in a boating capsize in a storm) or memorialising local dignitaries (a poem of farewell to Brunswick Station Master, Mr. C.Y. Ford, on his transfer to a remote location), are rhymed sentimental effusions, but Torrance's sense of control generally displays the aptness of such verse to occasion and audience.

In July 1919, the Melbourne *Advocate* recorded that 'a very tuneful and seasonable poem', 'The Dawn of Peace' had just appeared during the current peace rejoicings, and that 'Miss Torrance was the writer of a most patriotic song, entitled "Sons of the Southern Land"', which had 'caught on' not only in Australia, but also in Great Britain.

In 1915, Torrance's mother died in the Cheltenham Benevolent Asylum, and Torrance's brother Hamilton McMurdie, a company manager living at Windsor, enlisted in the AIF as a private on 12 July 1915, but was commissioned as a Second Lieutenant. He was discharged from the army on 30 July 1916. Torrance's son Charlie, who was living in Whangarei, New Zealand in 1914, enlisted in the New Zealand Army, serving in the Auckland Infantry Battalion until he was wounded in the shoulder on 19 August 1915 and discharged as medically unfit. He offered himself for enlistment in the Australian Army for service abroad in November 1916, and was instead assigned to home service (in the Permanent Guard Unit) through 1917 and 1918, being promoted to Corporal in October 1917 and, in 1920, Sergeant Driver until discharged in 1921.

§

Joan Torrance's character was not always equable. The Melbourne *Argus* reported on Monday 36 April 1909 that she had been charged with offensive behaviour as a result of an encounter with her publisher, Charles E. Glass. Glass, who had paid her one hundred pounds for the poems, had to call the police when Torrance arrived at his shop 'in an excited state' after she had 'evidently taken too much drink'. Torrance claimed that Glass had thrown a bucket of water over her—which he denied, though he stated he had a bucket of water and a mop when Torrance called, and she had pulled his hair and held his head down. Torrance stated that if given the opportunity, she would leave Melbourne, and that she felt very ill. The Police Magistrate remanded Torrance to the Gaol hospital for a week for medical treatment.

Torrance was modest about her own poetic accomplishments. In a letter to the *Record* newspaper in 1931, she remarked,

> I have, only recently, had brought to my notice a kindly reference to myself, in connection with the planting of memorial trees to Australian poets at Wattle Park by the Australian Literature Society. The account was published in 'The Record' last November. Mention is made of my connection with South Melbourne. I have memory of those happy days, and am proud to know that I am numbered with those entitled to fame, as a more or less illustrious citizen of your illustrious city.
>
> In relation to the poets honoured at the planting, it was my privilege to be well acquainted with them all. The late J. B. O'Hara, a fellow citizen of olden days, was one whose works I greatly admired, and I feel it an especial honour to be in a group with him as worthy to be classed 'poet,' even though my merits may be on a less exalted plane. With a tinge of sorrow, I realise that I am the only one of the little group of honoured poets who has not passed The Great Divide; but, having been so honoured in my lifetime, I shall endeavour to prove worthy of the honour.

Joan Torrance died of cervical cancer at the Abbotsford Convent, 52 Victoria Avenue, Albert Park, on 20 July 1943, and was buried with Presbyterian form the following day at Springvale Botanical Cemetery (in the Thomas Simmons Lawn, Row DB, Grave 45).

§

Torrance's single collection of poems, *'Twixt Heather and Wattle: Poems,* was published by George Robertson in Melbourne in 1904. The edition was illustrated by artists Tom Roberts, Archibald R. Colquhoun, and Henry J. Recknell. The book proved highly popular and was reprinted several times. The fifth and sixth editions were published by Robertson in Sydney in 1911.

The Call to Arms, included here, was printed on a single card, folded laterally, with the title and the Australian coat of arms and motto 'Advance Australia' on the front page. The publication bears no colophon or date on the back page, but was published by the Melbourne printing firm of McCarron Bird in 1915. The poem 'Christmastide 1919' was similarly published as a card.

Publications

Joan Torrance, *'Twixt Heather and Wattle: Poems*, Melbourne: George Robertson, 1903.

Joan Torrance, *'Twixt Heather and Wattle: Poems,* Sydney: George Robertson, 1911.

Joan Torrance, 'Heidelberg', *Weekly Times,* Saturday 18 September 1897, p. 9.

Individual poems cited:

'At the Sign of the Lyre. William Gay', *Bendigo Advertiser,* 18 June 1898, p. 2.

'Miss Torrance's Ode' ['All hail! Most gallant ship! Hail to our Southern Sea, / Ice-fighters bold, from Arctic cold, we honour such as thee'), *Weekly Times,* 24 December, 1898, p. 8.

'An Easter Hymn', *Herald,* Saturday 1 April 1899, p. 2.

'Miss Joan Torrance's Memorial Lines' ['O, Gordon! Though not all our own'], *Herald,* 23 June 1899, p. 2.

'Sons of the Southern Sea. New Patriotic Song', *Australian Star* (Sydney), Saturday 20 January 1900, p. 7.

'Welcome to Lord and Lady Hopetoun', *Herald,* Monday 26 November 1900, p. 3.

'Easter Tide', *Broadford Courier and Reedy Creek Times,* Friday 20 April 1900, p. 3.

'Lord Roberts Visits his Son's Grave', *Weekly Times,* Saturday 24 November 1900, p. 12; *Herald,* Monday 11 February 1901, p. 4.

'Baden-Powell', *Herald,* Saturday 19 May 1900, p. 4.

'An Australian Anthem. Dedicated to the A.N.A.', *Herald,* Monday 11 February 1901, p. 4.

'In Memoriam of the Members of the Mornington Football Team', *Standard* (Frankston), Thursday 9 May 1946, p. 9 [reprinted from *'Twixt Heather and Wattle: Poems*].

'Thy friends have gathered here tonight', *Coburg Leader,* Saturday 15 October 1904, p. 1.

'To Kendall', *Mirror* (Sydney), Saturday 7 July 1917, p. 5.

'A Tribute to the Late Archbishop, Thomas Joseph Carr', Advocate, Saturday 26 May 1917, p. 17.

'Lines in Memory of Sister Mary of St Gabriel', *Advocate,* Saturday 20 July 1918, p. 3.

'To the Rev. Fr. Robinson. The Vigil', *Advocate,* Saturday 2 November 1918, p. 16.

'The Triumph of Erin', *Advocate,* Thursday 2 March 1922, p. 18.

References

Marriage Notices from the Wigtownshire Press, The Wigtownshire Pages. http://freepages.history.rootsweb.ancestry.com/~ainsty/wfp/marriages/25.html accessed 10 January 2016 [Marriage of John Torrance and Janet Coulter]

SCT-Wigtownshire Press Archives, http://archiver.rootsweb.ancestry.com/th/read/SCT-WIGTOWNSHIRE/2008-11/1226599863 accessed 10 January 2016.

The AIF Project. https://www.aif.adfa.edu.au/showPerson?pid=203715 accessed 8 April 2018. [Information about Hamilton McMurdie].

'Presbyterian Concert', *Broadford Courier and Reedy Creek Times,* Friday 8 April 1904, p. 2 [Report on the Torance sisters' recitations, and other features of the concert].

Argus, Monday 26 April 1909, p. 11 ['Poetess and Publisher']

Age, Friday 22 March 1912, p. 6; 'Social', *Table Talk,* Thursday 28 March 1912, p. 30.

Bendigo Advertiser, 30 March 1919, p. 10 [Torrance's version of 'Who shall roll away the stone' sung at St Andrews Church].

Advocate, 12 July 1919, p. 12 [Torrance's poem 'The Dawn of Peace' featured in peace celebrations].

Record (Emerald Hill, Victoria), Saturday 23 March 1935, p. 6 ['Sth Melbourne Poetess': on Torrance's association with South Melbourne].

Stephanie Hume, Post-War Correspondence with Lord Birdwood, part 2. https://www.awm.gov.au/blog/2015/08/12/post-war-correspondence-with-Lord-Birdwood-part-2/ accessed 10 January 2016.

Online Cenotaph. Tamaki Paenga Hira Auckland War Memorial Museum. http://www.aucklandmuseum.com/war-memorial/online-cenotaph/record/C47633
accessed 10 January 2016. [Information about Charles Tennyson Torrance]

New Zealand's Roll of Honour. http://paperspast.natlib.govt.nz/cgi-bin/paperspast?a=d&d=NZH19150818.2.89 accessed 10 January 2016.

Genie's Jottings: World War One—Rolls of Honour. From the *Auckland Weekly News*. http://www.ozlists.com/genies/defence/ww1/rollhono/k2.htm accessed 10 January 2016.

NAA: MT1486/1 Kerr, Charles Tennyson, National Archives of Australia, soda.naa.gov.au/record/9527979/1-19 Accessed 7 June 2018 [Charles Kerr's enlistment record in Australian Imperial Force].

'Poetess and Publisher', *Argus*, Monday 26 April 1909, p. 11 [Charge against Torrance].

'A Troublesome Poetess', *Geelong Advertiser*, Monday 26 April 1909, p. 3 [Charge against Torrance].

'Poetic Frenzy', *Barrier Miner*, Saturday 1 May 1909, p. 3 [Charge against Torrance].

Joan Torrance, 'An Acknowledgment' (Letter to the Editor), *Record*, Saturday 14 March 1931, p. 1.

Victorian death Certificate No. 7335 [Deaths in the District of Melbourne in Victoria: Joan Kerr].

Joan Torrance
The Call to Arms

Australia is waiting now
The crown of freedom on Her brow,
And she will still the right defend
And fight for Britain to the end.

The call has come the call to War
And it is sounding near and far,
The hope of Peace, alas is o'er
And Britain lifts the sword once more;
But still the Union colours float
On lofty tower and British boat.

The hearts of men are just as bold
As they were in the days of old—
No traitor dare our trust betray
When Britain proudly leads the way.
The men we love will do their part
And live within the Empire heart.

And in this time of stress and need
The Word of God we all must heed;
Because we cannot see the light n
The skies are dark, that once were bright.

God bless the Nurses who will give
Their best, to help the Soldiers live,
And guard them in this time of dread
And over them thy mantle spread;
The fear shall vanish and the light
Of duty make their pathway bright.

We pray for our good King and Queen
Though surging oceans sweep between,
Our people trust their boundless love,
And pray for Peace to God above.

Source: 'The Call to Arms', Single card printed by McCarron Bird, Melbourne, 1915.

Joan Torrance
Lines Suggested on Viewing Mount Macedon

The orb of day, resplendent bright,
Crowns now the Mount with rosy light;
While o'er its green and fertile side
Fantastic shadows softly glide.
Now on the fleeting winds we hear
The wild birds anthem, strong and clear;
And there is something in the strain
Which tends to raise the song again,
And draw us nearer at this time,
Nearer to God and things sublime.
Our sad hearts yearn for those afar,
Our men and boys so brave in war,
Who on the shrine of duty place
Deeds which the years will not efface.
But in the future they shall hold
The pride of place among the bold,
When the great King, the King Divine
Shall cause the light thro' gloom to shine
And the true heralds of His love
Descend in triumph from above.
And when the trumpet voice shall call,
When men before their Maker fall,
Then we who trust may claim again
Our brave who were for freedom slain.

Source: *Gisborne Gazette*, Friday 24 August 1917, p. 3.

Joan Torrance
An Invocation

Oh, Queenly Mother, send us now thine aid;
The 'way' is dark, and we are sore afraid.
No kindly star sheds forth a shining ray.
Only dense shadows now obscure the way.
Help those who now despair with hope once more,
Guard thou our brave upon the sea and shore;

Comfort the mothers in their sad distress,
And the afflicted wife console and bless.
Plead with the King of Kings in realms above
Still to uphold our hearts with divine love.
Thou, the strong link which binds, Mother of All,
Trusting, we pray to thee; list to our call.

Thou art the 'Seamen's Star,' gleaming so bright,
All through the lonely hours of the long night,
And when fierce tempests sweep across the deep.
Watch by the helmsman's side and safely keep
Those who for honour fight by night and day.
Those whom we love so well, for whom we pray.

Advocate, Saturday 22 September 1917, p. 3.

Joan Torrance
Christmastide, 1919

Once more the season of goodwill,
    Once more the Angels' strain,
Is ringing down time's chancels clear
    To raise our hearts again.

And though we do not see the star,
    Nor yet behold the light,
We know the way unto the Lord
    Was made by Angels bright.

We know within a stable lay
    The Prophet, Priest, and King,
And that from year to year His praise
    The choirs of Angels sing.

And as we pray for clearer light
    To guide us day by day,
In thought we go towards the East
    To where the Saviour lay.

The star of God, the star of hope,
    Is scintillating still.
And on the wings of winds we hear
    The Anthem of goodwill.

War's cruel tide is o'er at last,
    But still we mourn the brave.
The gallant men who fearlessly
    Their lives for freedom gave.

And as we hear the Christmas hymn
    Faith draws the veil apart,
And the true Comforter gives balm
    To every aching heart.

> Goodwill to men, goodwill to all,
> Resounds from shore to shore.
> For Peace hath spread her shining wings
> Above the world once more.

Source: *Advocate*, Saturday 27 December 1919, p. 14. The newspaper added the following note: 'The gifted authoress has had these seasonable verses neatly printed on a card as a Christmas greeting. A few copies will, we understand, be available for sale to the public'.

Select Bibliography

Apart from the specific references noted in the main text of this book, some of my background reading includes the following, which other readers might find illuminating.

Checklists and bibliographies

Laird, J.T. 'A Checklist of Australian Literature of World War 1', *Australian Literary Studies,* vol. 4, no. 2, October 1969, pp. 148-163.
Laird, J.T. 'Australian Poetry of the First World War: A Survey', *Australian Literary Studies,* vol. 4, no. 2, May 1970, pp. 241-250.
Laird, J.T. 'A Checklist of Australian Literature of the First World War', *Australian Literary Studies,* vol. 12, no. 2, October 1985, pp. 275-287 [updated 1969 list].

World War One verse in anthologies: Australian

Note: John T. Laird and David Holloway are far and away the pioneers in representing a significant number of civilian women poets alongside the male poets of World War One. By and large, other anthologies listed here do not necessarily aim to represent poets of every State.

Abbott, Edith S., ed. *Violet Verses,* Adelaide: W.K. Thomas, 1917.
Barrett, Paul, and Kerry B. Collison, eds. *The Happy Warrior: An Anthology of Australian and New Zealand Military Poetry,* Hartwell, Victoria: Sid Harta Publishers, 2001.
Chittleborough, Anne, and Annie Greet and Sue Hosking, eds. *Hope and Fear: An Anthology of South Australian Women's Writing, 1894-1994,* Adelaide: Centre for Research in the New Literatures in English, 1994.
Galway, Maria Carola, ed. *Lady Galway Belgium Book*, Adelaide: Hussey and Gillingham, 1916.
Hansen, M.H., and D. McLachlan, eds. *An Austral Garden: An Anthology of Australian Verse.* Melbourne: G. Robertson, 1926.
Holloway, David, ed. *Dark Somme Flowing: Australian Verse of the Great War 1914-1918,* Malvern: Robert Andersen and Associates, 1987.
Laird, J.T., ed. *Other Banners: An Anthology of Australian Literature of the First World War,* Canberra: Australian War Memorial and Australian Government Publishing Service, 1971.
Murdoch, Walter, and A. Carson, A.T. Chandler and W. Siebenhaar, eds. *Westralia Gift Book To Aid Y.M.C.A. Military Work and Returned Nurses' Fund by Writers and Artists of Western Australia,* Perth: V.K. Jones & Co. Ltd., 1916.

Paterson, Franklin, ed. *Melba's Gift Book of Australian Art and Literature,* Melbourne: George Robertson, 1915.

Seal, Graham, ed. *Digger Folksong and Verse: An Annotated Anthology,* Perth: Centre for Australian Studies, Curtin University, 1991.

Seal, Graham, ed. *Echoes of Anzac: The Voice of Australians at War.* Melbourne: Lothian, 2005.

Turner, Ethel, and Bertram Stevens, eds. *The Australian Soldier's Gift Book,* Sydney: Voluntary Workers' Association, 1917.

Wilkinson, Mary E., ed. *Gleanings from Australian Verse: Poems of Manhood,* Sydney, 1919.

World War One Verse in anthologies and single-author volumes other than Australian

Blunden, Edmund. *Overtones of War: Poems of the First World War,* ed Martin Taylor, London: Gerald Duckworth and Co., 1996.

Gardner, Brian, ed. *Up to the Line of Death: The War Poets 1914-1918: An Anthology,* London: Methuen, 1964.

Higonnet, Margaret. R., ed. *Lines of Fire: Women Writers of World War I,* New York: Plume/Penguin, 1999.

Hudson, Edward, ed. *Poetry of the First World War,* Hove: Wayland, 1988.

Hussey, Maurice, ed. *Poetry of the First World War: An Anthology,* London: Longman, 1967.

Nichols, Robert, ed. *Anthology of War Poetry 1914-1918,* London: Nicholson and Watson, 1943.

Reeves, James, ed. *Georgian Poetry,* Harmondsworth: Penguin, 1981.

Reilly, Catherine W., ed. *Scars Upon My Heart: Women's Poetry and verse of the First World War,* London: Virago, 1981.

Wright, Sydney Fowler, ed. *An Anthology of Contemporary Dominion and Colonial Verse,* London: The Merton Press Ltd, 1924.

Studies and memoirs relating to women's writing during World War One (and other wars)

Bassett, Jan. '"Preserving the White Race": Some Australian Women's Literary Responses to the Great War', *Australian Literary Studies,* 12, 2 (1985): 223-233.

Bassett, Jan. *As We Wave You Goodbye: Australian Women and War,* Melbourne: Oxford University Press, 1998.

Boxwell, D.A. 'The (M)Other Battle of World War One: The Maternal Politics of Pacifism in Rose Macaulay's *Non-Combatants and Others', Tulsa Studies in Women's Literature,* 112, 1993, 85-101.

Buck, Claire. 'British women's writing of the Great War', *The Cambridge Companion to the Literature of the First World War,* ed Vincent Sherry, Cambridge: Cambridge University Press, 2005, pp. 85-112.

Casson, Marjory Rose. *The Secret of Poetry*, Adelaide: Hassell, 1920.

Cooke, Miriam. *Women and the War Story,* Berkeley: University of California Press, 1996.

Damousi, Joy. *The Labour of Loss: Memory and Wartime Bereavement in Australia*, Cambridge: Cambridge UP, 1999.

Elshtain, Jean Bethke. *Women and War,* New York: Basic Books, 1987.

Giordano, Margaret, and Don Norman. 'Helen Power (1870-1957)', in *Tasmanian Literary Landmarks,* ed Margaret Giordano and Don Norman, Hobart: Shearwater Press, 1984, pp. 91-97.

Goldman, Dorothy, ed. *Women and World War I: The Written Response,* St Martin's New York, 1993.

Higonnet, Margaret R. Jane Jenson, Sonya Michael and Margaret Collins Weitz, eds. *Behind the Lines: Gender and Two World Wars,* New Haven and London: Yale University Press, 1987.

Khan, Nosheen. *Women's Poetry of the First World War,* University Press of Kentucky, Lexington, 1988.

Lask, Berta. 'Selbstgericht' ['Self-indictment'], in Agnès Cardinal, 'Women on the Other Side', in Dorothy Goldman, ed, *Women in World War I: The Written Response,* Houndmills: Macmillan, 1993, pp. 31-50.

Longley, Edna. *Poetry in the Wars,* Newark: University of Delaware Press, 1987.

Manuel, Jacqueline, 'Australian Civilian Women's Poetic Responses to the First World War', *Journal of the Australian War Museum.* no. 29, November 1996. http://www.awm.gov.au/journal/j29/manuel.asp. Accessed 16 November 2011.

Mills, F[rederick].J[ohn]. *Cheer-Up: A Story of War Work,* Adelaide: Cheer-Up Society, 1920.

Markmann, Sigrid, and Dagmar Lange. *Women and the First World War in England / Frauen und Erster Weltkrieg in England: A Select Bibliographical Guide / Auswahlbibliographie,* Osnabrück: H.Th. Wenner, 1988.

Potter, Jane. *Boys in Khaki, Girls in Print: Women's Literary Responses to the Great War,* Oxford: Clarendon Press, 2005.

Shute, Carmel Mary. 'Australian women and the Great War: Aspects of ideological change, with particular emphasis on Queensland', B.A. thesis, University of Queensland: Department of History, 1973.

Shute, Carmel. 'Heroines and Heroes: Sexual Mythology in Australia 1914-1918', *Hecate, An Interdisciplinary Journal of Women's Liberation*, vol. 1, no. 1, 1975, pp. 6-22.

Stout, Janis P. 'The Great Grief: Women Poets of World War I', *Coming out of War: Poetry, Grieving, and the Culture of the World Wars,* University of Alabama Press, Tuscaloosa, 2005, Chapter 3, pages 59-82.

Tylee, Claire M. *The Great War and Women's Consciousness: Images of Militarism and Womanhood in Women's Writings, 1914-64*, Iowa City: University of Iowa Press, 1990.

Critical and general studies relating to writing of World War One (and other wars)

Caesar, Adrian. *Taking It Like a Man: Suffering, Sexuality, and the War Poets Brooke, Sassoon, Owen, Graves,* Manchester University Press, Manchester, 1993.

Campbell, James. 'Combat Gnosticism: The Ideology of First World War Poetry Criticism', *New Literary History,* vol. 20, no. 1, 1999, pp. 203-215.

Eby, Cecil. D. *The Road to Armageddon: The Martial Spirit in English Popular Literature, 1870-1914.* Durham: Duke University Press, 1987.

Evans, Martin, and Ken Lunn, eds. *War and Memory in the Twentieth Century.* Oxford: Berg, 1997.

Foulkes, A.P. *Literature and Propaganda,* London: Methuen: 1983.

Goldensohn, Lorrie. *Dismantling Glory: Twentieth Century Soldier Poetry.* New York: Columbia University Press, 2003.

Gregson, J.M. *Poetry of the First World War,* London: Arnold, 1976.

Heath, Gordon L. 'Passion for Empire: War Poetry Published in the Canadian English Protestant Press During the South African War, 1899-1902', *Literature and Theology,* vol. 16, no. 2, June 2002, pp. 127-147.

Hibberd, Dominic. *Poetry of the First World War,* London: Macmillan, 1981.

Hibberd, Dominic and Onions, John, eds. *Poetry of the Great War: An Anthology,* London: Macmillan, 1986.

Hynes, Samuel. *A War Imagined: The First World War and English Culture,* New York: Athenaeum, 1991.

Johnston, John Hubert. *English Poetry of the First World War: A Study in the Evolution of Lyric and Narrative Form,* Princeton: Princeton University Press, 1964.

Kellow, Henry Arthur. *Queensland Poets,* London: George Harrap and Co., 1930.

Rolfe, Patricia. *The Journalistic Javelin: An Illustrated History of the* Bulletin, Sydney: Wildcat Press, 1979.

Ross, Robert. *The Georgian Revolt: Rise and Fall of a Poetic Ideal 1910-22*, London: Faber, 1967.

Sharkey, Michael. '"But who considers women day by day?"': Australian Women Poets and World War I', *Australian Literary Studies,* vol. 23, no. 1, 2007, pp. 63-78.

Spargo, R. Clifton. *The Ethics of Mourning: Grief and Responsibility in Elegiac Literature,* Baltimore: Johns Hopkins University Press, 2004.

Spear, Hilda D. *Remembering, We Forget: A background Study to the Poetry of the First World War,* London: Davis-Poynting, 1979.

Tylee, Claire M. *The Great War and Women's Consciousness: Images of Militarism and Womanhood in Women's Writings, 1914-1964*. Iowa City: University of Iowa Press, 1990.

Williams, Linda M., and Victoria Banyard, eds. *Trauma and Memory*. Thousand Oaks: Sage, 1999.

Winter, J.M. *Sites of Memory, Sites of Mourning: The Great War in European Cultural History*, New York: Cambridge University Press, 1995.

Personal narratives

ABC Radio National. *Warriors, Welfare and Eternal Vigilance: The History of the Returned Services League. Program 1: The Beginnings*. ABC Radio Talks and Documentaries, 9 May 1982.

Donnell, Anne. *Letters of An Australian Army Sister*, Sydney: Angus and Robertson, 1920.

Freeman, Hilda. *An Australian Girl in Germany: Through Peace to War, Jan-Oct 1914*, Melbourne: Specialty Press, 1916.

King, Olive. *One Woman at War: Letters of Olive King. 1915-1920,* ed Hazel King. Melbourne: Melbourne University Press, 1986.

Neale, Clara [MBE, Military]. *Memories of France,* Sydney: R. Dey, Son and Co., 1921.

Robertson, Philadelphia N. *Red Cross Yesterdays,* Melbourne: J.C. Stephens for Australian Red Cross, 1950.

Tilton, May. *The Grey Battalion,* Sydney: Angus and Robertson, 1933.

Wyatt, Mary. 1914-1919: *Remembering those Years,* Adelaide: The author, 1920 [printed by W.K. Thomas & Co.].

Supplementary historical reference

'Australians at Zeebrugge'. Naval Historical Society of Australia. http://www.navyhistory.org.au/australians-at-zeebrugge/ Accessed 8 November 2011.

Frame, T.R. and G.J. Swinden. *First In, Last Out: The Navy at Gallipoli,* Kenthurst: Kangaroo Press, 1990.

'HMAS Encounter', Australian War Memorial. http://www.awm.gov.au/units/unit_10622.asp Accessed 13 May 2013.

Molkentin, Michael. *Fire in the Sky: The Australian Flying Corps in the First World War,* Sydney: Allen and Unwin, 2010.

Robson, L.L. *The First A.I.F.: A Study of Its Recruitment 1914-1918,* Melbourne: Melbourne UP, 1976.

www.ingramcontent.com/pod-product-compliance
Lightning Source LLC
Chambersburg PA
CBHW031058080526
44587CB00011B/728